W9-AAU-608

ABORTION IN
THE UNITED STATES

Selected Titles in ABC-CLIO's
CONTEMPORARY
WORLD ISSUES
Series

For a complete list of titles in this series, please visit
www.abc-clio.com.

Books in the Contemporary World Issues series address vital issues in today's society such as genetic engineering, pollution, and biodiversity. Written by professional writers, scholars, and nonacademic experts, these books are authoritative, clearly written, up-to-date, and objective. They provide a good starting point for research by high school and college students, scholars, and general readers as well as by legislators, businesspeople, activists, and others.

Each book, carefully organized and easy to use, contains an overview of the subject, a detailed chronology, biographical sketches, facts and data and/or documents and other primary-source material, a directory of organizations and agencies, annotated lists of print and nonprint resources, and an index.

Readers of books in the Contemporary World Issues series will find the information they need in order to have a better understanding of the social, political, environmental, and economic issues facing the world today.

ABORTION IN THE UNITED STATES

A Reference Handbook

Dorothy E. McBride

CONTEMPORARY WORLD ISSUES

A B C CLIO

Santa Barbara, California
Denver, Colorado
Oxford, England

Library of Congress Cataloging-in-Publication Data
McBride, Dorothy E.
  Abortion in the United States : a reference handbook / Dorothy E. McBride.
    p. cm. — (Contemporary world issues)
  Includes bibliographical references and index.
    ISBN 978-1-59884-098-8 (hard copy : alk. paper) —
ISBN 978-1-59884-099-5 (ebook)   1. Abortion—United States.
2. Abortion—Law and legislation—United States.   3. Pro-life
movement—United States.   4. Pro-choice movement—United States.
I. Title.
  HQ767.5.U5M3727 2008
  363.460973—dc22
                                         2007025876

12   11   10   09   08   1   2   3   4   5   6   7   8

ABC-CLIO, Inc.
130 Cremona Drive, P.O. Box 1911
Santa Barbara, California 93116-1911

This book is also available on the World Wide Web as an ebook.
Visit www.abc-clio.com for details.

This book is printed on acid-free paper ∞
Manufactured in the United States of America

Contents

Preface

Debate. Controversy. Argument. Conflict. Struggle. Clash. Battle. War. All of these terms have been used to describe the status of the abortion issue in American society and politics, and it has been this way for nearly a half century. The conflict affects our legislatures, political parties, courts, churches, schools, hospitals—and even our foreign policy. And there is no other country where the battles over abortion are so intense and pervasive. What is this conflict? What are people fighting about? Where did it come from? Who are the players and where do they engage each other? Why is it so hard to settle? What are the effects on society and politics? This book describes the origins and changes in the conflict over abortion; the major combatants; what they are fighting about; the arenas for the conflicts; and the effects on politics, policy, and social debate. The purpose is to provide timely information to readers and resources for further exploration of the topic.

We start with the basics in Chapter 1. That means looking at the public history of abortion since the founding of the American republic, especially the campaign to criminalize the procedure during the nineteenth century. Then we see how the criminal laws became out of date in the mid-twentieth century, provoking a new campaign, this time for reform and repeal of these criminal laws. *Roe v. Wade* was the turning point in 1973. This decision legalized abortion but did not end the debate; in fact, it gave birth to the clashes we live with today. The pro-choice and pro-life movements are the big story after 1973. Movements are a combination of ideas called *frames* and members called *activists*. Chapter 1 concludes with a full presentation of the frames of both great crusades.

After an understanding of the basics, we are ready in Chapter 2 to delve into the war itself, battle by battle, showing winners and losers over thirty-five years. One of these major conflicts pertains to the constitutionality of abortion law and the campaign to overturn *Roe v. Wade*. But there are also skirmishes over funding, administrative regulations, family planning, and emergency contraception. Included in the coverage is the all too real firefight over clinic access in the 1990s.

Chapter 3 takes a look at the rest of the world where, for the most part, people are born, grow old, and die without knowing anything about incessant public debates over abortion. In some of these places—Western Europe, for example—the issue has been settled for years, and there is a balance between access to contraception, legal abortion, and low abortion rates. In other countries, the issue has not been on the public agenda at all, despite the fact that abortion is illegal and there are high rates of maternal mortality as a result. In some places, the American struggles spill over to other countries where Western feminists face off against pro-life Roman Catholic activists.

Readers who want a capsule overview of the waxing and waning (mostly waxing) of abortion politics will find a chronology from 1803 to 2007 in Chapter 4. The remaining chapters provide supplemental materials to fill out the story of this conflict: biographies, a list of agencies and organizations, and print and nonprint resources. These do not exhaust the available materials by any means, but they are a good place to start.

After someone has devoted several decades to a job or project, it's usually time to retire. That certainly pertains to me. If I add up the years I have spent either involved with or studying abortion politics, it comes to more than thirty-five years. That's why it has been so interesting to me to work on this reference book: it has been a way to retrace my steps and take the measure of the journey I and others have made. It also makes me want to move on to another project, perhaps tracing my family's genealogy or gardening.

Do movements retire like people do? How long is long enough? Maybe they don't retire but transform themselves into some other form. This is a good time for a reference book on the abortion issue to come out because there is some evidence that we may be at another turning point in history of this standoff. For one thing, the biographies of the major players and their organizations show that most of them have devoted their lives to either the pro-life or the pro-choice cause. Their consciousness about choice and life matters was raised as a result of *Roe v. Wade* and its aftermath. Now a few have passed on, some have retired, and others taken the role of "senior advisers" to younger activists. This means that a new generation is about to pick up the battle flags. But this new generation may not be "true believers" in the same sense as the old, not having had their passions forged by the conflagration of *Roe* and its aftermath.

Second, there are hints of a weakening of the coalition between evangelical Christians and the Republican Party built in the 1970s. The right wing of the party grew by using moral issues—abortion and gay rights—as wedge issues to mobilize the voters, especially through the evangelical churches. Today the leaders of these churches are bringing other issues to the fore, showing that there is an expanding agenda that challenges the dominance of the Republican right.

Finally, a compromise may be brewing in the growing support for the idea of making abortion safe, legal, and rare by preventing unintended pregnancies through better sex education, counseling, and access to contraception. Hard-core abortion rights activists worry that such an approach will make abortion seem like a bad choice. The Roman Catholic Church opposes this approach as promoting immoral sexual behavior. Nevertheless, proposals such as the Prevention First Act are the first in a long time to attract the support of both pro-life and pro-choice members of Congress. Whether this approach settles the issue remains to be seen.

1

Background and History

Introduction

The practice of abortion is legal in the United States. This seems simple enough, but just like everything about the abortion conflict, there is no easy way to describe abortion law. The law has many sources—constitutions, legislative statutes, administrative regulations, court decisions—and to become an expert on abortion law one would have to become familiar with all of them. This book contains information about many aspects of abortion policy. But to begin, it is useful to have a clear reference point that can serve as the framework for looking at all the many forms of government action that compose U.S. abortion policy.

The foundation of abortion law is the U.S. Constitution as interpreted by the Supreme Court. Constitutional law does not directly regulate abortion. Rather, it sets limits on the powers of the states and the federal government to regulate abortion. The authority to regulate abortion has long been reserved to the states by the Constitution because Article I—which covers the legislative branch—does not give Congress explicit authority to regulate medical practice. However, Congress does get involved in abortion policy through its power to spend money and regulate interstate commerce.

The Court has established this constitutional law of abortion through a series of decisions, called *case law*, especially *Roe v. Wade, Doe v. Bolton,* and *Planned Parenthood v. Casey* (see Chapter 6). States do not have constitutional authority to prohibit the medical practice of abortion before the fetus is viable; any laws

that make abortion criminal before viability would be unconstitutional. After viability, that is, when an unborn child is able to
live on its own outside the mother, state governments have the
authority, but not the obligation, to prohibit abortion, except
when medical judgment decides that the abortion is necessary to
save the life or health of the mother. In other words, abortion is
legal in the United States without condition before the fetus is
viable. After viability, abortion is prohibited in some but not all
states except when the health or life of the mother is at risk.

At the same time, governments do have constitutional
authority to enact rules and regulations that may have the goal of
influencing abortion decisions by the woman or the doctor as
long as these are not an undue burden on the woman's right to
seek an abortion. In other words, state governments are permitted to enact requirements that may place hurdles in the path
toward abortion, such as twenty-four-hour waiting periods and
tests for viability, as long as they do not place a major, substantial, even insurmountable obstacle on the path.

The logic underlying this constitutional foundation is the
assumption that there are important differences in stages of pregnancy, specifically, before and after the fetus is viable. The point at
which a fetus is viable varies from pregnancy to pregnancy, but it
is generally thought to be after the twentieth week of gestation.
Experts disagree about the exact point of viability. The legal definition is that a viable fetus is capable of surviving outside the
mother's body on its own or with neonatal assistance but does not
include a specific week. Abortion law varies based on a division
of pregnancy into stages of "pre-viability" and "post-viability."

With this approach, current U.S. law is quite similar to abortion law in the eighteenth century when the Constitution was
drafted and ratified. Then, all the states had adopted English common law, which made abortion a crime only if it was performed
after quickening—what was also called animation. The definition
of a "quick" fetus was that the mother had felt it move inside her
uterus. The common law reflected an ancient debate (at least back
to the Greeks) about the moral status of a human embryo and
when the developing unborn child became possessed of a soul.
There was widespread belief that quickening, which takes place
in the second trimester of pregnancy, signaled that something
substantial had changed in the pregnancy, and the developing
fetus may be possessed of a selfhood, a soul, or even an independent life. At the same time, people believed that if they could see

the fetus at this stage, it would look more like a baby and less like a bunch of cells. Thus, it seemed to make sense to punish anyone who killed a quick fetus because it was similar to killing a baby.

The problem was that in those days there was no independent way to determine whether a woman was pregnant; the only one who knew was the mother and only when she could feel the quick movement. Therefore, anyone charged with performing an abortion—a very rudimentary and unpredictable procedure in the eighteenth century—could use the plausible defense that she did not know the woman was pregnant. Many women sought help when their periods stopped; the accused could claim he was just helping start the blocked "courses." In this era, therefore, people, especially women, considered the process of menstruation and early pregnancy to be very closely linked.

Both the eighteenth-century common law and the twenty-first-century constitutional law are periodic forms of abortion law: the law regulates abortion based on stages of pregnancy, either before and after quickening or before and after viability. Such periodic laws are found in a number of other countries, such as France and Austria (see Chapter 3). The other type of abortion law is conditional. Typically, in conditional laws abortion is criminalized except in certain conditions of pregnancy, such as to preserve the health of the mother, if the fetus is deformed, or if the pregnancy is the result of rape or incest. In the United States, the law allows states to enact conditional laws that come into force only after viability. Most countries have similar conditional limits on abortion in later stages of pregnancy. In the United States, as we see in the next section, a successful campaign in the nineteenth century changed the rather liberal common law to criminal laws with very limited conditions that remained in place until the *Roe v. Wade* decision in 1973.

Criminalization: The Nineteenth-Century Debate

When we talk about criminalization, what we mean is that governments declare that it is a crime to perform abortions or to help someone else perform them. In fact, under common law abortions after quickening were crimes. Yet there was a period of early pregnancy when performing an abortion was legal. Until the mid-

1800s, abortions were readily available. Women could perform them on themselves, and there were many practitioners who would help them. Most of these practitioners had little training; they learned through folk medicine or midwives and wise women. Others peddled herbs and concoctions that had little effect (see Mohr 1978). In the early days of the republic, these practices were tolerated primarily as "women's business." When the government tried to prosecute an abortionist, juries regularly acquitted because there was no way to prove the defendant knew the woman was pregnant and because there was widespread sympathy for those who found themselves in the predicament of needing to seek an abortion. Many believed they were helping poor and unfortunate girls and women to resolve a difficult situation.

James Mohr's book *Abortion in America* is the primary resource for those who want to learn about the process of criminalization in the nineteenth century. (However, for an alternative view, see Olasky 1992.) The process was gradual and followed changes in the economy, society, and especially, the practice of medicine over the 100 years. The issue of abortion practice and what to do about it became a public problem about mid-century. Before that there was a slow increase in writings about abortion; doctors especially began to document that abortions were not a sort of rare last resort for the desperate poor. More and more women were getting them, and they were women of the "respectable" white, Protestant, middle class. Abortion had also gradually become a business, and advertisements marked the commercialization of what was apparently a lucrative practice.

Abortion was not a practice dominated by physicians, as it is today. Back then, doctoring was not a "profession" in the sense that there were rules and regulations limiting who could practice. Some physicians were trained—although training was quite rudimentary by today's standards. Scientific knowledge was also rudimentary, but these physicians claimed they were the experts. The 1840s were not far removed from the days of barber physicians or patients being bled, and formally trained physicians had to compete with many other practitioners for patients and for status. For many of the trained physicians, or "regulars" as they were called, no issue demonstrated the problem of their profession better than abortion. Anybody could and did use all manner of means to end pregnancies; because of the law that reinforced the doctrine that abortions before quickening were not killing a human being but solving a female problem, the regulars could do nothing about it.

The social and economic modernization of the United States brought increasing attention to standards of education and the professions. To promote these ideas, professional organizations appeared, and the regulars formed the American Medical Association (AMA) in 1847. From the beginning many of the members called for change with respect to abortion. They claimed that their scientific knowledge completely refuted the idea that there were fundamental differences between quick and not quick pregnancies. The embryo and fetus were essentially the same throughout the pregnancy. Further, they argued that the reason there were so many abortions was that women were ignorant; they did not have this knowledge of fetal development. It was the doctors' responsibility to remedy this ignorance by declaring that all abortion killed human beings and prohibiting abortion except to save the life of a pregnant woman.

In 1859, the AMA enacted a resolution to that effect:

Resolved, That while physicians have long been united in condemning the act of producing abortion, at every period of gestation, except as necessary for preserving the life of either mother or child, it has become the duty of this Association, in view of the prevalence and increasing frequency of the crime, publicly to enter an earnest and solemn protest against such unwarrantable destruction of human life.

Resolved, That in pursuance of the grand and noble calling we profess, the saving of human lives, and of the sacred responsibilities thereby devolving upon us, the Association present this subject to the attention of the several legislative assemblies of the Union, with the prayer that the laws by which the crime of procuring abortion is attempted to be controlled may be revised, and that such other action may be taken in the premises as they in their wisdom may deem necessary.

Resolved, That the Association request the zealous co-operation of the various State Medical Societies in pressing this subject upon the legislatures of their respective states (reprinted from Dyer 1999, 14–15).

This resolution reflects the official concern with "saving human life" and "sacred responsibilities," but there was another motive in the campaign against abortion: eliminating competition from the "irregulars." Providing help to women seeking abortions was big business, and it kept those the regulars called "quacks" in business. Criminalization would deny the competition business. Thus, prominent physicians contacted their friends in the state legislatures and urged that they not only prohibit the quacks from performing abortions but also develop licensing requirements to deny the irregulars the right to practice any medicine without proper credentials.

The debate over abortion policy began in the 1840s (although some states changed their laws as early as the 1820s) and continued until 1900. In this public debate, physicians led the way, defining the issue of abortion as first a moral one and second a question of health, science, and medical standards. What was exceptional about the debate was that these often competing ideas were intertwined. The doctors defined abortion as a crime (despite the law at the time) that killed human life—a moral stance. But at the same time they placed themselves as the saviors of that life—their sacred duty—through their scientific knowledge and expertise. They saw their duty to persuade the public, and especially women, that even tiny embryos were human lives, not some blockage of menstrual flow.

In the 1870s, doctors got a substantial boost in their campaign from the antiobscenity movement led by Anthony Comstock of New York. In those days, many leaders considered sex and childbirth to be inseparable and guided by religious moral principles. Thus, growing interest in contraception and the public discussion of abortion led Comstock and his Committee for the Suppression of Vice to include them in their crusade against the moral degradation of society. Comstock successfully lobbied Congress in 1873 to pass the Comstock Act, which made importation, trade, and commerce in "obscene materials" federal crimes. Among the materials defined as obscene were information and materials that induce abortion. Comstock also made it his business to arrest abortionists by masquerading as a poor husband looking for remedies to his wife's "problem." Comstock had the support of evangelical reformers and allied with some feminists in the social purity movement. He brought important resources to the physicians' campaign.

In contrast to today's abortion politics, in those days two perspectives were not part of the terms of debate in the state legislatures: that of the women's movement leaders and that of the

Roman Catholic Church. The feminists said little about abortion, but they tended to condemn it as evidence of the way men and male lust victimize women. Generally, women's rights advocates, such as Elizabeth Cady Stanton and Susan B. Anthony, viewed the women who sought abortions as desperate because their husbands took little heed of the effects of frequent pregnancies on their health or the well being of the family. The way to prevent abortion was for men to exercise sexual restraint and to adopt the moral standard of purity they placed on their wives. To the nineteenth-century feminists, abortionists were another class of men who preyed on women. Later in the century "voluntary motherhood" became their cry. Recall that in this period contraception was primitive (abstinence being the most reliable), married women had few legal rights, marital rape was permitted under common law, and both abortion and pregnancy were routinely life threatening. To their advocates, the status of married women would improve if abortion were suppressed.

Similarly, quiet were voices from the Roman Catholic Church. Although today the official view of church history is that the Roman Catholic Church has always condemned abortion, formal church policy dates only to the late nineteenth century. In the abortion conflict, different sides select different parts of church history to support their contemporary points of view. It is more accurate to say that, like others, Catholic theologians wrote tracts about abortion, but there was no official church doctrine. Some turned to St. Augustine, who maintained that the soul enters the body only after it is formed—at 40 days of gestation for males and 80 days of gestation for females. Before that point, presumably, abortion did not kill a human being. Not surprisingly, the pronouncements of theologians and church leaders fit the knowledge of the time. The view that abortion before quickening was acceptable because there was no child formed until then also fits the Augustinian pronouncements.

The distinction between the ensouled (animated) and the nonanimated fetus began to lose support among Catholic theologians as early as the seventeenth century, yet it was not until 1869 that Pope Pius IX made it official, declaring that the embryo was a being with a soul from conception and abortion was a sin leading to excommunication. Another papal decree in 1884 declared that abortion, even to save the mother's life, was prohibited among Catholics. Some of the same social and scientific changes that influenced physicians likely also had an effect on church leaders, but until the early twentieth century, the church did not take a position on the public debate about abortion policy in the United States.

From 1820 to 1900, abortion prohibition proposals were on agendas of state legislatures. Before the AMA set out on its quest for criminalization, states had begun to adopt statutes, putting the common-law rules into their law codes. By definition, common law is not in a code but is found in the accumulated case law of England. William Blackstone prepared a summary in the 1700s that was often consulted, annotated, and reprinted. To make their laws clearer, U.S. lawyers urged states to enact legislative statutes to give the law formal legitimacy. Most of these maintained the features of the common law: abortion before quickening was not criminal, and a woman receiving an abortion was immune from prosecution. The AMA resolution and lobbying activities occurred at the end of what Mohr (1978) calls a transitional phase between the 1840s and the 1860s. After the 1860s, states came into line with the AMA plan and prohibited abortion from conception on; threats to the mother's life were the only exception. In 1873, the federal Comstock Act prohibited information and materials on abortion to be distributed through interstate commerce and mail. By 1900, all states had dropped the quickening distinction, revoked women's common-law immunities from prosecution (both the woman and the abortionist could now be sent to jail), and prohibited advertising of abortion services.

What had changed? Just about everything. The law was overturned—what had been legal, private, and available in 1800 was criminal, public, and penalized in 1900. The framework of abortion policy changed from the periodic model to an indications or conditions model—a severe model that allowed saving the life of the mother as the only defense for the crime. The terms of debate also changed. Before, when abortion was rarely discussed as a public problem, it was viewed as a symptom of poverty and victimization of the weak. By 1900, abortion was publicly defined as an immoral taking of a human life, an action so serious that it could take place only if the pregnancy threatened to take the life of another human being—the mother. Medical doctors were charged with the lofty responsibility of determining when that decision was warranted.

When the abortion reform movement rose up in the 1960s and 1970s, activists looked back at the history of the criminalization crusade. One of the issues in the 1960s was the dangers of illegal abortions. Activists learned that abortions had once been legal and abortions, like childbirth, constituted a real threat to women's lives. Looking at the methods of abortion used historically made it difficult for many to imagine that women in large numbers resorted to the procedure. Before the 1860s abortions were legal but not safe. Medical practice in the late nineteenth century improved dramatically, however. The invention of the speculum and the dilation and curettage, or D&C procedure; knowledge of the risk of bacterial infection; and new methods of anesthesia allowed for safe abortions for the first time. Yet just as these medical improvements came along, the legislatures and the doctors whose practice benefited moved to criminalize abortion. To many twentieth-century activists it seemed that the abuses women suffered from so-called back street abortionists were due to the fact that doctors had worked so hard to make it so.

One way to compare abortion policies across governments and over time is to classify them in terms of what some call the abortion triad (McBride Stetson 1996). Any abortion policy distributes powers and resources among the three main players: the government, the doctors with expertise to perform safe abortions, and women seeking abortions. The abortion policy from the eighteenth to the mid-nineteenth century in the United States empowered women. The state largely stayed out of the process of delivering abortion. Women were not only free to seek help from a variety of practitioners but they could also perform an abortion on themselves with no punishment. Further, they and only they could determine when criminal laws kicked in—at quickening. From the last decades of the nineteenth century, abortion policy shows an alliance between the government and doctors and the disempowerment of women. The new criminal laws had a loophole for acquiring an abortion—the life of the mother. Question: Who determined when that condition was met? Answer: medical doctors. Only they could judge when and if an abortion was warranted. Women who sought to end their pregnancies without a doctor's permission could go to jail. The next section of this chapter briefly summarizes how women coped with the new triad and how it broke down under the pressures of social, medical, and economic change in the mid-twentieth century.

Reform and Repeal:
The Road to Decriminalization

As in the nineteenth century, the twentieth century saw enormous social and economic changes; medical technology was no exception. The success of the AMA's criminalization campaign had placed the medical profession firmly in control of the practice of safe abortion. Apparently, the major legal shift had little impact on women's desire for abortion. Women sought abortions and many doctors provided them. This became women's secret (Reagan 1998). The motives of those who promoted the criminal laws may have been to "protest against such unwarrantable destruction of human life" but in practice medical doctors had varying opinions about when abortion was warranted. All the laws had the exception for therapeutic reasons—to save the life of the mother—but whether any pregnancy posed such a threat was determined by the doctor alone. He could perform an abortion in his office or the patient's home and no one would know about it. Women quietly told their friends about those sympathetic doctors; men left the whole business to women to sort out. Kristen Luker (1984) calls this period the "century of silence." However, antiabortion doctors made some attempts to expose their more liberal colleagues. None of these moved the issue to the public agenda for long.

As in the 1830s, the increase in abortion rates in the 1930s started the process toward new policy debates on the issue. The Great Depression of the 1930s took an enormous toll on families. People faced with extreme poverty became desperate to find ways to avoid bringing more mouths to feed into the world. At the same time, medical advances had greatly reduced the risk that pregnancy would lead to death; women began to seek to end pregnancies for other reasons. By this time, abortion procedures were conducted in hospitals, rather than doctors' offices. Some doctors began to stretch the therapeutic exception to include social conditions of the pregnancy, but most would not. Women increasingly sought solutions that were unsafe and ended up in hospitals, where many died. During the 1930s, as many as 17,000 women are estimated to have died each year (out of 800,000 abortions) from botched abortions (Garrow 1994, 272). In the hospitals where they worked, doctors saw first hand the effects of all these trends.

One response to the situation was that the police and prosecutors began to crack down on doctors and others who appeared to be performing abortions outside the law. Another was for hospitals to establish committees to oversee both doctors and patients; these were intended to bring an impartial judgment to the doctor/woman decision making that had characterized the early 1900s. Others reacted by thinking of ways to prevent abortion through family planning. Court decisions in the 1930s had overturned those aspects of the Comstock Act that prevented doctors from prescribing contraceptive devices such as diaphragms. In the early 1940s, Margaret Sanger's American Birth Control League changed its name to Planned Parenthood Federation of America (PPFA) and intensified its campaign to expand contraceptive information and use to prevent abortion. At the same time, Dr. Alan Guttmacher called for liberalization of the law at a Planned Parenthood meeting in 1942.

The nineteenth-century abortion laws had always caused some discontent, but most trace the origins of the movement to reform the law to a 1955 Planned Parenthood conference. It is understandable that this organization provided an arena for doctors and lawyers to discuss the abortion issue and express concern about the laws. Doctors and lawyers had been discussing the problems in professional journals for several years. They soon realized that if anything was going to change it would be necessary to bring the issue to a public agenda—that is, to awaken public opinion to the need for reform. When that time occurred in the 1960s, reformers were already prepared with a model reform statute that would answer all the concerns doctors and lawyers expressed.

In 1959, the American Law Institute (ALI) outlined a model that, in effect, would amend criminal laws to expand conditions for legal abortion. According to the proposal "A licensed physician is justified in terminating a pregnancy if he believes that there is a substantial risk that continuance of the pregnancy would gravely impair the physical and mental health of the mother or that the child would be born with grave physical or mental defects or that pregnancy resulted from rape, incest, or other felonious intercourse." (quoted in Davis 1985, 260). In the United States, then, abortion reform meant a slight increase in the number of indicators that would permit legal abortion while keeping most abortions criminalized. Many doctors agreed with this approach. Guttmacher and others in New York formed the

Association for the Study of Abortion in 1960 to try to drum up support for the reform.

At this time, most people in America had no idea that there were groups working to change abortion laws, that is, until two events brought the issue to public attention and the national agenda (from where it has not receded). In 1962, Sherri Finkbine, a mother of four, discovered that the sleeping pills her husband brought her from England contained thalidomide—a tranquilizer that causes terrible birth defects. (Thalidomide had not yet been approved for use in the United States.) She and her doctor quietly scheduled an abortion in an Arizona hospital on a Monday. On the Sunday before the procedure, Finkbine called an acquaintance in the news business and suggested she might warn others about the dangers of thalidomide. The next day Finkbine's scheduled abortion was headline news. As a result of the publicity, the hospital canceled her abortion, and she had to go to Sweden for the procedure. The national media picked up the story, focusing on the problems faced by women carrying deformed fetuses. Support for those women took on steam in the next year when a rubella epidemic (a form of measles that also causes birth defects) occurred. The spin in the media was that perhaps the nineteenth-century laws were too strict and out of date given all the social and medical changes in the twentieth century. The change in public opinion necessary for the abortion reform advocates to form a viable movement was finally underway in the early 1960s. Most professional organizations of doctors, lawyers, and health workers endorsed the ALI reform.

With the attention to proposals for limited reform, new voices joined the debate. Proposals for repeal of state criminal laws, not simply reform, arose. Some came from the ranks of the reformers in the law and medical communities. Changes in contraceptive laws had an impact on their views. In 1965, the Supreme Court ruled in *Griswold v. Connecticut* (38 U.S. 479, 1965) that states could not criminalize contraceptive use by married people because such laws interfered with their rights to privacy in their decisions and behavior with respect to sex and procreation. It seemed logical to many that laws that made it a crime for a woman to end a pregnancy would also interfere with her privacy. Many from population, family planning, and health organizations who had campaigned for reform now began to propose that states repeal their laws altogether. Some vowed to take the campaign nationally, holding the First National Conference on

Abortion Laws in 1969 in Chicago. At that conference, a few prominent leaders formed NARAL—the National Association for the Repeal of Abortion Laws.

Activists in California played an important role in developing the argument for repeal. This stemmed from their realization that the conditional ALI reform merely gave doctors a few more legal justifications to perform abortions. But those reasons—mental health, fetal deformity, and pregnancy by rape and incest—were only a very tiny percentage of the reasons women sought abortions. Such a reform would not decrease dangerous illegal abortions. And why should a woman have to prove she is crazy (to two psychiatrists) just because she does not want to be pregnant and bear a child for her own reasons? These ideas led women to see that the state was forcing them to remain pregnant against their will or face dangerous procedures. This was "compulsory pregnancy."

One who developed these ideas was Patricia Maginnis, who early in the 1960s had formed the Citizens' Committee for Humane Abortion Laws. Her claim was that abortion was a woman's business—and the government should have no control over this decision. Her demand previewed the mobilization, just a few years later, of the new feminist movement to the cause of repeal. At its second national conference in 1967, the newly formed National Organization for Women (NOW) endorsed repeal. But the real energy for the repeal campaign came from the more informal Women's Liberation Movement groups such as New York City Redstockings and the Chicago Women's Liberation Union. Black feminist groups joined the cause as well. All feminists advocating for repeal based their claims on women's own experiences as revealed in speak-outs and small group meetings, forming an ideology that linked the question of abortion to the lives of all women. To them, criminal abortion laws were a manifestation of the male medical establishment's control of women and their bodies. To repeal these laws would liberate women to control their own bodies. Slogans such as "My Body Belongs to Me" and "Get Your Laws Off My Body" went straight to the point. Black feminists told their stories of black women who sought abortions being forced to undergo sterilization as a condition. The feminist demands became: "Repeal all anti-abortion laws! No Forced Sterilization! No Restrictive Contraceptive Laws!"

Activists in the movement for repeal used a variety of tactics in their efforts to change the laws nationwide. They used conventional approaches by lobbying state legislatures and filing

lawsuits to have nineteenth-century state laws declared unconstitutional. The feminists, especially, used nonconventional tactics. Consciousness-raising groups—which were an essential
feature of the larger women's liberation movement—encouraged
women to learn about their bodies and to develop the self-confi-
dence to confront the doctors who had life-or-death authority
over their reproductive lives. Some of the groups took direct
action, by setting up self-help feminist clinics, referral services
for abortions inside and outside the United States, and even
learning how to perform early-pregnancy abortions—the famous
"Jane" in Chicago is an example (Kaplan 1996). In 1970, tens of
thousands marched in Washington, DC, and San Francisco in
huge demonstrations for their goals. Most scholars agree that the
mobilization by the feminist movement in the late 1960s and
early 1970s turned the reform movement into an abortion rights
movement (e.g., Staggenborg 1991). At the same time, the feminist activism for repeal became the foundation for the women's
health movement that has accomplished a revolution in women's
health care (Morgen 2002).

By 1971, a majority of Americans supported legalization; by
early 1973, a stunning 57 percent of Americans, including 54 percent of Roman Catholics, agreed that the abortion decision should
be left to the woman and her doctor (Gallup poll quoted in Garrow 1994, 539). At this time there was little organized opposition
to the new abortion rights movement. Most of the opposition in
the states came from Roman Catholic doctors and other professionals, largely taken off guard by the speed with which the
reform and then repeal bandwagon grew. Black nationalists
opposed both liberal birth control and abortion services for black
women, claiming it was part of a long-standing effort by the white
establishment to reduce the size of the African-American population. Still, although the opposition was weak and the repeal
movement growing, many state legislators were opposed even to
modest reforms of their laws, let alone repeal. As the pressure
grew, the antiabortion forces gained strength in some states where
they organized to maintain criminalization.

By far, the most significant accomplishment of the movement
for changing abortion laws was their success in dramatically
changing the terms of the debate on the abortion issue. Since the
late nineteenth century and even through the early years of the
movement for reform, the issue was considered a matter of negoti-
ating the rights of doctors to prescribe abortion for their patients.

Groups concerned about family planning and population control defined abortion as something that must be available to serve their larger goals of reducing unsafe illegal abortions, in the case of the family planners, and to allow parents to reduce the size of their families, in the case of the zero population activists. Neither of these perspectives was enough to light any fires for change in the population overall. What did get their attention was the unprecedented, but finally obvious, claim that abortion was a women's issue and legal abortion was a women's rights issue. In this, they shifted the terms of debate from a contest between doctors and the government to a rebellion of women against the medical/government establishment that controlled their reproductive capacity and their bodies. To them, criminal abortion meant compulsory pregnancy— a form of oppression enforced by the state. To the feminists of the early 1970s, by women controlling their own bodies through abortion on demand they would find liberation from that oppression.

By 1973, the campaign for changes in abortion laws had achieved legislative victories in fifteen states. Beginning with California, Colorado, and North Carolina in 1967, twelve states adopted some version of conditional abortion patterned after the ALI model statute (Arkansas, Delaware, Georgia, Kansas, Maryland, New Mexico, Oregon, South Carolina, and Virginia). Four states repealed their laws—Washington by referendum and Alaska, Hawaii, and New York by legislative action. By 1973, however, the opposition to reform was also gaining strength. In Michigan and North Dakota, referendums for abortion without condition up to 20 weeks of pregnancy failed by large margins. Lobbying efforts in state legislatures stalled, especially those promoting repeal. Because of the New York repeal, many women traveled there to obtain abortions through referrals operated by Planned Parenthood and other organizations. Perhaps this alleviated the pressure presented by illegal abortions. Pope Paul VI's 1968 encyclical, *Humanae Vitae* (Human Life), which reiterated the church's absolute opposition to abortion as well as all forms of contraception and sterilization, may also have stimulated the Roman Catholic Church to support a more organized antiabortion presence in the various state and local debates. In any event, although today some claim that the Supreme Court's 1973 decision interrupted a wave of abortion reform that would have solved the abortion conflict, there is little evidence to support that notion. Reform was quick at first, but it was very limited and did not answer demands from the feminist movement to get the government out of the business of regulating the practice of abortion altogether. At the same time, the speed of the early ALI-style reforms mobilized opposition to further reforms. In New York, the antiabortion forces were successful in getting the legislature to overturn repeal—which was only stopped by Governor Nelson Rockefeller's veto of the bill to recriminalize.

Reform and repeal activists in the legal profession were well aware of the difficulties of changing laws nationally by trying to pass reforms in fifty state legislatures. They opted for a litigation strategy that would at least undermine the nineteenth-century criminal laws and force the legislators to consider reform and at most extend the guarantees of privacy won in *Griswold v. Connecticut* to a woman's decision to seek an abortion. Thus, in the late 1960s and early 1970s, many cases were brought challenging the constitutionality of state laws. As litigation spread, the debate over the law spread as well and revealed a wide range of disagreement over the respective rights and responsibilities of government, physicians, and women. Opponents of legal abortion spoke for the rights of the unborn to prevail; many equated all abortion with murder.

Finally, the Supreme Court agreed to consider the constitutional issues and issued its decisions on the status of both the nineteenth-century criminal laws and the more recent ALI-style reform laws in 1973. These cases—*Roe v. Wade* (410 U.S. 113) and *Doe v. Bolton* (410 U.S. 179)—mark the end of the movements for reform and repeal and the beginning of the contemporary abortion conflict in the United States. The impact of these movements has been enormous and will be the subject of Chapter 2. Here we review the cases in terms of how they answered the various demands of the reform and repeal movements and how the opinions in the cases affected the terms of public debate on the abortion issue.

Roe v. Wade and Doe v. Bolton

Roe v. Wade was a challenge to the constitutionality of the criminal law that Texas enacted in the 1850s. The law prohibited anyone to "procure" or "attempt" an abortion except, based on medical advice, "for the purpose of saving the life of the mother" (410 US 113, 118). "Jane Roe" was the pseudonym for Norma McCorvey, who had sought an abortion because she could not afford to raise a child. Two feminist attorneys, Sarah Weddington and Linda Coffee, had been developing a plan to challenge the Texas law and recruited Norma McCorvey to be their "Roe."

Doe v. Bolton was a challenge to Georgia's 1968 reform that criminalized abortion except when the pregnancy endangered the life of the mother, there was grave fetal deformity, or the pregnancy was the result of rape. The Georgia reform, like many of the ALI-inspired laws, was very restrictive. In this case the Georgia legislature had added stringent and cumbersome rules including a requirement that the abortion decision must be approved by a committee and the medical judgment must be confirmed by two doctors in addition to the woman's own physician. "Jane Doe" was the pseudonym for Sandra Bensing, a victim of domestic violence, who, like McCorvey, sought the abortion because she could not take care of another child. She was represented by Margie Hames and other feminist attorneys who were keen to challenge the restrictive law because efforts to convince the Georgia legislature repeal the law had stalled.

The justices treated the two cases as a single decision, but it is *Roe v. Wade* that has become the most famous, the symbol for what is right and wrong (depending on your point of view) with abortion law in the United States. Justice Harry Blackmun wrote the decision, which was supported by seven of the nine justices. The feminists got what they wanted from both cases: both the nineteenth-century criminal laws and the 1960s ALI-inspired reform laws were declared unconstitutional violations of the right to privacy as outlined in the precedent *Griswold v. Connecticut* 8 years earlier. Although the term "privacy" is not mentioned in the Constitution, justices in these and other cases have recognized that the Constitution does guarantee areas or zones of privacy and that personal privacy, especially, is a fundamental right. What the justices did in *Roe* was to rule that "a woman's decision whether or not to terminate her pregnancy" is in one of those zones of privacy where the government cannot interfere. Included in that zone was also the physician's right to practice medicine. Most of the U.S. state laws at the time prohibited abortions and thus invaded, unconstitutionally, that zone.

At the same time, the Court acknowledged that the right to make the abortion decision was not unlimited, because the state (government) has legitimate interests in regulation and in protecting the fetus. These interests—the woman's, the physician's, and the state's protection of the fetus—seemed to be irreconcilable. The difficulty in finding a compromise among these interests had stymied peaceful reform in many state legislatures since the mid-1960s. To reconcile these interests, the Court divided pregnancy into trimesters marking the changes in the growing fetus and the complexity of abortion techniques. As pregnancies progress through 40 weeks, the fetus gets closer to viability, and abortion procedures become increasingly dangerous to the woman. Based on this framework, the Court issued constitutional guidelines to the states:

Before the beginning of the third trimester, the state may not prohibit abortions; the woman's decision with her doctor is in the zone of privacy and is paramount. After the beginning of the third trimester, the "State in promoting its interest in the potentiality of human life may, if it chooses, regulate, and even proscribe, abortion except where it is necessary, in appropriate medical judgment, for the preservation of the life or health of the mother." In addition, the state may enact regulations after the first trimester in "ways that are reasonably related to maternal health" (410 U.S. 113, 164). What this means is that state governments *may* but are not required to prohibit abortions in the late stages of pregnancy.

The immediate effect of these rulings was that most states had to revise their statutes to get them in line with the Supreme Court's guidelines. But most realized these were just the first of many cases that would be necessary to determine the limits of state power in this area, a process of litigation that continues as legislatures test the limits of the case law. The content of the decision had a great impact on the abortion conflict. As we have seen, before the 1960s the abortion issue was a medical issue in official debate, placed in the hands of doctors to decide within limits set by state governments. In the 1960s, many new views came to the fore and competed for attention. In succession, people argued that abortion law was a public problem because of illegal abortion; limits on medical professional judgment; the need for ways to plan families and limit population growth; invasion of personal privacy; women's rights to control their bodies; and threats to the humanity of the fetus, a person due constitutional protection. Not all of these perspectives could become part of the official terms of debate.

The *Roe* opinion set forth the new terms of debate. The abortion issue was to be a question of the rights to privacy of women and their doctors against the government's interest in protecting potential human life—the fetus. No longer a medical issue, abortion became a privacy issue related to a fundamental right to decide whether to bear a child and the reasonable limits on that right to protect both the woman and the unborn child. The Court ruled that abortion pertains only to private morality and that the state could not promote one view over another of, for example, when human life begins. "We need not resolve the difficult question of when life begins. When those trained in the respective disciplines of medicine, philosophy, and theology are unable to arrive at any consensus, the judiciary, at this point in the development of man's knowledge, is not in a position to speculate as to the answer" (410 U.S. 113, 159), As to the question of fetal personhood deserving protection under the Fourteenth Amendment, the Court ruled "the word 'person' used in the Fourteenth Amendment does not include the unborn" (401 U.S. 113, 157).

The new U.S. abortion law shifted the balance of power significantly in the abortion triad—women, physicians, and government. Before, the state had empowered doctors to control the decision making about abortion with restrictions. For the most part, they were largely unfettered by state interference until the early years of the reform movement. After 1973, however, the Constitution, as interpreted by the Supreme Court, empowered women, along with doctors, to make decisions about abortion. The government lost authority to make even the most limited restrictions on the abortion decision for the first six months of pregnancy.

After *Roe:* Pro-Life and Pro-Choice Movements Face Off

According to sociologists, a social movement happens when "ordinary people join forces in contentious confrontation with elites, authorities and opponents" (Tarrow 1994, 1). This refers to collective action—through groups and organizations—bound by common purposes and solidarity through recognition of common interests. Movement thinkers construct collective action frames as a way of defining their common purposes. They use these frames to mobilize support, organize activists, and communicate with the public. After a brief review of the movements' origins, the following sections describe the collective action frames of the pro-life and pro-choice movements as presented by writers and activists claiming to speak on behalf of the movement. The frames are presented as though they were coming from pro-life and pro-choice spokespeople. People use a variety of terms to identify the movements in the abortion conflict, depending on their perspective (such as proabortion, antiabortion, antichoice). Here we use the terms used by the activists themselves.

Pro-Life Movement

Origins

In the debates leading up to *Roe v. Wade,* antiabortion individuals and groups opposed efforts at reform and repeal. But it wasn't until after *Roe* that a pro-life movement mobilized. Before *Roe,* Catholics had taken the lead in testifying against reform and repeal. The Vatican's renewed interest in the issues of contraception and abortion as signified by *Humanae Vitae* encouraged clergy to speak out. After *Roe,* the church hierarchy and organizations on behalf of official doctrine began to take a more active role in leadership in reaction to legalization of abortion. However, Catholics were by no means in agreement on how to proceed or even if it was appropriate for the church to be active in the political arena.

But a movement needs more than leaders and doctrine from on high. It needs "ordinary people." In her study of pro-life activists in California in the late 1970s, Kristin Luker (1984) found that many were "stunned" by the Court's decision to declare an unborn child a nonperson under the Constitution. Many said they had never considered that this was possible. In fact, they had assumed that everybody agreed with them that an embryo was a human being from conception and equal to all other human beings. Luker also discovered that most of the post-*Roe* activists were married women with children who lived in traditional marriages and did not work outside the home. By deciding that women's choices came first, even if that meant that women could decide to get an abortion for convenience, the Court undermined the value of mothers putting their children ahead of their own lives.

Some other forces were at work in building the pro-life movement. In the 1970s, some conservatives in the Republican Party saw an opportunity to recruit supporters for their candidates if they could link economic conservatism to social conservatism.

This New Right worked closely with leaders of evangelical churches, including Pat Robertson and Jerry Falwell. The fundamentalist and Pentecostal religions strongly opposed abortion; Republican strategists promoted an antiabortion platform and candidates in the Republican Party to attract the support of these groups that had typically stayed away from politics. Legalization of abortion without condition was a threat to their fundamental values, and the effect was to politicize religious faith. From their perspective, fundamental beliefs were under attack, so evangelical Christians became fully committed to fighting the evil of abortion.

Pro-Life Collective Action Frames

Abortion is the murder of an innocent human being. This is so because from the moment the sperm fertilizes the egg—conception—a human being exists, even though it is just one cell. We know that conception creates a human being in two ways. First, from the Bible we know God creates life by bringing the sperm and egg together. Everyone can see the law of God in nature's law. God created everything to have a purpose. In his plan, men and women marry and have sexual relations. The purpose of those relations is to procreate—to create a new life that is a gift from God. It is evil to destroy that precious gift through abortion.

Second, even people who are not religious know that human life begins with conception. Advances in genetic science prove that at the moment of conception, a new human being exists with all the genetic information that he or she will have when reaching maturity. The fertilized egg is very tiny, but it is an independent life. No real difference exists between that one cell and an adult human. Killing a human being is wrong; that is a value everybody accepts. Because abortion kills an unborn human being, abortion is wrong by definition (Beckwith 1993).

The current law is nothing more than abortion on demand. Women have no limits on their "rights" to kill their babies at any stage. Even after viability, the courts have allowed for an exception for health. This exception is always interpreted so generally that just about any reason can be related to a woman's health. *Doe v. Bolton* defined health as including: "physical, emotional, psychological, familial, and the woman's age—relevant to the well-being of the patient. All these factors may relate to health." This health exception can justify anything. So, the law legalizes killing human beings—children.

This "slaughter of innocents" has been like the Holocaust. Since *Roe v. Wade* a million babies a year have been killed in the abortion factories—that's more than 35 million children! An unborn baby is a person, just like her mother, and she has to be treated equally. A woman does not have a "right" to kill her baby; doctors don't have a "right" to kill babies. Babies have rights to life. Abortion takes the life of another, and it is never, never justified. Even when it may occur to save the life of the mother—if both would die otherwise—it is an evil.

This plague of abortion is the mark of a society that has lost its way: it treats children like garbage. It has come about because of the so-called sexual revolution; abortion is almost a sacrament of that revolution. Sex has been completely separated from its purpose, which is to create life. Our sex-saturated society teaches kids that sex is for fun, for pleasure, for self-expression, or for conquest. Abortion is a no-fault sex insurance policy. This has made a mockery of any attempt at maintaining strong families—the love and responsibility people have toward each other. Now society is full of rampant individualism. If you get pregnant or if your girlfriend gets pregnant—just get rid of it! The abortion holocaust is part of the growing culture of death. If it is okay to kill an unborn child, why not kill sick people, old people, or the handicapped? They have no more "right" to live than unborn children.

Our opponents—the proabortion people—claim that women have the right to control their bodies. They do, but they do not have the right to kill their babies. The law now allows self-indulgent women to do anything they want and to go to the abortion factory just for convenience. These women deny their bodies and the wonderful capacity to nourish life that God has given them. They also deny the life path that will give them the most joy and will make the best contribution—that is to marry and have children. Most women agree with this at heart; they don't want to kill their babies. Once they learn that their little embryo dances in their womb, has a beating heart, has its own blood and organs, feels pain, and suffers terribly from abortion, they want to do the right thing.

Many of our opponents claim they are feminists, but they do not work for the best interests of women. Our opponents want to deny that they are women and to live like men. The true feminist is pro-life and realizes abortion is really a threat to women, not a choice. Proabortion people focus on autonomy and individual choice; but this view denies the fact that humans have to live in relationships to survive, and the most important relationship is the one between parent and child. "A woman, involuntarily pregnant, has a moral obligation to the now-existing dependent fetus whether she explicitly consented to its existence or not" (Callahan 2001, 171). Women have the moral obligation to use their life-giving potential. Today, abortion practices often victimize women who are pressured by men or even their own families to kill their babies. They have lifelong guilt that destroys their health and even their lives; many turn to crime and drug addiction. Abortion has to be halted to protect both women and the children they bear.

Finally, the *Roe v. Wade* decision must be overturned. If not, we must amend the Constitution to protect unborn life. *Roe v. Wade* is one of the worst Supreme Court decisions ever. Even those who are not religious or as passionate as others about protecting unborn children find this case to be deplorable. The activist, liberal judges on the Court created a so-called right to privacy out of thin air! Nothing in the Constitution suggests that governments have to stay out of matters relating to sex and procreation. This is "legislating from the bench" of the worst kind. The last time the Court tried something like this in the name of individual rights was when it said slavery was okay because people had a right to own slaves and do what they wanted. The government couldn't interfere.

Apparently, some of the judges who signed on to *Roe v. Wade* thought they were helping settle an issue. Some claimed that the legislatures were making a mess out of the efforts to change abortion laws. But what they did was to make the whole thing much worse. They launched the culture wars that have rent our society. They deprived pro-life people from having any say at all in the law and took the issue out of the legislatures. This is not a compromise: it is dictating one theory of life—that a woman has the right to make any choice she wants about her baby—on all the rest of us who think unborn babies are sacred.

Pro-Life Framing Tactics

Collective frames are "meaning makers." Their goal is to construct reality in such a way that they will mobilize supporters of movements and defeat their enemies. Some tactics of the pro-life collective action frames are worth pointing out.

1. Portray the fetus as a little human. The frames rarely if ever use the term "fetus" or "embryo." It is nearly

always unborn child, human being, human entity—"a new tiny individual with its own genetic code" (Beckwith 1993, 42).

2. Refer rarely to woman or mother as a whole body but to the womb, not uterus. Isolate the fetus from the mother's body through ultrasound images and language that portrays the unborn child in "space" or a "cradle."

Pro-Choice Movement

Origins

The advocates for liberal abortion laws had already formed a social movement before the decision in *Roe v. Wade*. Originally, the leaders for reform were doctors, lawyers, and professionals associated with population control and family planning. The rise of the women's liberation movement gave these leaders the "ordinary people" who mobilized to gain repeal of the old criminal laws. By the early 1970s, many organizations from the women's rights movement, sometimes referred to as the "older branch" joined to support the idea that women should have the right to choose whether or not to have a child.

Immediately after the *Roe* decision, there was some slump in the activity of the pro-choice organizations while, one suspects, they enjoyed the unexpected triumph of their goals and their frame of the issue in the courts. But they soon began to pick up the banner when faced with the immediate pro-life efforts to amend the Constitution to change the Court's decision. They also saw the mobilization of many individuals and organizations throughout the country to overcome the sudden legalization of abortion nationwide. NARAL led the way; its first action was to change its name to reflect the new challenge. It became the National Abortion Rights Action League in 1973 pledging to "develop and sustain a constituency which effectively uses the political process at the state and national level to guarantee every woman in the United States the right to choose and obtain a legal abortion" (quoted in Wilder 1998, 79).

Pro-Choice Collective Action Frames

The issue of abortion affects every woman because women are the ones who give birth. Unlike men, they cannot walk away from a pregnancy; each pregnancy not only affects a woman's body but also her life. Because pregnancy has such a major effect on women's lives, it is essential that women be able to make the decision to become pregnant and to terminate a pregnancy. When women are unable to get safe and legal abortions, it means that if they are pregnant against their will, they are forced to remain pregnant—what some have called "compulsory pregnancy." For many women, finding out they are going to have a child is a joyous event. But for others, it is a tragedy—the end of their hopes and desires. Because it is their bodies and their lives at stake, they must have the choice.

It is not just a question of legal abortion; it is a matter of reproductive freedom and liberty. Legal abortion does not guarantee freedom if there is no information or services for contraception. Freedom includes contraception but also the right to say no to sex. It includes safety from forced sterilization but also access to surgical sterilization if desired. It means the right to have children and raise them with sufficient child care, health care, education, and income so they won't be in poverty. Although much of the pro-choice movement's political activism focuses on abortion laws and practices, the overall goal has a much broader context of bearing wanted children and raising them to be happy and healthy citizens.

We wish we could spend more time on the larger reproductive freedom issues, but we are aware that *Roe v. Wade* and the legalization of abortion are under assault from the antichoice forces. *Roe* is the law of the land. The antichoice people think they know better and do not have to respect what the Court ruled. They want to turn back the clock to a time, not so long ago, when desperate women resorted to the humiliation of illegal abortions. In those days, many young women were ignorant about birth control; when they found themselves pregnant they would get into bad marriages and be subject to frequent pregnancies; their lives—from their education to their maturity—were cut short. They were children raising children. Others sought illegal abortions in terrible conditions, and thousands of women died from the butchering.

The antichoice forces want to make all abortions illegal, which will make women suffer more. Criminalized abortion laws don't eliminate abortions; they never have and they never will. Women will continue to seek abortions—in other countries, in back alleys, from friends—or they can try to cause themselves to miscarry. Many of these procedures will mean women will end up in hospitals with damaged uteruses and life-threatening infections. Those who want to make abortions illegal want to put their moral views about human life into the law. In fact, theirs is a minority view. A majority of Americans want to keep abortions legal. In addition, despite what our opponents say, most religions, even the Catholics, have pro-choice traditions (Maguire 2001).

Our opponents want to impose an absolute "moral" standard that the fertilized egg is more important than the woman who conceives it. They dismiss any complications or tragedies that result from this rule. In fact, matters of sex, contraception, pregnancy, and abortion are complex. Real women, and their families, face such problems every day: through ignorance, failed contraception, economic deprivation, and victimization. Women need all the resources possible to be able to make good decisions about their bodies and their lives. Making them into criminals will not help them or their children.

Trusting women to make decisions about their pregnancies is our bottom line. Women are moral agents, and they are capable of making complex decisions. In addition, women may not agree with the moral stand taken by our opponents. In fact, many people believe there is a difference between a fertilized egg in the body of a woman and a child who has been born. To treat them as equal is to ignore the woman's body and her life altogether. We staunchly oppose this position.

We are convinced that our opponents have an agenda even larger than reversing *Roe v. Wade* and criminalizing abortion. They want to eliminate contraception as well. Through some clever twists in definition, they claim that all contraceptives, except condoms and diaphragms, are actually abortifacient—that is, they stop a pregnancy. The trick is that they do not discuss pregnancy but talk about conception: they say the fertilized egg is a human being. But there is no pregnancy until the fertilized egg attaches itself to the wall of the uterus and begins to draw nutrients. Doctors can only tell if a woman is pregnant after implantation. This other definition is just a way to claim that contraceptives—which are officially opposed by many in the so-called pro-life movement—can be criminalized along with abortion.

Pro-choice is the real "pro-life" movement (Page 2006). We believe contraception use can prevent abortions and must be not only encouraged, but also supported by the government. We also believe sexuality is a value that should be nurtured to achieve intimacy and pleasure. Our opponents follow the dictates of the

Roman Catholic Church that all sex outside of marriage is wrong and that the purpose of sex is procreation. They believe nothing should be permitted to interfere with this view. The crusade to criminalize abortion is just the first step in a campaign to attack contraception and, ultimately, sex itself. By this, they will have accomplished the primary goal: to force women to be dependent, to limit their lives to bearing children, and to control women's lives and choices.

Pro-Choice Framing Tactics

The collective action frames of the pro-choice movement are shaped by the fact that they are in the form of responses to the frames of the opponents in the pro-life movement. Some of these tactics include the following:

1. Portrayals of the hardships of individual women with problem pregnancies in the old days before legalization and in more recent days because of problems of access. In this they seek to undermine the absolute assumptions of fetus = human being; abortion = murder.
2. Combat pro-life efforts to eliminate images of woman from the debate on abortion. Pro-choice frames claim that equality for zygotes means turning women into incubators. At the same time, they use medical terms like zygote, embryo, and fetus, never terms such as baby or unborn child.

Frames and Framing: Tools for Understanding Abortion Debates

The next chapter describes the range and depth of the abortion conflict in the United States by tracing several policy debates from the early 1970s to the present. A policy debate is a structured discussion that takes place in public arenas for the benefit of policymakers in government. Usually these debates focus on a particular proposal for a law; at other times the debates may pertain to the general approaches to public problems. On the agenda of U.S. federal and state governments are several issues that provoke debates that don't go away. Even though from time to time some government entity—a legislature or a court—makes a formal decision, the debate is not out of the picture and comes back. As long as there are substantial disagreements among groups with sufficient resources to make their views known, such debate will continue over new proposals as well as old proposals that are revisited. The abortion conflict is just this type of conflict. The question is firmly on the government's agenda, powerful activists who are interested in the issue disagree on what the issue is about and how to solve it, and the government has thus far not found a solution that will send the parties home.

Policy debates occur in arenas. Most policy arenas are attached to government institutions at the federal and state levels, such as legislatures, bureaucratic agencies, the courts, or the executive leaders. The arenas are large enough to encompass the expression of views by media, formal organizations, and mass publics. But individuals and organizations, as well as policymakers, are the major participants in these arenas when issues they are interested in or have responsibility for come up. Think of them as "policy actors." They could be spokespersons for movement groups like NARAL and the National Right to Life Committee; they could also be legislators and public intellectuals, for example. Their give and take on a topic reveals several things of interest in trying to understand what is going on. We can make sense of what they say by using the idea of "frames." We have already discussed collective action frames of social movements in which they present their comprehensive view of the problems and their solutions. Two other kinds of frames are important: strategic frames and issue frames.

Strategic frames show the way policy actors present their claims and goals for the policy debate. They usually consist of two types of statements. One is a definition of the problem showing there is something wrong and why government should act to fix it. This is sometimes referred to as the "diagnosis" part of the frame. The other part is the solution offered to the problem: what should be done, sometimes called the "prognosis." For social movements such as pro-choice and pro-life, strategic frames are excerpts from the more comprehensive collective action frames. However, the movement leaders adjust their frames to fit a particular policy debate and specific proposal. At times, for example, the pro-choice movement may choose not to emphasize a woman's right to control her body and instead talk about the dangers of criminalizing abortion. The latter frame may be more effective in winning support.

Issue frames show how the policy actors who are regular participants on the issue see the problem and solution. Often the issue frame is in the form of a confrontation. For example, we have seen that *Roe* established an issue frame that defined abortion as a question of women's privacy against the state's legitimate interest in protecting fetal life. So *Roe* not only settled, for a time, the policy outcome of the abortion repeal/reform campaign, but it also officially stated what the terms of debate about abortion would be: a matter between a woman and her doctor except for the period after viability. After that, the goal of the pro-life movement was to change that issue frame by presenting its own strategic frame about abortion. Before too long, the dominant issue frame changed and the issue was defined as a conflict between women's right to privacy and the right of the fetus to life.

As you can see, the goal of many activists is to have their diagnosis and prognosis of the matter, that is, their strategic frame, be adopted as the official frame by the policymakers. A lot is at stake in these frames. Probably most evident is that the decision that results from a policy debate stems directly from the way the issue is defined by the policymakers. If a prognosis is ignored, there is little chance activists will get what they want. Equally important, however, is that the issue frame has a profound effect on who gets access to the policy arenas. By defining abortion as a medical matter in the nineteenth century, for example, women had no claim to be consulted or have a voice on the question of legal abortion because it was not "about them." However, when the repeal movement successfully claimed that abortion was a woman's issue and pertained to her rights and privacy, women were now part of the debate and guaranteed a place at the table. In the next chapter we will follow the developing issue frames in various abortion debates stopping to note the official actions (cases, statutes, orders) along the way.

References

Beckwith, Francis J. *Politically Correct Death: Answering the Arguments for Abortion Rights*. Grand Rapids, MI: Baker Books, 1993.

Blackstone, William. *Commentaries on The Laws of England:* in four books by William Gladstone. New York: Harper Bros, 1872.

Callahan, Sidney. "Abortion and the Sexual Agenda." In *The Ethics of Abortion: Pro-Life vs. Pro-Choice,* 3rd ed., edited by R. M. Baird and S. E. Rosenbaum, 167–178. Amherst, NY: Prometheus Books, 2001.

Davis, Nanette J. *From Crime to Choice: The Transformation of Abortion in America.* Westport, CT: Greenwood Press, 1985.

Dyer, Frederick. "Horatio Robinson Storer M.D. and the Physicians' Crusade Against Abortion." *Life and Learning IX,* 1999. www.uffl.org/vol%209/dyer9.pdf (accessed 11/10/06).

Garrow, David J. *Liberty and Sexuality: The Right to Privacy and the Making of* Roe v. Wade. Berkeley: University of California Press, 1994.

Kaplan, Laura. *The Story of Jane: The Legendary Underground Feminist Abortion Service.* New York: Pantheon Books, 1996.

Luker, Kristin. *Abortion and the Politics of Motherhood.* Berkeley: University of California Press, 1984.

Maguire, Daniel C. *Sacred Choices: The Right to Contraception and Abortion in the World's Religions.* Minneapolis, MN: Fortress Press, 2001.

McBride Stetson, Dorothy. "Abortion Policy Triads and Women's Rights in Russia, the United States and France." In *Abortion Politics,* edited by Marianne Githens and Dorothy McBride Stetson, 97–117. New York: Routledge, 1996.

Mohr, James C. *Abortion in America: The Origins and Evolution of National Policy.* Oxford: Oxford University Press, 1978.

Morgen, Sandra. *Into Our Own Hands: The Women's Health Movement in the United States, 1969–1990.* New Brunswick, NJ: Rutgers University Press, 2002.

Olasky, Marvin. *Abortion Rites: A Social History.* Wheaton, IL: Crossway Books, 1992.

Page, Christina. *How the Pro-Choice Movement Saved America: Freedom, Politics, and the War on Sex.* New York: Basic Books, 2006.

Reagan, Leslie J. *When Abortion Was a Crime: Women, Medicine, and Law in the United States, 1867–73.* Berkeley: University of California Press, 1998.

Staggenborg, Suzanne. *The Pro-Choice Movement. Organization and Activism in the Abortion Conflict.* New York: Oxford University Press, 1991.

Tarrow, Sidney. *Power in Movement: Social Movements, Collective Action and Politics.* Cambridge, England: Cambridge University Press, 1994.

Wilder, Marcy J. "The Rule of Law, the Rise of Violence, and the Role of Morality: Reframing America's Abortion Debate." In *Abortion Wars: A Half Century of Struggle, 1959–2000,* edited by Rickie Solinger, 73–94. Berkeley: University of California Press, 1998.

2

Problems, Controversies, and Solutions

Introduction

The abortion conflict in the United States takes many forms. It is not a simple face-off between pro-life and pro-choice forces over whether abortion should be legal. That is one of the major clashes, to be sure, but there are many more manifestations of the abortion wars. This chapter will cover the range of topics that make up the abortion conflict and describe the arenas of these many battles. What are the participants fighting about other than *Roe v. Wade?* The list includes parental notification, clinic access, and all forms of government funding and support, and it extends to the personhood of the fetus, birth control, sex education, and embryonic stem cell research. The battles take place in federal and state courts, congressional committees, federal executive agencies, political parties, election campaigns, foreign policy and international organizations, as well as in clinics and doctor's offices. This chapter portrays the course of these disputes with special attention to the frames of the debates as well as the outcomes—who won, who lost, and the decisions to date. Given the persistence and widespread impact of the abortion conflict in American law, politics, and society, numerous authors have offered solutions to the problem. This chapter will conclude with summaries of several proposals inviting the reader to assess the feasibility and effectiveness of each.

Constitutional Legality of Abortion

The Supreme Court's decision that the Constitution includes a right to seek abortion was a tremendous shock to the opponents of abortion. Even before the pro-life movement mobilized, leaders sought to do whatever they could to put things back the way they were before January 23, 1973. When the Supreme Court, the highest court in the land, rules on the meaning of the Constitution, those who oppose its ruling have only two options. Neither is quick or easy. The first is to work to pass an amendment to the Constitution itself. The founders who drafted the document made it very difficult to change. It takes two-thirds approval of both the House of Representatives and the Senate and ratification by three-fourths of the states—thirty-eight state legislatures. There is another method—never used successfully—whereby two-thirds of the states would call for a convention to amend the Constitution.

The second option is a litigation strategy to convince the Court to change its ruling. This is difficult because of the importance of precedent or stare decisis in U.S. law. This means official interpretations of laws by the Supreme Court are the law of the land and all courts, including the Supreme Court itself, decide other cases that come before it following the way the courts did it before. Of course, the Supreme Court does occasionally overturn a precedent, but that is often many years after the initial decision. The justices accept that conditions and times change and that their rulings must also change. A major condition for overturning precedent is that the members of the Court have changed and the newer justices feel less bound by the decisions of their predecessors. At least this possibility was important as the pro-life movement developed a strategy to upend legalization of abortion.

Amending the Constitution

Before September 1973, in an immediate response to *Roe v. Wade*, members of Congress submitted eighteen proposals to amend the Constitution to supersede the ruling and a couple of regular bills to prohibit abortion (Packwood 1992). Some form of the Human Life Amendment has been introduced in every Congress to this day. These proposals have taken three forms:

1. to outlaw abortion directly except to save the life of the mother;
2. to extend the constitutional definition of person to all human beings from conception;
3. to give the states the power to criminalize abortion, the so-called "states' rights" amendments.

Most of the congressional consideration of these amendments took place in the 1970s and early 1980s. Congress briefly considered the amendments right after the *Roe* decision, heard presentations from pro-life and pro-choice advocates, but was reluctant to act. Anxious pro-life leaders even started a backup campaign in states to request a constitutional convention "for the sole purpose of proposing an amendment to the Constitution of the United States which would more effectually protect the lives of unborn human offspring." (Florida State Senate, 1979)

Pro-life activists kept pressure on Congress all through the 1970s. They staged an annual "March for Life," where they would distribute roses to all members as symbols of the babies they claimed were murdered by legal abortion. When Republicans took the Senate and the presidency in 1981, pro-life supporters held key positions in both the administration and the Senate committees. Senator Jesse Helms's bill got the first attention: "The paramount right to life is vested in each human being from the moment of fertilization without regard to age, health, or condition of dependency" (97th Cong., 1st Sess. [1981]). This was followed by Senator Orrin Hatch's constitutional amendment proposal: "A right to abortion is not secured by this Constitution. The Congress and the several States all have the concurrent power to restrict and prohibit abortions" (97th Cong., 1st Sess. [1981]).

The extensive hearings on the Helms bill gave leaders of both the pro-choice and pro-life movements the opportunity to present their views on abortion and whether it should remain legal. But the most important effect was to focus the debate on the status of the fetus. When is a fetus a human being? Or, as the question is more commonly reported in the press, When does human life begin? To address this difficult and some say eternal question, the pro-life strategy was to claim that it is a scientific rather than a moral question, and science can provide the answer. They wanted that answer to be codified into law.

According to the pro-life frame, modern biology had discovered that every human life begins at the moment of its conception. Through genetic research, scientists can trace to fertilization the stage at which the cells form an individual with complete genetic information to become a member of a particular species. The tiny conceptus formed by sperm and egg of a mouse becomes an individual mouse. Similarly, the conceptus of the sperm and egg of human parents becomes a human being—a member of the human species. Because of ultrasound technology scientists can observe a child as he or she develops.

> "The baby plays, so to speak, on a trampoline! He bends his knees, pushes on the wall, soars up and falls down again. Because his body has the same buoyancy as the amniotic fluid, he does not feel gravity and performs his dance in a very slow, graceful, and elegant way, impossible in any other place on the Earth . . . We now know what he feels, we have listened to what he hears, smelled what he tastes and we have really seen him dancing full of grace and youth. Science has turned the fairy tale of Tom Thumb into a true story, the one each of us has lived in the womb of his mother" ("When does human life begin?" Testimony of Jerome Lejeune at the U.S. Senate Judiciary Committee 1981; available at www.californiaprolife.org/abortion/whendoes.html).

Thus, it is no longer a matter of opinion, or moral ambivalence—we know that actual human life begins at conception and the unborn baby is equal to all other human beings.

Since the pro-life strategic frame moved to the terrain of science, the pro-choice advocates moved to counter their claim by appealing to scientists such as Leon E. Rosenberg, a professor of genetics at Yale. He did not quibble with Lejeune's observations, but rather pointed out that the phrase "actual human life" used by the pro-life advocates is not a scientific term. It is true that the fertilized egg is a potential human life, but when it becomes "actual" is not determined by science. Some say it is conception, others say when there is brain function, and still others when the fetus moves and looks like a baby or when it can live outside the uterus. The embryo development process is continuous. No definite break exists where one can say it is actual human life after and not before. Although there are scientists that argue the other side, they are not doing it as scientists but are expressing their religious views: "I maintain that the concepts such as humanness are beyond the purview of science because no idea about them can be tested experimentally" (Rosenberg testimony, reprinted in *The Miami Herald,* May 3, 1981, p. 1).

Although the Judiciary Committee recommended both pieces of legislation to the full Senate, neither the Helms bill nor the Hatch amendment passed. Senator Bob Packwood filibustered until both of them were withdrawn. The Hatch amendment did get a full floor debate in 1983, but it was defeated 49–50. The pro-life forces could, nonetheless, claim a victory. They were successful in bringing the issue of fetal personhood—recently ruled by the Supreme Court as a nonlegal matter—to the highest levels of government. The result was that the frame of the abortion debate, which the Supreme Court established as a matter of the privacy of woman in *Roe,* now became a matter of the personhood and thus life of the fetus versus the privacy of women.

Changing the Court

On the problem "What to do about *Roe?*" the activists from the pro-life movement have agreed on the diagnosis that abortion on demand is wrong. They have not always agreed on the solution or prognosis, however. While some were promoting a constitutional amendment, others took a more political approach. They mobilized their followers to become active in the Republican Party, adopt a pro-life plank in the Republican platform, and give their support to Ronald Reagan for president. When Reagan took office in 1981, he was indebted to the pro-life movement and responded to their demands to appoint pro-life justices to the federal courts, especially the Supreme Court. At the same time, pro-life activists worked in various states, lobbying legislatures to enact restrictions that would take away convenient access to abortion services. When these restrictions were challenged by pro-choice organizations, each case provided an opportunity for the courts to whittle away *Roe* as well. From 1973 until 1989, the Court struck down most of these restrictions and reiterated its ruling that states could not interfere in any way with women's right to privacy in securing abortions. However, after 1981, the majorities supporting *Roe* got smaller and smaller.

In 1981, President Reagan fulfilled his campaign promise with his first nomination to the Supreme Court—Sandra Day

O'Connor—who became the first woman to serve. Her answers about abortion cases in the hearings were vague, and most assumed she would support the pro-life position. And indeed, in the first abortion case after her appointment, she joined the minority opposing the *Roe* position. In *City of Akron v. Akron Center for Reproductive Health* (462 U.S. 416, 1983), the Court struck down five sections of a city ordinance, including requiring parental consent and a twenty-four-hour waiting period, because they restricted a woman's right to obtain an abortion. In her dissent, O'Connor said that given the changes in technology and improvements in neonatal care, *Roe's* trimester approach was "on a collision course with itself." The antiabortion tally on the Court was now three.

In 1986, Reagan nominated Justice Antonin Scalia to replace William Rehnquist, who was named Chief Justice after Chief Justice Warren Burger's resignation. Although Scalia had a well-known antiabortion record as an attorney and as an appeals court judge, his nomination provoked little controversy. But his influence was soon felt. In *Thornburgh v. American College of Obstetricians & Gynecologists* (476 U.S. 747, 1986), the Reagan administration, for the first time, presented a brief asking the Court to reverse its position in *Roe v. Wade*. They made the point that they were not opposed to a constitutional right of privacy as put forth in *Griswold v. Connecticut* but that abortion was a special case because it involved the killing of an unborn child and was not a matter of privacy. The *Thornburgh* decision invalidated several regulations aimed at discouraging women from choosing abortion as interfering with their rights. But this time the majority was 5–4, showing that the Court was one heartbeat away from reversing the *Roe* decision and issue frame.

The next opportunity to staff the Supreme Court came quickly in 1987. The pro-choice movement had certainly counted the votes, reviewed the Scalia confirmation process, and raised the stakes for the next candidate. Reagan nominated Robert Bork, someone who was not only antiabortion but who had written extensively against the rulings in *Griswold* and *Roe*, and against the entire idea of a constitutional right to privacy. The battle during the confirmation hearings was intense and widely publicized (for more on the Bork nomination see Gitenstein 1992; Craig and O'Brien 1993). The abortion issue was at the center of the debate because Bork would replace a "swing" justice, Justice Lewis Powell, who had supplied the crucial fifth vote to protect the right of abortion.

The Senate refused to confirm Bork by a vote of 52 to 48. President Reagan then nominated Anthony Kennedy who won confirmation with little trouble. Kennedy, like Scalia, is a Roman Catholic; thus, the pro-choice forces feared that the pro-life forces had finally achieved the majority that would undo *Roe*. Attention turned to the next challenge to state abortion restrictions to make its way to the Court for review: *Webster v. Reproductive Health Services* (492 U.S. 490, 1989). At issue was another set of hurdles women would have to face to obtain services. In addition, the state decreed that life begins at conception and that "unborn children have protectable interests in life, health, and well-being."

Once again the Justice Department, this time in the administration of President George H. W. Bush, urged the Court to overturn *Roe v. Wade*. Unlike *Thornburgh*, however, this time there was also a majority in favor of sustaining the restrictions in the Missouri statute: Rehnquist, Scalia, Kennedy, and O'Connor as well as Justice Byron White; all but White were Reagan appointees. Yet they did not speak with one voice about the status of the parent decision *Roe v. Wade*. Scalia clearly asserted that he wanted to overturn the previous ruling and invited direct challenges from the states. O'Connor continued to question the trimester framework but said there would be time to reconsider *Roe* in the future. But the dissenting justices, especially Justice Harry Blackmun, who had written the *Roe* decision, sent out the warning that "a plurality of this Court implicitly invites every state legislature to enact more and more restrictive abortion regulations in order to provoke more and more test cases, in the hope that sometime down the line the Court will return the law of procreative freedom to the severe limitations that generally prevailed in this country before January 22, 1973." He went on: "I fear for the future. I fear for the liberty and equality of millions of women who have lived and come of age in the 16 years since *Roe* was decided" (492 U.S. 490, 539).

The *Webster* opinions stimulated both pro-choice and pro-life groups into action. Pro-choice groups sent out the word that the Supreme Court now had the dreaded pro-life majority. The next case could easily rob women of their rights. The pro-life groups doubled their efforts at the state level, competing to pass a state law that would directly challenge the *Roe* decision by outlawing abortion in the first trimester of pregnancy. This was not all that easy, however. The *Webster* ruling had mobilized many to the pro-choice organizations because their leaders claimed that abortion would soon become a crime. For the first time, many women were aware that they could lose rights they had come to take for granted.

Pro-life activists, for their part, got busy in the states, pushing sympathetic legislators to enact laws that would violate the *Roe* ruling to give the Court a chance to do what some justices promised—overturn *Roe v. Wade*. This was more successful in some states than others. Utah, for example, passed a very strict conditional law—abortion only for health of woman or fetal deformity. In Florida, Montana, Alaska, and California, on the other hand, pro-life proposals ran counter to guarantees of privacy in the state constitutions. Governors in Louisiana and Idaho vetoed new restrictions as probably unconstitutional. Pennsylvania's governor, Robert Casey, signed that state's new law, which put in place five new hurdles for women seeking abortions:

- Special informed consent of woman seeking abortion
- Parental consent for minors with judicial bypass
- Notification of husband
- Compulsory antiabortion lecture by a doctor 24 hours in advance of the procedure
- Stringent reporting requirements for facilities providing abortions

A challenge to this Pennsylvania law by Planned Parenthood made its way to the Supreme Court. And it was this case—*Planned Parenthood v. Casey*—that many thought would be the crucial test for *Roe*. This was especially likely when Clarence Thomas replaced Justice Thurgood Marshall—one of the *Roe* majority in 1991. Thomas was questioned during his confirmation hearings about his views on the abortion case, but he had no written record and claimed he had never discussed *Roe* with anyone. Nevertheless, because he was a conservative attorney appointed by the pro-life Bush administration, pro-choice activists counted the votes on the Court to add up to an anti-*Roe* majority for the first time.

Facing the inevitable, the attorneys for Planned Parenthood formally asked the Court to take the opportunity in this Pennsylvania case to either affirm the right to abortion as a fundamental constitutional right or overturn the *Roe* decision altogether. They wanted to confront what they feared might be a gradual chipping away of abortion rights. The Bush administration lawyers were not as keen to make this case the final test of *Roe*. One reason was their awareness of pro-choice strategy leading up to the 1992 presidential elections, where President Bush would be challenged by Governor Bill Clinton—a pro-choice politician. Pro-choice movement leaders had joined with allies in Congress to promote the Freedom of Choice Act (FOCA). If passed, this act would codify the ruling in *Roe:* "a State may not restrict the right of a woman to choose to terminate a pregnancy (1) before fetal viability; or (2) at any time, if such termination is necessary to protect the life or health of the woman." If the Court reversed its ruling about women's right to seek abortions, then they would push this act through Congress. They figured that there would be sufficient support once people realized that otherwise abortion would become criminalized again. They also planned to make this a major issue in the presidential campaign, especially if President Bush vetoed the FOCA.

Both sides looked to the Court's decision in the Pennsylvania case with anticipation and some dread. When the Court announced the outcome, neither side could claim a victory. Pro-choice was disappointed that the Court upheld all but one—the requirement of husband's notification—of the administrative hurdles and invited the states to enact more. Pro-life was unhappy that the Court did not overturn the *Roe* ruling; even more frustrating was that the plurality upholding it included Justice O'Connor, one of Reagan's appointees, and Justice David Souter, one of President Bush's appointees. Both sides publicly criticized the ruling. Perhaps that meant the Court had struck a compromise between the women's rights and liberty and the fetus's right to life. The ruling and the opinions were complicated. No opinion was signed by a majority of the justices, but there was an outcome:

1. A majority of the justices confirmed the Court's central ruling in *Roe v. Wade:* "a recognition of the right of the woman to choose to have an abortion before viability and to obtain it without undue interference from the state" (505 U.S. 833, 846).
2. A plurality of the justices agreed that the trimester framework was no longer in force. The place to draw the line with respect to states' power to prohibit abortion would be viability.
3. Justices agreed that prior to viability the state could put administrative hurdles in place as long as these did not

constitute an "undue burden" on a woman's liberty. "A finding of an undue burden is a shorthand for the conclusion that a state regulation has the purpose or effect of placing a substantial obstacle in the path of a woman seeking an abortion of a nonviable fetus" (505 U.S. 833, 877).

The *Planned Parenthood v. Casey* decision cooled the turmoil over *Roe v. Wade* for more than a decade. Pro-choice leaders pursued the FOCA, but many members of Congress did not want to go on record for a woman's right to choose. At the same time President Bill Clinton appointed two pro-*Roe* justices to the Court: Justices Steven Breyer and Ruth Bader Ginsburg. The movements went on to other debates until another pro-life president, President George W. Bush, took office in 2001. Activists calculated the ages of the justices, thinking about who would be likely to retire during the second Bush administration.

The Contemporary Debate over *Roe v. Wade*

In 2005 it turned out that one justice from each side of the divide—Justices O'Connor and Rehnquist—left the Court. The Senate Judiciary Committee held public hearings that drew wide attention because the nominees—John Roberts and Samuel Alito—once again, had the potential to shift the Court to an anti-*Roe* majority. Even before the new justices were confirmed, state governments were preparing to pass laws that would violate the *Roe* guidelines. The first to do so was South Dakota. The governor signed legislation in late 2005 that criminalized all abortions except to save the life of the mother.

Ever since *Roe*, the central goal of the pro-life movement has been to somehow override, with constitutional amendment, or overturn, through changes in the Court, this constitutional law. Today, 35 years after this decriminalization of abortion, the pro-life strategic frame focuses on the number of abortions that have occurred, saying that babies are dying, and they vow to protect babies from what they see as a grisly practice. Linking unborn or "pre-born" children with those who are born, they demand protection for all human beings. In addition, pro-life attorneys represented by Americans United for Life charge that the decision was an "unconstitutional usurpation of people's right to self-government."

While there remains widespread agreement among activists on the diagnostic pro-life frame, there is disagreement on the policy solutions, that is, the prognostic frame. Some pro-life activists follow the South Dakota approach—direct confrontation and an early ruling by the new Court. Others fear that this is premature because there is no guarantee that the Court, even with the new justices Roberts and Alito, will rule against *Roe*. And if they don't, there could be another reaffirmation like the decision in *Casey*. These pro-life organizations want to stay with the plan of pushing laws that make access to abortion services more and more difficult through regulations on clinics and administrative hurdles for patients.

The strategic frame of the pro-choice movement with respect to the status of *Roe* is that any ban on abortion is an attack on women's health. Activists vow to stand up for women's freedom and privacy, but emphasize women's health as the issue of paramount importance. They have long claimed that legal abortion is in jeopardy, and the pro-life campaign to make direct challenges to *Roe v. Wade* underscores the threat. The prognostic pro-choice frame shows a shift toward activism in the policy arenas in state legislatures.

The issue frame that dominates the debate over *Roe v. Wade* remains the question of whether the Constitution guarantees privacy to women and doctors in making decisions about abortion and how these rights can be balanced with the government's interest in protecting fetal life (McBride Stetson 2004). In the Court, the frame focuses on whether specific abortion regulations constitute an undue burden on women's liberty, especially with respect to their lives and health, and deliberations are limited to this rather narrow question. Thus, the frame favors the pro-choice position because it keeps the legalization of abortion itself off the table, but the pro-life attack on *Roe* is intended to change this frame to define the issue in terms of the equal personhood of an unborn child and the Court's powers, which would work against pro-choice goals.

The debate over the direct attack on *Roe* is still unfolding. The South Dakota governor signed a statute that criminalizes abortion in all cases except when the pregnancy is a direct threat to the mother's life. The statute declares that life begins at conception and that the "guarantee of due process of law under the

Constitution of South Dakota applies equally to born and unborn human beings, and that under the Constitution of South Dakota, a pregnant mother and her unborn child, each possess a natural and inalienable right to life" (South Dakota 2006, sec 1). Throughout the act the fetus is referred to as an "unborn human being." Persons who perform abortions may be prosecuted but the woman seeking the abortion may not.

Most observers expected that pro-choice organizations, such as Planned Parenthood and the Center for Reproductive Rights would immediately challenge the constitutionality of the statute, which is in direct conflict with current constitutional law. Instead, they first organized a campaign for repeal within South Dakota, which was successful in November 2006 elections. Repeal squashed this opportunity for pro-life activists to get a chance at the new Court. In the meantime, the annual legislative sessions in the states continue to be busy with abortion-related issues, considering new bans on the procedure, and national organizations are organizing state campaigns to resist these proposals.

State Regulation of Abortion Practice and Access

Ever since states were prohibited from criminalizing abortion in 1973, a central strategy of the pro-life movement has been to lobby states to enact laws that would limit the practice of abortion and women's access to the procedure. As we saw in the *Planned Parenthood v. Casey* decision, the Court has ruled such regulations to be constitutional unless they place an "undue burden" on women's liberty in seeking abortions. This section reviews the debates and outcomes relating to several of the administrative hurdles the states have enacted and concludes with a section on the major battle over clinic access and pro-life violence and militancy in the 1980s and 1990s.

Administrative Hurdles

From the beginning, pro-life legislatures tried to test the limits of *Roe v. Wade*. In the early cases, when pro-choice enjoyed a strong Court majority, the Court tended to see most of these requirements as designed to interfere unconstitutionally with women's privacy. But as time passed and the membership in the Court changed to reflect the pro-life perspectives of the administration and Congress, the hurdles passed judicial scrutiny.

Parental Notification and Consent

One of the first pro-life victories was agreement, even among many pro-choice legislators, that doctors should not perform abortions on minors (usually considered to be those younger than 18 years) without their parents at least knowing about it, if not consenting. While the motive of pro-life activists in promoting these requirements was to discourage or prevent minors from getting abortions, some framed the issue as a matter of parental rights and responsibility. Doctors couldn't prescribe an antibiotic to a minor without a parent's permission. They certainly shouldn't be performing abortions on children without their parents at least knowing about it.

Pro-choice activists countered that these laws deprived young women of their constitutional rights to privacy and equality. They were also a hardship for many girls from dysfunctional homes. How can a young girl tell her parents that she is pregnant and wants an abortion if the father of her child is her older brother or her own father? Other girls, they claimed, would be so frightened that they would seek illegal abortions or even try to abort themselves and suffer drastic health consequences. A strategic pro-choice frame in this debate usually included examples of individual girls who had suffered such a fate. One such story that gained national attention in 1990 was about Becky Bell who fled to another state when the Indiana law required her to gain consent of one of her parents. She got a botched abortion and died of infection.

In the end, the Court has been persuaded that both parental consent and notification laws are constitutionally permitted, as long as they provide the option to get permission from a judge for hardship cases, the so-called "judicial bypass." In 1979, *Bellotti v. Baird* stated: "We therefore conclude that if a State decides to require a pregnant minor to obtain one or both parents' consent to an abortion, it also must provide an alternative procedure whereby authorization for the abortion can be obtained" (443 U.S. 622, 643). Today a majority of states require some parental involvement for minors to get an abortion. All follow the Court's requirement to have judicial bypass procedures.

Some states, including California, Illinois, New York, Oregon, and Washington have no parental notification or consent requirements. Thus, minors from states with restrictions may travel, often with the help of friends and relatives, to those states to obtain abortions. To prevent this, the National Right to Life Committee has, since 2000, promoted the Child Custody Protection Act, which would make it a federal crime for anyone who is not the parent to transport a minor across state lines to obtain an abortion. The pro-life supporters argue that it is primarily adult men, probably the ones who impregnated the minors, who take the girls to get the abortions, thus circumventing the parental notification laws in place to protect those minors from victimization. The pro-choice groups oppose this bill because it hurts young women who may be victims of family violence or who, becoming desperate, obtain illegal abortions. The most effective argument has proved to be the warning that it would be grandmothers who are helping their granddaughters who would be arrested under this law. In fall 2006, Congress rejected this act.

Informed Consent

Another means of slowing down abortion practice promoted by the pro-life movement is to require women to receive counseling from doctors or others about the pregnancy, fetal development, or alternatives to abortion to be sure that their decision is based on complete information. Often this counseling is required at least twenty-four hours before the procedure, ostensibly to allow the woman to think about what she has learned, but also to add another hurdle that might deter her from proceeding. In some states the legislatures specify the information that the women must receive and when they do, in most cases state health departments provide a script to doctors. The Supreme Court has ruled that such requirements are not undue burdens and thus constitutional. In any event more than half the states mandate that women receive counseling before an abortion.

The pro-life people, not unlike the American Medical Association in the 1800s, argue that women who seek abortions are ignorant about the fetus as an unborn child. They are convinced that when women know about what kind of operation is involved, and its effects on the fetus and on themselves, they will be reluctant to choose to go ahead. They believe women are also unaware of the terrible psychological toll abortion has on women who have them, what some call a "postabortion syndrome." Pro-life promotes the use of "pregnancy crisis centers," which do not even mention abortion as a choice.

The pro-choice people respond that these requirements are a way to harass women who are facing the difficult decision to end their pregnancies and scare them away. In addition, there is some evidence, they claim, that in many states women receive incorrect information about fetal pain during abortion, the psychological effects of abortion on women, or the link to breast cancer. Further there is no scientific evidence that women who have abortions suffer psychological trauma any more than women who give birth or women in general. They criticize the increased federal funding of the pro-life crisis centers.

Spousal Notification and Consent

In the 1970s, the pro-life activists lobbied for regulations that required a woman, if married, to receive her husband's consent to obtain an abortion. They argued that the father has an interest in the life of his unborn child. The pro-choice response was that because pregnancy had a major impact on women's lives and health, a woman should not have to inform or gain the consent of anyone. The Supreme Court has agreed with the pro-choice position. In the 1970s, the justices ruled that because the only time the husband's consent would be significant would be to deny a woman the right to choose abortion, and because even the state did not have that authority, it could not give such an authority to a husband.

Another strategy was to promote spousal notification. Along with this, pro-life groups joined with father's rights groups that encouraged men to file restraining orders when they believed a woman was trying to terminate a pregnancy that they had fathered. None of these efforts was successful. In *Planned Parenthood v. Casey,* the justices rejected only one of the five administrative hurdles in the Pennsylvania statute: the requirement that a wife notify her husband before obtaining an abortion. The justices noted: "It is an inescapable biological fact that state regulation with respect to the child a woman is carrying will have a far greater impact on the mother's liberty than on the father's . . . The court has held that, when the wife and the husband disagree on this decision, the view of only one of the two marriage partners can prevail. In as much as it is the woman who physically bears the child and who is the more directly and immediately affected by the pregnancy, as between the two, the balance weights in her favor" (505 U.S. 833, 896).

Clinic Access

After *Roe v. Wade* most hospitals surrendered to pressures from the pro-life movement and stopped performing first-trimester abortions. For a long time, therefore, most abortions have been performed in clinics established for this purpose and in a few doctor's offices. Moving the practice to the private business sector also moved it into a public space—the marketplace—where those seeking abortions can be observed. Some leaders in the pro-life movement have long advocated a direct approach to stop abortions by harassing the clinics and their patients with the goal of shutting them down. In 1980, Joseph Scheidler formed his own organization, the Pro-Life Action League (PLAL), which would be devoted to direct action against clinics. His work inspired Randall Terry to form Operation Rescue, which took the tactics to new levels. While Scheidler was a former Roman Catholic priest, Terry mobilized his troops among the Christian fundamentalists forming a new wave of "Christian soldiers."

Operation Rescue proclaimed a war against what they called the "child-killing industry." Their mission was to rescue America from moral decline by preventing women from aborting their children. They compared abortion to the Holocaust. Their goal was to save lives, and their crusade was more important than any laws; they were following a "higher law," what they called "Bible disobedience." Their tactics included blocking access to facilities, conducting sidewalk counseling with clients to persuade them not to kill their babies, tracing license numbers and phone numbers of clinic visitors and confronting these women at home, and sending threatening letters and making phone calls to doctors and clinic personnel. To teach these tactics Operation Rescue ran training programs in Florida.

Clinic owners and personnel sought to fight back by forming alliances with pro-choice groups to protect their businesses and their clients. The pro-choice organizations went to court to seek injunctions against the antiabortion protesters. But the protesters were relentless in defying injunctions and often seemed to invite arrest despite facing fines and potential jail time. They challenged these injunctions in federal court claiming that the injunctions violated their First Amendment rights. In 1994, the Supreme Court ruled against the antiabortion protesters saying that an injunction limited their conduct, not their speech. In the same year, pro-choice activists also won a victory when Congress passed the Freedom of Access to Clinic Entrances (FACE) Act, which makes it a federal offense to use force or threats of force against an organization that provides reproductive services and counseling. Other pro-choice litigation efforts were not successful. The Supreme Court has ruled that neither the federal anti-racketeering nor the nineteenth-century Ku Klux Klan civil rights statute could be used to bring federal charges against the pro-life clinic obstructionists.

Operation Rescue soon faded from the scene, but the militancy they inspired did not. During the 1990s, a new wave of antiabortion violence arose, what pro-choice called "pro-life terrorism." Direct action took a deadly turn with murders and attempted murders of doctors and other clinic personnel, fire-bombing of clinics, anthrax and fake anthrax attacks, and all sorts of harassment (Baird-Windle and Bader 2001). What ideas justified such violence? Those who advocated and defended violence saw abortion as the devil's work that brought down the wrath of God on America. (Pat Robertson even blamed the terrorist attacks of September 11, 2001 on feminists and abortionists.) They claimed they were an Army of God waging war with the devil and fighting as Lambs of Christ (Mason 2002).

The turn toward deadly violence demanded responses from police and the courts, and eventually most of those who murdered doctors were arrested, tried, and convicted. One, Paul Hill, was executed by the state of Florida. The Army of God named him a martyr for Jesus. Although the incidence of bombings and attacks on personnel has declined, the pro-life campaign at clinics continues. The pro-choice movement is concerned that the patterns of intimidation have severely reduced the number of doctors trained to perform abortions and have kept others from staying in the practice. Some state legislatures continue to enact new regulations, including special building codes, to make it more and more expensive for clinics to stay in business. The result, some fear, will be that abortion will be legal but no one will be able to get one.

Government Support of Abortion

As part of their strategy to prevent as many abortions as possible, the pro-life movement has worked with their allies in Congress, Republican administrations, and state governments to eliminate any government support to women seeking abortions. Usually this means looking carefully at all funding of health care for the poor and government employees and through public health plans such as family planning services. The general pro-life argument is that many people who oppose abortion do not want their tax dollars to pay for or facilitate abortion. This frame has limits because the government does many things some tax-payers don't like and could hardly justify not funding all of them. In framing the proposals, pro-life activists seek to define the problem as the government using tax dollars to kill unborn human beings. Pro-choice leaders respond by asserting the government's responsibility to ensure the equal rights of all citizens.

Hyde Amendment

Since 1976, Congress has attached the so-called Hyde Amendment, named after Republican Congress member Henry Hyde of Illinois, to the annual appropriations bill that provides funds for the Medicaid program. Medicaid is the publicly funded health care program for the poor, that is, those on welfare—mostly women with children—or those who are destitute. It is funded jointly by the federal government and the states. The Hyde Amendment prohibits the use of the federal funds to pay for abortions of women who receive Medicaid, even though the program is required to pay for "medically necessary" procedures. Thirty-two states follow the federal standard and provide Medicaid abortions only for life endangerment, rape, or incest (South Dakota pays only for life endangerment and a few states also pay for fetal abnormality). That leaves seventeen states that use Medicaid funds to pay for medically necessary abortions.

The amendment always provides an exception for those few cases where pregnancy threatens a woman's life. Sometimes Congress also allows funding for abortions when pregnancy is due to rape or incest, although these exceptions are considered difficult to administer. Those supporting the Hyde Amendment claim that abortion is never medically necessary unless a woman's life is threatened. Pro-life activists have been suspicious of exceptions for medical necessity or maternal health ever since the Supreme Court's ruling in *Doe v. Bolton*, which gave a very liberal definition of these exceptions. Further, some believe women can lie about the rape/incest exception and oppose this exception as well.

The amendment was introduced for the first time in 1974, right after the decision in *Roe v. Wade,* and was part of the pro-life campaign to reverse the effects of legal abortion. Pro-life activists took their efforts to the state level as well, proposing that states also ban the use of their Medicaid funds for abortion. The debates brought the place of the fetus as a human being to the fore, making it part of the issue frame. This challenged the frame put forth in *Roe v. Wade* that abortion is a matter of women's privacy to decide. Pro-life proponents asserted that the time for a woman to control her body is before conception; after conception she becomes the natural protector of her unborn child. They portrayed women who seek abortions as selfish, denying their offspring for their own convenience. In this, they did not recognize that the women who benefited from Medicaid were usually poor parents who received welfare to support their families.

The pro-choice opponents of the Hyde Amendment did not forget the poor women; they made them the center of their strategic frame during the debate. They argued that *Roe v. Wade* gave women a constitutional right to abortion. However, abortions cost money and women of means were better able to afford them than poor women. Denying them those funds, they claimed, was an unconstitutional discrimination against the poor. Without Medicaid, poor women would be forced to bring children into the world they could not raise and who would sink their family further into deep poverty. Or they would have to take desperate measures seeking cheap abortions from back-alley practitioners with all the attendant risks of infection and death. And all this, because they were poor! President Jimmy Carter made pro-choice advocates furious when he responded to their claim that cutting Medicaid support was unfair to the poor. "There are many things in life that are unfair," he responded (McBride Stetson 2001).

The pro-life campaign to cut Medicaid support was successful. The federal government has not paid for Medicaid abortions since 1976, except to save women's lives. Many state governments enacted similar restrictions. At first pro-choice forces fought back by challenging these laws in federal courts, claiming that they unconstitutionally discriminated against the poor and violated the intent of Medicaid to pay for health care for the poor. The Court rejected their claims, ruling the Hyde Amendment a constitutional use of government spending power and ruling that there is no constitutional responsibility to pay for health care. Further, poor women have no constitutional right to have an abortion—

only to seek abortion. Denying them Medicaid funding does not interfere with this right to seek abortion. Finally, the Constitution does not prohibit governments from passing laws that affect the poor differently (*Beal v. Doe* 432 U.S. 438, 1977; *Maher v. Roe* 432 U.S. 464, 1977 reviewed federal powers; *Harris v. McRae* 448 U.S. 297, 1980 addressed states' powers).

Pro-choice activists have not given up. Sometimes there is a glimmer of hope, as when President Clinton took the office in 1993. His first budget did not include the Hyde Amendment. In addition, he included abortion services ("medically necessary reproductive health services") in his plan for comprehensive health reform. Such actions mobilized the pro-life forces, especially the Christian coalition, to pressure legislators to oppose these measures. Again, they warned that the government was facilitating evil by requiring millions of citizens to pay for abortions, "forcing us to finance the deliberate destruction of human lives" (quoted in Hendershott 2006, 48).

When Henry Hyde retired from Congress at the end of 2006, the National Network of Abortion Funds launched a new campaign to repeal the restrictions on funding called "Hyde: 30 Years is Enough!" Women forgo food, security, and their possessions to pay for abortions or they are forced to continue pregnancies and stay trapped in poverty, they argue. "We call for full public funding of abortion as part of comprehensive health care for all, and support for low-income women to care for their children with dignity. We stand for reproductive justice, a world in which all women have the power and resources necessary to make healthy decisions about their bodies and their families" (www .hyde30years.nnaf.org/index.html).

Domestic and Global Funding Restrictions or "Gag" Rules

The questions at issue in funding restrictions come from policies first enacted in the Reagan administration in the 1980s. The federal government has, since the 1970s, funded private and public agencies that provide family-planning information and services to the poor. The law forbids these funds to be used to perform abortions for family-planning purposes. However, the family-planning programs are supposed to provide information to clients about their options. President Reagan used his executive authority to issue a rule that agencies receiving federal funds for family planning could not discuss abortion at all, even to give neutral information about options. They were only to discuss adoption or abstinence. Even if they received nonfederal funds, they could not use them for counseling either. Pro-choice activists labeled the policy a "gag" rule. They challenged the constitutionality of the rule, but the Supreme Court upheld it as a constitutional use of executive power to set guidelines on the expenditure of public funds (*Rust v. Sullivan* 500 U.S. 173, 1991).

President Reagan also ordered a rule pertaining to foreign aid, what pro-life activists call the Mexico City policy, after the Population Conference where it was announced in 1984. Pro-life advocates welcomed this policy, which banned U.S. aid to American and foreign family-planning organizations that provided abortions or abortion counseling or that advocated for legal abortion access anywhere in the world outside the United States. Reagan's rationale was that even if an agency involved in both family planning and abortion were given funding only for its family-planning functions, it would release funds within the organization for its abortion activities. The problem with aid to family-planning organizations, he maintained, is that it is used to promote abortion as a form of birth control and amounts to taxpayer funding of abortion in foreign countries. Many countries, especially in Latin America, have laws criminalizing abortion; funding what pro-life activists call "population-control" organizations allows them to harass these governments to legalize abortion against the countries' cultural norms and traditions. These population-control organizations attack human life and human dignity by encouraging women to seek abortions that endanger their health. The prognosis in the pro-life frame is for the U.S. government to continue and expand the Mexico City policy.

The pro-choice movement frames this debate and policy as the "Global Gag Rule." The problem is the policy itself, which pro-choice activists see as a terrible blow to efforts of nongovernmental organizations (NGO) to improve the health and status of women around the world. Removing support for family-planning organizations and the education and services they provide leads to an increase in unwanted pregnancies and thus the number of abortions, many of which will be unsafe. For some pro-choice advocates, the policy is not only an antiabortion measure but an attack on family planning itself. The results can be tragic because family planning educates and empowers women to take better care of themselves, their families, and communities. It will also undermine efforts to stop the spread of HIV/AIDS because many of the NGOs that promote family planning also educate about and promote safe sex. Finally, the problem with the Global Gag Rule is that it impinges on free speech by penalizing groups for the counseling and information they provide; pro-choice activists argue that such a ruling would be unconstitutional if instituted in the United States (although this is probably not true). They want the government simply to remove the rule and commit U.S. resources and energies to advancing health and development through family planning.

The issue frame in the debate over domestic family-planning funds and foreign aid boils down to whether the United States should use financial resources to support family planning and women's health or prevent resources from being used to support abortion in this country and others. These rules are at the discretion of the president. In 1989, President George H. W. Bush retained Reagan's approach but President Bill Clinton reversed both policies in 1993. When Republicans took control of Congress in the 1995, pro-life legislators were unsuccessful in introducing legislation to reinstate Reagan's ban. Then, in 2001, immediately after his inauguration, President George W. Bush put the Mexico City policy back in effect but not the domestic gag rule. Since 2001, pro-life senators have introduced bills to reinstate the prohibition on funds for family-planning organizations that perform or counsel abortions but none have passed to date.

Other restrictions on government funds for abortion depend on the position of the president who is in office. Under the Reagan administration, for example, in addition to the restrictions on family planning funds and the Mexico City policy, there were prohibitions on funds for abortions for military personnel and dependents, in military hospitals, for federal employees, and for Peace Corps volunteers. When President Clinton took office, he reinstated abortions for military personnel and their dependents in military hospitals (although Congress reinstated the ban in military hospitals in 1995).

Abortion Procedures

Abortion procedures, for the most part, are medical matters outside the purview of public policy and thus are rarely up for debate. There have been two exceptions. The first, the so-called abortion pill, was developed outside the United States and like all forms of medication was subject to approval by the U.S. Food and Drug Administration (FDA) before it could be prescribed and sold. Pro-choice activists sought to bring the pill to the United States. Because the FDA is a government agency, it is subject to control by Congress and influenced by the president. The pro-life movement brought the other procedure, which they called "partial birth abortion," to the public agenda because they claimed it was not a medical procedure but a form of infanticide that was subject to criminalization by both federal and state governments. This section surveys the terms of debate and the fate of these two very controversial procedures.

RU-486—Mifepristone

The French government was the first to accept RU-486—the drug mifepristone—as an abortion procedure in the 1980s. Pro-choice Americans were very interested in the medication, which induced abortions in the first 7 weeks of pregnancy by pills rather than the surgical removal of a fetus. Roussel-Uclaf, the Swiss manufacturer of the drug treatment, was nervous about antiabortion activism from the beginning. And the pro-life groups made their opposition known from the start, threatening to boycott all Roussel-Uclaf products. At one point the company withdrew RU-486 from the French market until the French government ordered it returned.

Thus, Roussel-Uclaf had no plans to apply to the FDA to offer the drug in the United States. It took a long campaign led by the Feminist Majority Foundation and the Population Council to persuade the Swiss company to donate its patents to the Population Council in 1994, which allowed the council to make the application and conduct the necessary tests. At one point Lawrence Lader and his group, Abortion Rights Mobilization, sponsored their own clinical trials. For the pro-choice movement, it was important that this work went on under the Clinton administration because it was highly doubtful that the FDA would have welcomed their proposals under the first President Bush.

As expected, the debate over RU-486 was lively. Pro-choice advocates framed the issue as a major breakthrough in technology that would benefit women's health and their privacy. First of all, French women who had had abortions using RU-486 reported that it was much more natural and less traumatic than a surgical abortion. All a woman had to do was take two pills and then wait for a miscarriage that was very similar to their menstrual periods. Pro-choice activists also welcomed this pharmaceutical procedure because it could take place between a woman and her doctor, in the doctor's office. There was no need to go to a clinic, often surrounded by pro-life protesters. This, they hoped, would reduce much of the clinic violence in the 1990s.

The pro-life activists likened RU-486 to chemical warfare on the unborn, a form of baby poisoning. It's not just like a woman's period, they claim; it's killing a human baby. Looking at the procedure as simply a way of starting up menstruation trivializes the taking of an unborn baby's life. Another concern is that the procedure is not safe. It looked as if the FDA was rushing through the testing because they relied on the fact that the drug had been used in Europe. Finally, pro-life activists were worried that the "pill" would make abortion too easy, too convenient. You could have abortions in every bedroom, they said.

The FDA approved RU-486 for use in the United States in 2000, during the last few months of the Clinton administration. It has taken some time for doctors to be trained in its use and for women to learn about the option. Little information about the pill was in the public arena until 2006, when it was reported that four women had died of infections after taking RU-486. Although health officials pointed out that such infections occurred during miscarriage and childbirth and more had died who had never taken the abortion pill, pro-life forces moved to take advantage of the publicity. They sponsored "Holly's Law," named after one of the women who died. This bill would suspend the approval of RU-486. Pro-life advocates claimed that because the approval process in the 1990s was slipshod, RU-486 has not been definitively proved to be safe for women and more testing should be done.

Ban on Partial-Birth Abortion

In 2000, the Supreme Court gave pro-choice forces a policy victory by ruling that state laws banning the procedure called "partial-birth" abortion without an exception for the woman's health were unconstitutional (*Stenberg v. Carhart* 530 U.S. 914, 2000). This outcome was a direct result of pro-choice influence in bringing women's health into the issue frame of the debate (McBride Stetson 2001). In the early 1990s, the pro-life movement had developed a strategy to ban abortion procedure by procedure rather than launch a frontal attack on all legal abortion. Their success depended on gaining Republican control of the Congress and inserting a new frame that excluded women from the discussion. The pro-life strategic frame separated the fetus from the woman's body and presented the procedure as a form of infanticide performed by doctors. They accomplished this with their definition of the banned procedure as killing a baby outside the womb, a baby who would otherwise be born alive. Pro-choice activists, with the help of President Clinton, who vetoed all partial-birth bans passed by Congress in the 1990s, successfully reinserted women into the issue frame by focusing on the need for this procedure to preserve women's health. None of the bans enacted so far in the United States have allowed exceptions for a woman's health, only for her life. This includes the federal ban enacted in 2003 and signed by sympathetic President George W. Bush.

The Court's ruling did not end the debate, however, which has continued since 2000. Pro-choice activists try to challenge the pro-life frame that has proved immensely effective in attracting political and public support. Pro-choice activists claim that the term "partial-birth abortion" itself is misleading—a term manufactured by pro-life strategists to gain support but which in fact is not a medical term. This deception is intended to be a smoke screen that will hide the true motives of pro-life activists on this issue: to criminalize abortion procedure by procedure with the goal of making abortion unattainable in the United States. The bans are written in such general terms that they extend to more than one procedure and threaten safe procedures for second-trimester abortions. Pro-choice activists denounce the pro-life argument that the law bans just one procedure and that alternatives are available to women in need as a myth promoted to disguise the true goal of criminalizing any abortion practice.

To pro-choice movement actors, a "renegade Congress" in 2003 flaunted the Supreme Court by enacting a national ban without a health exception—the type of law already ruled unconstitutional (Center for Reproductive Rights 2003). Congress, based on a deluge of "legislative findings," claimed that a health exception is never necessary. The pro-choice frame charges that Congress has shown a complete disregard for women's health and medical judgment, pointing to the opposition of most medical associations to the federal interference in medical judgments represented by the law. Most voters oppose "abortion bans," they claim.

Pro-life strategic framing has changed little in the partial-birth abortion debate. Having defined the procedure as killing a "living baby" outside the womb, activists are content that most people will see graphic drawings of the procedure as infanticide, not really abortion. The child no longer resides in the mother and the horrible procedure kills a child just "three inches" from full citizenship and personhood. Pro-life activists warn their supporters not to be fooled by proabortionists' use of the term "dilation and extraction" or D&X, which is, they say, "pseudo-medical jargon"; partial birth is the term used by doctors. They go on to give "facts" about the situation: this brutal procedure is performed thousands of times each year in the United States, generally doctors oppose the practice, and the majority of these abortions are performed on healthy babies of healthy mothers. Most of these babies would live, they claim, if allowed to be born instead of brutally killed.

So, according to pro-life advocates, the pro-choice claim that these abortions are performed for health reasons is a myth. Quoting medical doctors and other health professionals they assert that performing a partial-birth abortion for health reasons is never necessary. They caution that the health exception is typically very broad, includes mental health, and thus can allow abortions at any stage. The frame asserts that convenience is the primary reason women and their doctors decide to perform partial birth "atrocities." It's time for the Supreme Court to treat human life with dignity by upholding the congressional ban.

The issue frame in the policy debate over partial-birth abortion procedures has remained unchanged since the mid-1990s: whether the ban limits infanticide or threatens women's health and fertility. For a time, the frame favored efforts by pro-choice advocates to eliminate the bans, but only by moving the debate to policy arenas in federal courts and away from state and federal legislatures. As stated earlier, Congress enacted a law in 2003 similar to the state laws already declared unconstitutional in 2000. The Planned Parenthood Federation and the Center for Reproductive Rights immediately challenged the new law. In October 2006, the Supreme Court heard the case on the constitutionality of the federal ban. In the presentations, the two sides switched roles in a way. At issue was the contention by the congressional majority that the exception for women's health is not necessary because partial-birth abortions are never medically necessary and other procedures are available. During the congressional debate, the pro-choice side claimed the procedures were rare, and the pro-life side said they were frequent and gruesome. Yet before the Court, the defenders of the ban said the procedure was rare and never necessary for a woman's health, and the plaintiffs claimed that the procedure was often used to protect the health and fertility of women with dangerous pregnancies.

In April 2007, the Court which now included the two new justices—Chief Justice Roberts and Justice Alito—appointed by President Bush with the support of the pro-life movement upheld the congressional ban on what it called the "intact dilation and evacuation" (Intact D&E) procedure by a 5–4 decision (*Gonzales v. Carhart* No. 05-0380 April 18, 2007). The majority opinion, written by Justice Anthony Kennedy, justified departing from the precedent in *Stenberg v. Carhart* by arguing that the federal law had remedied the vagueness found in the state laws the Court declared unconstitutional in 2000. There were two startling claims in the majority opinion that resonated in the pro-life/pro-choice debate. One was that, although the federal law banned a procedure with no exception for a woman's health, Congress acted within its constitutional authority because medical opinion was divided on the question of medical necessity. The other was that banning the procedure was not an undue burden on women's right to decide about abortion but in fact would protect women from the emotional effects of the procedure. Justice Ruth Bader Ginsburg's dissent called the majority opinion "irrational" with no saving explanation for the ruling. Her dissent focused on the Court's shift away from promoting women's reproductive rights and liberty.

The pro-life forces hailed the decision as a victory—the desired effect of appointing the new pro-life justices to the Supreme Court in 2005–2006. At the same time, some state right-to-life activists claimed the decision did not save a single life because it allowed other procedures. The pro-choice leaders were appalled at what they claimed was a stinging rebuke of women's rights and autonomy. At the same time, the immediate effects of the ruling on medical practice are likely to be minimal, given the small percentage of second trimester abortions and the loopholes in the decision. Further, the opinion confirms the precedent in *Planned Parenthood v. Casey* that the Constitution prohibits legislatures from placing undue burdens on the path for women seeking abortions. However, what is more significant for the abortion controversy is the extent to which Justice Kennedy and the majority adopted the pro-life strategic frames in their rhetoric. The Court gives Congress the authority to place moral concerns about a medical practice above health concerns. It adopts the argument that abortion is a threat to women's mental health promoted by the pro-life Justice Foundation. In addition, it refers to "abortion doctors" rather than obstetricians, the "unborn child" and "baby" rather than the fetus, and describes a still legal D&E as "ripping" the fetus apart. This shift in the issue frame of the abortion debate in the Court is likely to be the most important victory for the pro-life campaign.

Fetus as a Person

The debate relating to partial-birth abortion is part of a more general pro-life strategy to establish the independent personhood of the embryo and fetus. Schroedel (2000) makes the point that technically an unborn human organism is not a fetus until the fourth month of development. Before that, it is a fertilized egg, or embryo. But in general use the fetus can refer to the entire period of prenatal development. From the moment the *Roe v. Wade* ruling was known—that the fetus was potential human life but not a person in the meaning of the Fourteenth Amendment—pro-life activists have fashioned many ways of overcoming this denial of legal personhood. Pro-life activists have been helped in this goal by advances in prenatal technology since the 1970s. Today it is no longer necessary to imagine the fetus in the womb, the photographs and ultrasound pictures are part of everyday life. With these images, the pro-life leaders describe the fetus as a tiny person, a new individual human. In this view there is no difference between a fertilized egg and an adult human man or woman. They are just at different stages of development. In addition to such images, a branch of medicine has developed called "fetal embryology" where doctors treat fetuses as patients in a way that is separate from their treatment of pregnant women.

Debates over proposals to codify the personhood of the fetus separately from the personhood of the woman who carries the fetus began in earnest in the 1980s and have continued to the present. Pro-life advocates assert that since there is no difference between a single-cell embryo and an adult, a woman has no right to disregard the status of the fetus; instead, as a mother, she has the responsibility to be sure that her child is born in good health. The law should recognize the equal rights of the fetus.

Pro-choice advocates reply that the interests of a woman and her fetus cannot be separated because they are a biological unit. The fetus is not a separate being; it exists in the pregnant body of a woman and the woman must make decisions for both. The embryo is just a collection of cells, even though it has the potential to become a child. Pro-choice leaders call the pro-life campaign for the personhood of the fetus just another means of opposing abortion with the ultimate goal of having abortion declared illegal. If the fertilized egg is considered a legal person equal to the woman, then they think it would be impossible to sustain support for legal abortion.

Prenatal Drug Laws

In the 1980s, the media brought to light the growing incidence of babies born addicted to drugs because of their mothers' drug use. Widespread evidence indicated that use of "crack" cocaine had become an epidemic. Reporters told stories about the strength of these drugs and how addicted women would do anything to get more crack. They had sex, they had babies, and there was an alarming increase in drug-exposed infants or "crack babies." To many, the women themselves were responsible for this; they were depicted as heedlessly harming their own children.

Some state legislators filed bills to make such behavior a crime and put the mothers in jail. These proposals did not get very far because there was overwhelming evidence that incarceration would deter the women from seeking help and getting prenatal care and not help their babies. States began to enact other laws such as requiring drug tests of pregnant women receiving state assistance such as welfare, requiring drug treatment to collect welfare benefits, and declaring drug addiction to be a form of child abuse. Others opted for more service-oriented approaches such as expanding public education and drug treatment programs for addicts. Overall, the pro-life campaign has supported such laws and has been successful: Thirty-five states have some form of prenatal drug laws (Schroedel 2000). Only two are purely punitive against the pregnant woman. The others include public health approaches either alone or in combination with regulations on pregnant women receiving public support.

Pro-choice activists and feminists have been very critical of many of these laws, primarily because they are based on the pro-life frame that a woman's main responsibility is to protect her unborn offspring and in the process lose her own rights. While they agree that drug addiction needed to be addressed, they have urged state authorities to take the women's lives into account. Studies show, they assert, that crack addicts typically are also victims of child abuse and woman battery; they take drugs to avoid the pain these experiences have caused. To put them in jail or charge them with child abuse without considering the mitigating circumstances adds even more pain to their lives. Feminists also point out that the focus on the fetus as a separate "patient" invites everyone to criticize a woman's behavior while pregnant. A pregnant woman is no longer carrying her own child in private. Instead, others think they have the right to intervene to criticize a woman for smoking, drinking a glass of wine, or riding on a motorcycle while pregnant. What's the next step, they wonder: confinement of all pregnant women to home? In fact, some admonitions to pregnant women have been extended throughout their reproductive years, whether they are pregnant or not. Health officials today advise "preconception care"—that is, abstaining from smoking, alcohol, and drugs and taking prenatal vitamins as long as women have the possibility of pregnancy. (See Centers for Disease Control and Prevention at www.cdc.gov/ncbddd/preconception/default.htm.)

Fetal Homicide Laws

Although the pro-life movement was one of the leaders in promoting prenatal drug laws, at first they were less involved with bringing the problem of third-party fetal killing to the public agenda. The media did not make much of the statistics that showed an increase in fetal injury and death as a result of violence against pregnant women in the 1980s and 1990s. In 1998, Ruth Schroedel conducted a study of thirty-two pro-life organizations and found only one, Americans United for Life (AUL), which considered the issue of fetal death worth promoting. AUL focuses on legislation and offers model statutes to states and Congress for bills they advocate.

This lack of interest changed soon after Schroedel's survey when the National Right to Life Committee (NRLC) launched a five-year campaign for fetal homicide laws. In fact, about half the states had already criminalized third-party killing of a fetus. What was different with the new campaign was that NRLC and AUL promoted laws that explicitly defined when the fetus was a person—from fertilization—and explicitly defined the crime as involving two separate victims—the pregnant woman and the embryo/fetus. Thus, someone who attacks a woman who does not know she is pregnant because the fertilized egg has not yet implanted in the uterus could be charged with murder.

Pro-choice activists opposed these new proposals as part of what they claimed was the pro-life strategy to dismantle the guarantees for women's choice in abortion in *Roe v. Wade* by legally defining the fertilized egg as a human being. By establishing the "two victims" approach, the pro-lifers actually give the fetus preference over the woman, thus inflating the status of the fetus. The pro-choice prognosis for the problem of fetal homicide is for states to define the crime as injuries inflicted on a pregnant woman—one victim—and increase the penalties to take into account that injury to the fetus has occurred.

Pro-life activists have responded to the pro-choice frame of the issue by pointing out that their proposals will not affect women's rights because they exclude abortion explicitly. Others admit, however, that once the fetus is considered a separate human being it is harder and harder to justify laws that allow doctors and pregnant women to kill them. Pro-life frames also reject the idea of stiffer penalties for crimes against pregnant women claiming that an assailant will get a longer prison term for a crime with two victims rather than one.

This campaign got a boost in the early 2000s when the murder of Laci Peterson, who was seven months pregnant, was followed closely in the news. When her body was discovered in San Francisco Bay separate from her fetus, whom she had planned to name Connor, the issue of fetal homicide was on the national agenda. California already has a fetal homicide law dating from the 1970s, so Laci's husband, Scott Peterson, was tried and convicted for two murders—those of Laci and Connor. The pro-life activists convinced Laci's family to let them name their bill, the Unborn Victims of Violence Act (UVVA), "Laci and Connor's Law." All this publicity sealed the fate of the UVVA, and it was passed and signed by President Bush in 2004. Although as a federal criminal law it has limited application, the national debate spurred the passage of identical laws in several states. Today thirty-seven states have fetal homicide laws, twenty-four of them defining the fetus as a person or human being at any stage, many modeled after the federal law covering embryos and fetuses from the earliest stages: "As used in this section, the term 'unborn child' means a child in utero, and the term 'child in utero' or 'child, who is in utero' means a member of the species *homo sapiens*, at any stage of development, who is carried in the womb" (18 USC 90A Sec 1841, d).

Embryonic Stem Cell Research

Medical research in genetics and embryology has shown that the cells and tissues in human embryos and fetuses have special qualities that could be used in treating diseases such as diabetes, Parkinson's disease, and spinal injuries. Since the 1970s, fetal tissue research has been conducted on aborted embryos, and fetuses have been used for transplants to replace diseased or damaged tissues. Further, the discovery that embryonic stem cells—those that have not yet differentiated into specific tissues—can be grown to be used in a variety of diseases and injuries has stimulated interest in more research.

From the beginning, the pro-life movement has opposed the use of fetuses and embryos for research and treatment. They have linked this research with abortion and have been concerned that after legalization people would have abortions just to provide such tissue for family members. In the 1980s, they convinced the Reagan administration to impose a moratorium on federal funds for research on the use of human fetal tissue in such transplants; the moratorium was extended by the first Bush administration. When Bill Clinton became president, one of his first acts was to lift the moratorium, and in 1993, Congress passed the National Institutes of Health (NIH) Revitalization Act, which permits the use of fetal tissue from abortions, but NIH has strict guidelines to avoid abuse and misuse of the tissue.

The debate over embryonic stem cell research has grown with the advances in the technology. Thus far, there have been few stories of cures, but scientists claim that if they had access to federal funds, they could move the research toward effective therapies for diseases that are now incurable. Proposals so far have focused on using embryos developed but not used for in vitro fertilization (IVF) and that are currently in frozen storage. The pro-life movement opposes this research because, in their view, the research kills human beings—the embryos. The Roman

Catholic component of the movement opposes any form of artificial conception such as IVF. Further, they are concerned that such research devalues human life and encourages people to conceive just to obtain cells for research and treatment. The next step would be cloning human beings. Pro-choice organizations generally support such stem cell research, primarily because pro-life groups are opposed. Feminists disagree over the whole matter of new reproductive technologies. While some focus on the choices such technologies open for women who want children, others are concerned that women, especially low-income and minority women, will be exploited for their eggs—turned into sources of biological material.

The issue frame of the debate over stem cell research is not, however, a fetus versus women's rights frame like the abortion issue frame. In fact, it is primarily defined as a medical and health matter. Researchers hold out the promise of cures for incurable diseases. Many people have relatives and friends who could benefit if the research promise is fulfilled. Thus, some voters and members of Congress who otherwise vote with the pro-life position have voted to fund stem cell research. In 2006, Congress passed a bill to fund embryonic stem cell research by substantial majorities in both houses, but not enough to overcome President Bush's veto, his first. He signed the veto at a White House ceremony flanked by "snowflakes"—children who were adopted while they were still frozen embryos. At the same time, he signed the Fetus Farming Prohibition Act, which prohibits the use of fetal tissue when that fetus was conceived just for that purpose.

Other Debates Relating to Fetal Personhood

The UVVA was not the first time the federal government defined the fetus as a person from conception. In 2002, Tommy Thompson, secretary of the U.S. Department of Health and Human Services, issued a regulation that allows states to define fetuses as unborn children and extend health care to them under the Children's Health Insurance Program (CHIP). CHIP was established in 1997 to cover health care for low-income children who were not eligible for Medicaid and whose families could not afford insurance. Before this ruling, CHIP allowed states to seek permission to cover pregnant women, but not the fetuses separately. This new rule excluded pregnant women from coverage and applied only to fetuses at any stage of development.

Pro-choice organizations attacked the move as part of the series of "backdoor" efforts to advance an antiabortion agenda and establish a federal legal precedent that the fetus is a person. By denying pregnant women coverage, the Bush administration acts as though women did not exist or were, at the very most, containers for fetuses. A fetus cannot be treated apart from the pregnant woman's body that carries it; thus, CHIP and other health care programs should expand prenatal care to all women. The Bush administration and pro-life activists responded that the only goal was to protect the health of unborn children and had nothing to do with abortion.

Another pro-life statute passed in 2002 prompted less controversy: the Born Alive Infants Protection Act. Congressional committees heard testimony from nurses and other health workers that in some late-term abortions babies survived. The medical personnel were instructed not to treat these infants but to let them die. Congress responded by giving all infants at any stage of development born alive the full protection of the law. That means doctors and hospitals must do what they can to save their lives. Pro-choice organizations took no position on this law, and many congressional abortion rights advocates voted for it because it did not change the legal status of the fetus. It applied to infants who had left the womb and were still alive.

The brief calm over the Born Alive Infants Protection Act did not last long. Pro-life members of Congress began to promote the Unborn Child Pain Awareness Act. Some physicians testify that a fetus feels pain at 20 weeks and that an abortion performed at that time results in an excruciating death. Pro-life activists suppose that if women knew about the suffering their abortions would cause, they would be less likely to have them. On the other hand if they go ahead, they should be able to provide anesthesia. The proposal before Congress would require doctors to read a statement written by Congress to a woman undergoing an abortion at 20 weeks after fertilization or more, give her a pamphlet that informs her that her unborn child feels pain, and give her the option to request anesthesia before going ahead with the procedure. Failure to comply would bring fines of $100,000 to $250,000.

Pro-life advocates define this issue as a simple matter of providing information to women so they can make an informed decision about the abortion. It's not fair to keep women in the dark, they say. It also gives pro-life advocates a chance to talk about late-term abortion procedures in graphic detail—a tactic that was successful in banning partial-birth abortions: dismemberment, crushing the fetal skull, and poisoning in utero. Pro-choice advocates respond by accusing the pro-life side of using the rhetoric of pain when the issue is not about pain but about trying to harass women and prevent more abortions. In fact, they assert, the medical profession does not agree about when or even whether a fetus feels pain—there is an ongoing debate. Pro-life groups want Congress to take sides and silence opinion that disagrees with the pro-life approach. Many doctors have opposed the idea of letting Congress determine what doctors must say to patients. They say the requirement to offer anesthesia to a fetus overlooks the difficulty in administering such drugs and the dangers to women in doing so. Pro-choice activists go on to point out if Congress is so concerned about pain for the unborn, why not examine the pain they suffer in ordinary childbirth and in neonatal treatments. The fact that this bill says nothing about these conditions supports the charge that it is, like the other proposals discussed in this section, part of a campaign to undermine abortion services and limit the number of abortions.

Birth Control and Sex Education

Pro-choice and pro-life movements have fundamental disagreements about sex, birth control, and abortion. A major component of the pro-choice movement came from family-planning and population-growth organizations. They promoted values that while individual choice and privacy are constitutionally protected, all people, especially the young, should have sex responsibly. That means that they should take action to plan when they want to have children and only have the children they can afford to bring up to be healthy, educated, and happy. Knowledge about and services for contraception provide the means for them to plan their families. Legal abortion is necessary to take care of cases where contraception fails or people lapse in their responsibility.

When feminists joined the pro-choice movement, at first they tended to place less emphasis on responsibility and focused on rights and removing the limits of access to abortion. In the 1980s, however, they promoted a collective action frame of reproductive freedom for women. This meant support for liberty and resources for women in the full range of their reproductive lives—from sex education, the right to decide when to have sex and with whom, contraceptive information and services through prenatal care, abortion access, health care, child care, and adequate income. Nelson (2003) attributes this expansion of the feminist pro-choice frame to the influence of women of color. In 1994, to reflect this expansion of what it meant to be pro-choice, the National Association for the Repeal of Abortion Laws (NARAL) changed its name to the National Abortion and Reproductive Rights Action League "to develop and sustain a constituency that uses the political process to guarantee every woman the right to make personal decisions regarding the full range of reproductive choices, including preventing unintended pregnancy, bearing healthy children, and choosing legal abortion" (quoted in Wilder 1998, 87). When pro-choice activists found themselves put on the defensive to protect *Roe v. Wade*, they had fewer resources to work for this expanded agenda. Nevertheless, in the early 2000s, they discovered that the pro-life movement had moved to attack birth control and sex education policies that had been in place since the 1970s.

One of the original components of the pro-life movement was the Roman Catholic Church, but the movement attracted other components brought together by their aversion to legal abortion and desire to overturn *Roe v. Wade*. Since the 1980s, however, the official Catholic values regarding sex, birth control, childbirth, and abortion have found a more central place in the agenda of social conservatives in the pro-life movement. It's not just a matter of stopping abortion. Some had hoped that if it were, there would be common ground with pro-choice groups in preventing abortion through greater knowledge and use of contraception. Instead, the pro-life frame also opposes contraception.

This is due to a particular view of sex and morality held by many in the pro-life movement. In their view, availability of contraception is both cause and consequence of a general moral decline in America. With the invention of the birth control pill, individuals and even married couples began to separate sex from reproduction and engaged in sex as an end in itself. Along the way they devalued the wonder of sexual relations in creating life and devalued each other. When husbands use contraception, they turn their wives into whores. No matter who uses it, contraception increases sexual promiscuity and, rather than preventing unwanted pregnancies, leads to more abortions.

It's not just contraception in general that is opposed according to these ideas. Some so-called contraceptives actually cause abortions because they destroy a fertilized egg which is a human being. Among these are intrauterine devices and birth control pills that prohibit implantation, not conception. In this section we review two debates that have arisen from this conflict when demands for reproductive freedom meet conservative ideas about sex and morality: emergency contraception and sex education.

Emergency Contraception

Most policymakers believe that although abortion remains very controversial Americans generally accept financial support for birth control methods and services as important and legitimate public policy. In the pro-choice collective action frames, unintended pregnancies represent serious harm to the health of women and their children. (It is important to note that for many years, the pro-choice activists used the term "unwanted pregnancy," which pro-life activists challenged by arguing that with adoption, no baby is unwanted. The change to "unintended" leaves it open whether the baby is wanted or unwanted.) Because unprotected sex and even rape continue to occur, women must be able to obtain emergency contraception (EC) to solve the problem and prevent abortions. Intense challenges over access to EC, sometimes called the "morning-after pill," came as a surprise to pro-choice activists. In their strategic frames, this effort by opponents of EC to restrict its use is a serious problem because it reflects a broader pro-life strategy to promote abstinence and limit birth control generally (Shorter 2006). Worse, the pro-choice actors claim that these dangerous efforts are led by political appointees inside the executive agencies in the Bush administration, especially at the FDA, which has been reluctant to allow EC to be available without a doctor's prescription or over the counter.

In the pro-choice frame, the prognosis or solution to the problem is to expand access to EC, making it readily available in hospitals for rape victims and in drug stores to help women whose contraception has failed. Planned Parenthood recommends that every woman have EC in her medicine cabinet. They argue that EC *prevents* pregnancy; it does not *end* a pregnancy. Therefore, it is not an abortifacient, as pro-life opponents claim, and its use presents no moral choice. In addition, EC is most effective when taken within 24 hours of sexual intercourse so it is imperative that women be able to obtain the drug over the counter. Research shows that having EC available does not lead to risky sexual behavior or increased sexual promiscuity among teens, according to pro-choice strategic frames.

Like most pro-choice/pro-life debates, the strategic frames of the two movements mirror each other with respect to access to EC. For the pro-life activists the problem with EC is that it is an abortifacient. Conception occurs when the sperm fertilizes the egg, and they assert that the result is an embryo and a pregnancy. Because EC works to prevent an embryo from implanting in the uterus it destroys the embryo, the same as an abortion. In fact, for many religious pro-life advocates, all birth control pills have the same effect by making the uterus unsuitable for implantation. Some claim that scientists who maintain that pregnancy results only after implantation are "medically dishonest" (Wilks 1998).

Not only does EC result in an abortion, but access to EC also promotes unsafe sexual behavior goes the pro-life frame. With access to drugs that quickly abort any pregnancies, people don't have to show restraint. The result is an increase in promiscuity and sexual disease. In short, the pro-life movement places EC as an immoral threat to traditional marriage and its relation to procreation. Thus, like abortion, use of EC presents a moral dilemma for policymakers, doctors, and pharmacists. The solution is to restrict availability and access to EC and, for some activists, to limit access to all birth control pills as well. Pharmacists for Life International are among those who argue that pharmacists must have the right to decline to fill prescriptions for EC, and policymakers at the FDA are correct in keeping restrictions on access to the pills.

The issue frame of the debate among policymakers centers on contradictory claims over the safety and effects of EC, whether it is a necessary means of reproductive choice or an immoral means to sexual promiscuity, abortion, and disease. At first, it was available only by prescription. The drug company that makes EC, many doctors, and pro-choice activists demanded that the FDA allow it to be sold over the counter. Science advisory committees to the agency recommended approval but FDA policymakers deferred action until it became clear that nominees for FDA director would not be confirmed by the Senate. Critics charged that the FDA nonaction was based on ideological attachment to pro-life notions about EC and not based on the science. Senators Hillary Rodham Clinton (D-NY) and Patty Murray (D-WA) blocked confirmation until the FDA made a decision about the status of EC. In September 2005, Susan Wood, director of the Office of Women's Health at the FDA, resigned accusing the FDA of using abortion politics in its failure to make a decision. Finally, in late 2006, FDA approved over-the-counter sales of EC except for those under the age of 17. In April 2006 and January 2007 Senate Democrats introduced the Prevention First Act to link birth control to preventing abortion, to expand education about all contraception, and to require EC to be offered to victims of assault.

Policy action on this issue is taking place in state arenas as well as at the federal level (Guttmacher Institute 2006). Nine states have policies that expand access to EC, including eight that allow pharmacists to dispense EC without a prescription under certain conditions. The governor of Illinois, Rod Blagojevich, has ordered that Illinois pharmacists who stock birth control must dispense EC despite any moral qualms. Around the same number of states have policies restricting access, including four that allow pharmacists to refuse to dispense contraceptives, including EC, on moral grounds. Bills are pending in other states, some that would require hospitals to make EC available to rape victims. The Federal Office of Violence Against Women did not include any mention of EC in its recent hospital protocol for victims of sexual assault.

Sex Education

The debate over the place of abstinence in publicly supported sex education programs brings pro-life and pro-choice movements to policy arenas in Congress, the executive branch, and the states. The diagnostic strategic frame of the pro-life advocates is that American culture is saturated with sex and sexually explicit messages that encourage adolescents to engage in too much sexual activity. The problem with this is that teen sex is responsible for serious social problems: increasing the incidence of sexually transmitted diseases (STDs), emotional and psychological injury, promiscuity, and high levels of out-of-wedlock childbearing (Rector 2002; Maher 2006.) Taken together, these effects render many young adults incapable of committing to marriage and family responsibilities.

Most sex education programs promote the use of condoms and other contraceptives to solve the problems caused by teen sexual activity. First of all, pro-life advocates claim that contraceptives are often ineffective in preventing pregnancy and that condoms provide only limited protection against STDs. Giving contraceptives to teens encourages risky sexual activity and leads to higher rates of disease, pregnancies, and abortions. Many of the so-called "safe sex" or "comprehensive sex education" programs claim to include a discussion of abstinence, but in fact they do not. The solution or prognosis in the pro-life frame is that abstinence-only programs are desirable and effective. They promote personal responsibility and commitment to marriage while reducing out-of-wedlock births among young adults. Pro-life advocates claim that a growing number of studies show the effectiveness of these programs, which have become highly popular among teens.

On the other side, pro-choice strategic frames diagnose the problem to be the expansion of abstinence-only programs in schools. Such programs are steadily replacing what they call the real sex education curricula that had become widespread in the 1970s (Feldt 2004). The abstinence-only approach teaches the young that sex is dangerous and contraception is ineffective to protect them, and it silences teachers who would like to give students information about how to prevent pregnancy and disease effectively through knowledge and contraceptive use. Instead, young people are told to sign pledges of virginity and engage in sexual activity only upon marriage. Yet most young people do have sex in their teens and wait until they are 25 years or older to marry. The effect of the decline of real sex education includes increases in unintended pregnancy and STDs in the United States, which has the highest rates among postindustrial democracies, because people aren't getting real information and abstinence-only programs do not work. The policy solution in the pro-choice frame is to eliminate the abstinence-only approach in favor of comprehensive sex education in the schools—favored by most parents—which would provide all available information, including abstinence as an option. Pro-choice advocates believe such courses should be based on the belief that sexuality is natural, normal, and healthy, not something to fear or feel guilty about. Such courses should provide accurate information about birth control and how to use condoms, promote the lifelong consistent use of contraception, and cover topics like abortion, masturbation, and sexual orientation.

The issue frame in the sex education debate places abstinence against other forms of sex education; both sides contend that to follow the other side's plan leads to disease and abortion. Abstinence has become more central to the issue frame since the late 1970s, and this has favored the pro-life movement. The federal government has been funding abstinence education since the Adolescent Family Life Act was passed in 1981. The winners in the conflict over the definition of the issue are religious and conservative organizations that benefit from grants to the detriment of those favoring secular sex education and freedom. The 1996 Welfare Reform Act authorized matching grants to states for abstinence education aimed at groups prone to out-of-wedlock births (about $50 million per year). The push to replace more general sex education with abstinence-only programs in the schools has strengthened during the Bush administration. Since 2001, Congress has spent $779 million on abstinence programs through grants to schools and not-for-profit groups. Some of the latter are part of the Bush strategy to engage "faith-based" (religious) groups in administering social policy. State legislatures have adopted similar programs to limit conventional sex education in favor of abstinence education. In response, some parents and health professionals are challenging these trends in the states and have proposed their own comprehensive sex education bills.

The Abortion Conflict in Political Parties and Elections

If you polled members of the Democratic and Republican parties before 1973, you would very likely find no differences between the parties in their views about abortion. That is, in both parties, you would find those opposed to legalization of abortion and those in favor of reform and repeal. That changed in the 1970s when the Republican Party became the "pro-life party" and the Democratic Party became the "pro-choice party." The first change came with the Republicans. When the economic conservatives formed an alliance with the evangelical Christian Right to rebuild the Republican Party in southern and western states, they brought a substantial number of pro-life voters and party activists. With a new group of voters, candidates began to appeal for their support, and the Republican strategists used the abortion debate as a wedge issue in state and national elections. In the 1970s, passing a Human Life Amendment to overcome the *Roe v. Wade* ruling was a top priority for the Christian Right, and they found their candidate in Ronald Reagan, governor of California.

Pro-choice Republicans started to lose elections, even those who were incumbents of long standing (Packwood 1992). To get the Republican nomination in 1976, President Gerald Ford had to switch and declare support for the Human Life Amendment. George H. W. Bush became a staunch opponent of legal abortion to be acceptable as vice president to Reagan in the 1980s.

Pro-choice movement activists, many of them feminists, became increasingly active in the Democratic Party. They were not happy with President Jimmy Carter, however, who as a born-again Christian had been able to win the presidency in 1976, but who consistently opposed pro-choice proposals for such policies as Medicaid funding. After that the Democratic Party adopted a pro-choice plank in its platform and nominated only pro-choice candidates for president. These candidates were not successful in gaining the White House, however, until 1992 when Bill Clinton defeated the incumbent George H. W. Bush, partly on the abortion issue. This election took place in the wake of the debate over the unsuccessful 1987 Supreme Court nomination of Robert Bork and the 1989 *Webster* decision that mobilized millions of pro-choice voters.

The parties remain officially divided on this issue today. The platforms in 2004 presidential election reflected the differences:

The Democrats:
"We will defend the dignity of all Americans against those who would undermine it because we believe in the privacy and equality of women, we stand proudly for a woman's right to choose, consistent with Roe v. Wade, and regardless of her ability to pay. We stand firmly against Republican efforts to undermine that right. At the same time, we strongly support family planning and adoption incentives. Abortion should be safe, legal, and rare" (Source: "Strong at Home, Respected in the World." The 2004 Democratic Platform for America." p. 38. http://a9.g.akamai.net/7/9/8082/v002/www.democrats.org/pdfs/2004platform.pdf; accessed March 27, 2007).

The Republicans:
"We support a human life amendment to the Constitution and we endorse legislation to make it clear that the Fourteenth Amendment's protections apply to unborn children. Our purpose is to have legislative and judicial

protection of that right against those who perform abortions. We oppose using public revenues for abortion and will not fund organizations which advocate it. We support the appointment of judges who respect traditional family values and the sanctity of innocent human life" (Source: "2004 Republican Party Platform: A Safer World and a More Hopeful America." p. 84. www.gop.com/media/2004platform.pdf; accessed March 27, 2007).

It is important to keep in mind that the platforms do not reflect the views of all party activists, nor do they bind legislators to vote a particular way. For example, there are organizations such as Republicans for Choice and Pro-Life Democrats. And while most Republican legislators have high marks from the National Right to Life Committee for the pro-life voting, there are Republicans in Congress who are pro-choice. Similarly, Democrats do not all have perfect scores on the NARAL Pro-choice America Choice index. In fact, in 2007, NARAL can rely on only 38 percent of the House and 35 percent of the Senate to vote consistently pro-choice despite a majority for the Democrats.

Research has shown a close relationship between party identification, voting, and opinion on the abortion issue (Jelen and Wilcox 2003). However, it is not clear whether people vote Democratic and Republican because of their views on the abortion issue or whether their views on the abortion issue are shaped by their identity with the Republican or Democratic Party. Public opinion on abortion has been fairly stable since the 1970s. A minority intensely adhere either to the pro-choice idea of abortion based on woman's choice alone or the pro-life idea of criminalized abortion and complete fetal rights, but in the middle most have more moderate views. We see, then, that despite 30 years of supporting a Human Life Amendment, no Republican president has put his political capital in a campaign to pass it. And despite 30 years of support for a woman's right to choose, Democrats have voted for bans on partial-birth abortion and against the Freedom of Choice Act.

Solutions to the Abortion Conflict

This chapter has described how the abortion conflict between pro-life and pro-choice movements has played out in several policy issues ranging from the legality of abortion to embryonic stem cell research. This discussion is not exhaustive because the stand-off between the two movements can appear in other policy debates: welfare reform, education funding, and anything to do with health care. Looking across these various debates, it is easy to see why some fear that the debate is unending and irresolvable. Nevertheless, various scholars, analysts, and journalists have proposed solutions that would end the divide between the fetus's right to life and the woman's right to liberty, at least in the public policy arenas. To conclude this review of the abortion conflict, this section gives a summary of several of these proposals with references for further reading. Based on what you have read about the conflict, what is the likelihood that any of these proposals will "get traction" to reach enduring solutions to the "abortion wars"?

Changing Pro-Life and Pro-Choice Frames

As the collective action frames and the strategic frames derived from them seem to permit no compromise, some writers suggest that one side or the other change its position to permit some neutral ground. Hendershott (2006), a sociologist with sympathies for the pro-life perspective, claims that pro-life movement frames are on the ascendancy in the debate over the meaning of the abortion issue because most abortion debates favor protecting the fetus from conception as a human being. Having achieved this redefinition of the issue, she suggests that pro-life activists could help end the abortion wars by moving away from the philosophic absolutism of the past debates and move toward some real dialogue with pro-choice counterparts who also want peace. They could, for example, give more attention to providing public services to pregnant women and not spend all their time on changing abortion laws. To bolster her argument, she quotes Marvin Olasky, who says pro-life advocates should exert "steady pressure through all the means that worked a century ago to reduce abortions and are beginning to work anew: education about abstinence, refuges for the abandoned, provision of adoption and many other services" (Olasky 1995; quoted in Hendershott 2006, 144).

Naomi Wolf, writing as a pro-choice feminist, agrees that pro-choice has lost out to the pro-life movement in the debate. The reason is that the pro-choice focus on women's privacy and rights has abandoned the moral argument, leaving it to the pro-life side to charge that abortion is an immoral choice. Wolf (2001) points out that pro-choice rhetoric completely ignores the fetus, as if it means nothing. Abortion rights need to be placed into a moral framework that admits that abortion leads to the death of a fetus and that this is a bad thing and an immoral thing, but sometimes a necessary thing. It is up to women to make the judgment, but they also have to face that it is a failure to have to choose abortion. The pro-choice argument should recognize the responsibilities of women—to use contraception, for example—as well as the right to make the choice: "We need to contextualize the fight to defend abortion rights within a moral framework that admits that the death of a fetus is a real death; that there are degrees of culpability, judgment, and responsibility involved in the decision to abort a pregnancy; that the best understanding of feminism involves holding women as well as men to the responsibilities that are inseparable from this country's high rate of abortion" (Wolf 2001, 180).

Common Ground

A hope among those who wish to calm abortion battles is that both sides agree on some common goals that could form the basis for a compromise. In 1990, in the midst of the furor over *Webster v. Reproductive Services,* Laurence Tribe, a Harvard professor of constitutional law, labeled the abortion conflict as "the clash of absolutes" between the absolute right of the fetus to life and the absolute right of a pregnant woman to liberty. He also noted that each side ignores the worth, if not the very existence, of the other side in their frames. Pro-life activists show photos of fetuses at antiabortion rallies with no image of where these fetuses actually live. Pro-choice activists rarely acknowledge the being that is aborted; the photos of wire coat hangers focus on injury done by self-abortion; no attention is paid to the injury to the embryo or the fetus. "Giving voice to the human reality on each side of the 'versus,' keeping both the woman and the fetus in focus at the same time, may be the only way to avoid the no-win battle that mercilessly pits women against their unborn children and leaves us all impoverished" (Tribe 1990, 6).

Tribe attempts to make the case that there is common ground between the sides, and that is to avoid abortion as much as possible. Both sides should envision a world where there are only wanted pregnancies and women don't have to make a decision about abortion. The goal then would be to reduce the number of abortions, not to make them illegal. Public policies that could advance this goal include better sex education, such as attention to abstinence; contraceptive services; and programs to help families raise children that focus on health care, education, and reconciliation of work and family responsibilities.

This compromise has some appeal for pro-choice politicians. Bill Clinton picked up this idea when he said abortion should be safe, legal, and rare (a phrase still in the Democratic Party platform). In 2005, Hillary Rodham Clinton got media attention when she said that abortion was a tragedy:

> This decision, which is one of the most fundamental, difficult and soul searching decisions a woman and a family can make, is also one in which the government should have no role. I believe we can all recognize that abortion in many ways represents a sad, even tragic choice to many, many women. Often, it's a failure of our system of education, health care, and preventive services. It's often a result of family dynamics. This decision is a profound and complicated one; a difficult one, often the most difficult that a woman will ever make. The fact is that the best way to reduce the number of abortions is to reduce the number of unwanted pregnancies in the first place (Clinton 2005).

Some analysts claimed that Senator Clinton was fielding a more conservative position in the abortion debate to move to middle ground in advance of a run for the presidency.

William Saletan (2003), on the other hand, has noted that pro-choice activists have been most successful when they find common ground with conservatives in a privacy framework. The pro-choice movement had been hurt by its association with feminism and the sexual revolution. In several elections in the 1990s, opponents of criminal abortion laws were able to frame the issue as a problem of government intrusion into the privacy of families. This approach bundles a number of issues together: freedom from government intrusion, family, parental rights, opposition to funding abortions, and the right to abortion in some circumstances such as rape. NARAL picked up the idea with their slogan "Who Decides?" which leaves ambiguous the context of the decision but can be interpreted to mean: Who decides? You and your family or the government? This type of solution would search for specific policy proposals that include something for each side.

New Collective Frames for Legal Abortion

Eileen McDonagh (1996), a professor of political science, has proposed a rethinking of the entire basis for legal abortion. Up to now, the main argument has been based on privacy and women's rights. At the same time, the pro-life strategy of advancing the humanity of the fetus has been gaining ground. For each step forward for the fetus, there has been a backward step for woman's rights and choice. McDonagh sees that the collective action frame of choice has led to a battle over the moral status of the fetus— Tribe's clash of absolutes. McDonagh, in a sort of "if you can't beat 'em, join 'em" approach, advocates accepting the pro-life view. Yes, the fetus is a human being with equal rights to all other humans including the woman where it lives.

Based on this assumption, then, the fetus will have the same rights as other humans—but also the same responsibilities. In fact the fetus is the result of a fertilized egg that implants itself in a woman's body—with or without her consent. With her consent, it is welcomed, loved, and cared for. Without her consent, then there is no obligation for the woman to welcome or protect it. Just like with rape, a woman's body is violated against her will. The fetus has the potential to injure the woman, cripple her, or even kill her. In any case, it will change her life utterly. No human being has the right to do that to another human without her consent, and the state has the obligation to protect persons from being hurt by other persons. Even now, pro-life and pro-choice agree that abortion should be legal when a pregnancy threatens a woman's life. Similarly, a pregnant woman has a right to destroy the fetus to stop the danger and the state has the obligation to help her do it by providing funding. "It is how we think about pregnancy, therefore, not merely how we think about the fetus, that justifies abortion" (McDonagh 1996, 17).

For another approach, look at Alexander Sanger's 2004 book *Beyond Choice: Reproductive Freedom in the 21st Century.* As the title indicates, Sanger suggests a new collective action frame for those who favor legal abortion turning from the right to choose toward a guarantee of reproductive freedom. Using a foundation from the science of evolutionary biology, Sanger argues that reproductive freedom is essential to humanity: it allows each generation to reproduce in the best possible way. That is, freedom advances the creation of life and its survival to the next generation. Women who can control their childbearing have a better chance of surviving, and so do their children. With that freedom, people are able to find partners or not, give birth or not according to their circumstances, and ensure that if they have children they are raised to be healthy and well equipped to start the reproductive cycle over again. Reproductive freedom is not granted by government; humans have it naturally. What can happen, however, is that government can try to take that freedom away. "If a moral rule helps community survival, the rule will last. If it does not, it will wither away. Such is the case with moral rules against birth control and abortion. These practices help humanity survive and reproduce successfully and many humans use them. Moral rules forbidding them will not stand" (Sanger 2004, 85).

Sanger writes that the pro-choice movement should start using these scientific arguments to advance their goals of legal birth control and abortion. Pro-life made substantial gains with their biological arguments to support the humanity of the fetus. Pro-choice actors could do the same to justify reproductive freedom. For example, the argument that every fertilized egg should be protected goes against the scientific laws of natural selection. Human beings must have some control over the reproductive process to advance the overall well-being of humanity. Efforts to deny this control will either not work and be ignored or they will work to the detriment of the health of the human community, says Sanger.

References

Baird-Windle, Patricia, and Eleanor J. Bader. *Targets of Hatred: Anti-Abortion Terrorism.* New York: Palgrave, 2001.

Center for Reproductive Rights. "Unconstitutional Assault on the Right to Choose: Federal Abortion Ban Is an Affront to Women and the Supreme Court." 2003. www.reproductiverights.org (accessed April 11, 2006).

Clinton, Hillary Rodham. "Remarks by Senator Hillary Rodham Clinton to the NYS Family Planning Providers." January 24, 2005.

http://clinton.senate.gov/~clinton/speeches/2005125A05.html (accessed November 27, 2006).

Craig, Barbara Hinkson, and David M. O'Brien. *Abortion and American Politics.* Chatham, NJ: Chatham House, 1993.

Feldt, Gloria. *The War on Choice: The Right-Wing Attack on Women's Rights and How to Fight Back.* New York: Bantam Books, 2004.

Gitenstein, Mark. *Matters of Principle — An Insider's Account of America's Rejection of Robert Bork's Nomination to the Supreme Court.* New York: Simon & Schuster, 1992.

Guttmacher Institute. "State Policies in Brief: Emergency Contraception." 2006. www.guttmacher.org (accessed April 6, 2006).

Hendershott, Anne. 2006. *The Politics of Abortion.* New York: Encounter Books

Jelen, Ted G., and Clyde Wilcox. 2003. "Causes and Consequences of Public Attitudes toward Abortion: A Review and Research Agenda." *Political Research Quarterly* 56 (2003): 489–500.

Maher, Bridget. "Why Wait: The Benefits of Abstinence Until Marriage." Family Research Council. 2006. www.frc.org (accessed April 4, 2006).

Mason, Carol. *Killing for Life: The Apocalyptic Narrative of Pro-Life Politics.* Ithaca, NY: Cornell University Press, 2002.

McBride Stetson, Dorothy. "US Abortion Debates 1959–1998: The Women's Movement Holds On." In *Abortion Politics, Women's Movements and the Democratic State: A Comparative Study of State Feminism,* edited by D. McBride Stetson, 247–266. Oxford: Oxford University Press, 2001.

McBride Stetson, Dorothy. *Women's Rights in the USA: Policy Debates and Gender Roles.* 3rd ed. New York: Routledge, 2004.

McDonagh, Eileen L. *Breaking the Abortion Deadlock: From Choice to Consent.* New York: Oxford University Press, 1996.

Nelson, Jennifer. *Women of Color and the Reproductive Rights Movement.* New York: New York University Press, 2003.

Olasky, Marvin. *Abortion Rites.* Washington, DC: Regenery, 1995.

Packwood, Senator Bob. "The Rise and Fall of the Right-to-Life Movement in Congress: Response to the *Roe* Decision, 1973–83." In *Abortion, Medicine, and the Law,* 4th ed., edited by J. Douglas Butler and David F. Walbert, 629–647. New York: Facts on File, 1992.

Rector, Robert E. "The Effectiveness of Abstinence Education Programs in Reducing Sexual Activity Among Youth." The Heritage Foundation. 2002. www.heritage.org/Research/Family (accessed March 23, 2006).

Saletan, William. *Bearing Right: How Conservatives Won the Abortion War.* Berkeley: University of California Press, 2003.

Sanger, Alexander. *Beyond Choice: Reproductive Freedom in the 21st Century.* New York: Public Affairs, 2004.

Schroedel, Jean Reith. *Is the Fetus a Person? A Comparison of Policies across the Fifty States.* Ithaca, NY: Cornell University Press, 2000.

Shorter, Russell. "Contra-Contraception." *New York Times Magazine.* May 7, 2006: 48.

Tribe, Laurence H. *Abortion: The Clash of Absolutes.* New York: W.W. Norton & Company, 1990.

Wilder, Marcy J. "The Rule of Law, the Rise of Violence, and the Role of Morality: Reframing America's Abortion Debate." In *Abortion Wars: A Half Century of Struggle, 1959–2000,* edited by Rickie Solinger, 73–94. Berkeley: University of California Press, 1998.

Wilks, John. 1998. "The Pill—How It Works and Fails." *Pharmacists for Life.* www.pfli.org. (accessed April 5, 2006).

Wolf, Naomi. "Our Bodies, Our Souls." In *The Ethics of Abortion: Pro-Life vs. Pro-Choice,* 3rd ed., edited by Robert M. Baird and Stuart E. Rosenbaum, 179–192. Amherst, NY: Prometheus Books, 2001.

3

Worldwide Perspective

Introduction

Debates about abortion and abortion law are global phenomena. Since the 1960s, liberalization has almost been like a wind blowing from one country to another, especially in the postindustrial democracies. Beginning with Great Britain in 1967, long-standing criminal laws prohibiting abortion have fallen in the context of demands for reform. The forces that brought the issue to the top of the policy agenda in the United States—population growth, worries about illegal abortions, demands for women's rights and liberation—pushed legislators in Western democracies to take up the issue, however reluctantly in many cases. The effects of existing laws on population growth and women's health have also come to attention in developing countries. The Roman Catholic Church's opposition to the practice of abortion forms a global countermovement to the demands for change. At the same time, pro-life and pro-choice movements in the United States have connected with transnational organizations to promote their collective action frames in other countries and in international forums.

There are nearly 200 independent nation states, and it is very difficult to generalize about their responses to the abortion issue. While there have been many changes in the law, the process and direction of change have not been uniform. The issue frames of debates often put women's self determination against the protection of unborn life, but the balance between these arguments varies as well as the significance of other issue frames, such as health, family traditions, population growth, or modernization.

Several important characteristics of countries are likely to affect their abortion politics and policy. First of all, the type of legal system is important. The United Nations (UN) classifies legal systems as common law, civil law (also called code law), and Islamic law. Common law, or judge-made law, is found in the former colonies of Great Britain, including the United States. Civil-law systems are fashioned after the Roman law code and later the Napoleonic Code. Countries in Europe and Latin America, as well as some in Africa and Asia, have the civil system. Finally, the third form is Islamic law or sharia, which is prevalent in countries in North Africa, the Middle East, and West Asia. Each system has different origins, sources, and methods of lawmaking that may affect abortion law. Another important factor affecting abortion policy is the status of women in society and culture. Social scientists sometimes refer to this as the "gender regime," that is, the norms, rules, and positions of women compared with men. These can range from egalitarian to patriarchal, that is, from a pattern where women and men have equal legal status and similar roles to one where men dominate in every sphere of life.

A third important component of the environment for abortion policy involves religion, not only the particular denomination and its beliefs about conception, pregnancy, and abortion, but also the degrees of religiosity and the political influence of religious leaders. For example, most of the people in a country like France may identify as Catholics, but religion may not be very important in their lives—they have a low level of religiosity. Therefore, the strict prohibitions against abortion that are part of Roman Catholic Church doctrine would have little effect on policymaking about abortion. The particular pattern of religious affiliation may also be important. In some countries the population is affiliated with two or more religions, and the pattern of settlement will be significant. In the case of Germany, for example, access to abortion is quite restricted in the Catholic southern regions whereas it is much more open in the Protestant north and east.

Finally, the status of the abortion issue in a country may depend on the form of government and the level of political conflict. Stable democracies offer an environment for advocates to bring their demands out in public and have an influence on policymakers. Authoritarian governments are unlikely to offer such an environment and may respond only to international pressure. In the developing world, many people are still trying to establish stable and legitimate regimes; high levels of conflict push issues like abortion policy into the background.

This chapter takes a regional approach to sorting out the worldwide perspectives on the abortion issue, pointing out the general trends in politics and policy for each, and looking in some detail at a few countries in each region where there are particularly interesting debates and practices. A goal will be to place the U.S. conflict in the context of these regions, pointing out similarities and differences. The chapter begins with a survey of abortion policy in countries that are most similar to the United States—the Western democracies. Then we turn to Central and Eastern Europe, Latin America, East and South Asia, and Africa and the Middle East. The chapter concludes with a description of the impact of current abortion policies on world health and a look at debates at the UN.

Western Postindustrial Democracies

Western postindustrial democracies are the countries whose economies and political systems are most like the those of the United States. Western democracies (comprising Western European countries, Canada, Australia, and New Zealand) had criminal abortion laws until abortion reform movements developed in the mid-twentieth century. Since then their laws have taken a variety of forms; today, for the most part, the debates are settled but there are some exceptions.

Great Britain, Canada, Australia, and New Zealand

As a result of the expansion of the British Empire, the legal systems and institutions of Britain, Canada, Australia, and New Zealand remained closely associated throughout the twentieth century, and British policy on abortion applied in the other countries as well. Thus, British common-law rules that permitted abortion before quickening, which had also prevailed in the early days of the American republic, governed abortion policy in the colonies. This was superseded by Lord Ellenborough's Act, which made abortion before quickening a felony, and again in 1861 when the British parliament passed the Offenses Against the Person Act, which established complete criminalization of abortion.

The latter act was also in force in Canada, Australia, and New Zealand. The conditions under which abortion could be legally performed expanded a bit as the result of the English court ruling in the 1939 *Bourne* case, which allowed abortions for threats to the physical and mental health of the mother. This case was precedent in the other countries as well.

Thus, it is not surprising that the British campaign for reforming the abortion law, led since the 1930s by the Abortion Law Reform Association (ALRA), stimulated reform activism in the other countries. At first, the ALRA worked for repeal of the old laws, a goal supported by feminists. But when the Abortion Act finally passed in 1967, it was a compromise designed officially to "fix" the problem of illegal abortions, not to provide abortion on demand (for the fascinating story of this reform see Hindell and Simms 1970; Potts, Diggory, and Peel 1977; Cohan 1986). The formal wording of the act considers abortion a criminal procedure but allows for exceptions: when two medical practitioners agree that continuing a pregnancy would endanger the life, physical, or mental health of the woman or her children, or if there is risk of fetal deformity or handicap. In determining the risk of pregnancy to a woman, a doctor can consider the so-called "statistical argument," that is, whether pregnancy would be more risky than abortion. Statistics show that it is almost always more risky to proceed to childbirth. In addition, doctors can take a woman's environment into account. The effect of these two provisions is to give the medical profession wide discretion in responding to women's requests to end their pregnancies. There was some debate about late-term abortions until 1990 when the cutoff date for the statistical argument and the environmental conditions was firmly established at 24 weeks.

Because it was the first reform of criminal abortion laws in Western European countries, the 1967 act, strict in language but liberal in implementation, made Britain a destination for women from other countries. Antiabortion activists in Britain, those most closely connected to the Roman Catholic Church and American pro-life groups, found allies in Parliament to try to rescind or at least restrict access to legal abortion. Many bills have been filed in the decades since 1967, but none has been successful (McBride Stetson 2001). At the same time, the women's movement, which came along after the 1967 reform, has consistently demanded free abortion on demand with little success. Their goal is to remove the control of doctors over the practice of abortion, but they have spent the most energy, like their counterparts in the United States, in defending the status quo. Today in Britain, the abortion triad privileges doctors in controlling which women get abortions and under what circumstances with little interference from the government (Sheldon 1997).

The movement for reform came to Australia in the 1970s. As in the United States, in Australia abortion laws are the responsibility of the state governments or provinces. There has been no counterpart to U.S. Supreme Court decisions that set national standards, however. Australia has been influenced by events in Britain. Abortion provisions in the provinces vary from abortion on request up to 20 weeks in Western Australia, to restrictions in the provinces of Victoria and others where courts have interpreted the old criminal statutes modeled after the Offenses Against the Person Act very narrowly. South Australia and the Northern Territory passed reform statutes modeled after the 1967 British act. In 1979, the national parliament agreed to include abortion under the national health insurance.

Australian abortion policy also resembles the British policy because the rules are fairly stringent on paper but quite liberal in practice. In general, doctors are in control of access to abortion. Women may travel from restrictive locations to more liberal ones as well. After the 1970s, the abortion debate was off the public agenda, apparently settled to advocates' satisfaction. However, in 2003 some leaders in the Conservative government warned of the practice of late-term abortions, apparently hoping to stimulate a debate about the rate of terminations and the status of abortion practice. Both pro-choice and pro-life organizations began to publicize their positions on the Internet as the parliament considered RU-486, stem cell research, and cloning.

Canada was governed directly by British criminal law until 1969 when the national parliament adopted a new criminal code. Included was the criminalization of abortion except to save the life and health of the mother. Although the debate over this provision coincided with abortion reform in Britain, the medical profession largely controlled the debate and came away with total control over the procedure. The law placed abortion practice exclusively in hospitals where therapeutic abortion committees determined who got abortions and for what reasons. Advocates for women's rights had not been influential before the new law; instead, the effect of the new law on women's choices stimulated them to action. Unable to gain much traction in the parliament, they found new access as a result of the 1982 Canadian constitution, which separated Canadian law from British law. Women's rights advocates joined with activist doctors in bringing a case to the newly empowered constitutional court, the Supreme Court of Canada. In 1988, the court ruled that the Canadian law was unconstitutional because it denied women's rights to liberty and security established in the 1982 constitution.

According to the Canadian constitution, the national federal government has the power to set criminal law, and because abortion regulation is considered part of criminal law, the provincial governments may not enact their own statutes. A Conservative government attempted to enact a restrictive national law, supported by pro-life groups, but failed in 1990 by one vote in the upper house. Thus, Canada presently has no criminal law regulating abortion; it is, essentially, abortion on request. Still, access to abortion depends to a great degree on the operation of the health care system and health insurance (Haussman 2005). The court has empowered women to exercise their liberty and doctors to provide abortions; the triad that results is that women and doctors negotiate abortion with little interference from the state.

New Zealand's abortion statute dates from 1977; before that time, policy conformed to the model Offenses Against the Person Act. The conditional statute allows abortions up to 20 weeks of pregnancy to safeguard the life and health of the mother, for fetal deformity, if the pregnancy is the result of incest or through a supervisor's intercourse with a minor, or if the woman is mentally subnormal. Two doctors are required to approve the procedure (United Nations 2001). Doctors remain in charge in New Zealand as in Australia resulting in regional variation in access to the procedure.

The Abortion Law Reform Association of New Zealand has sought decriminalization of abortion since its founding in 1971, but it has had little success in reaching the public agenda with the proposal. The most recent debate, which the group lost, was to require notification to parents and guardians before abortions can be performed on minors. Among these Western common-law countries, New Zealand has the most restrictive abortion policy.

France

The French case provides an interesting contrast to the British-influenced common-law countries. Most nations in Europe have some form of civil-law codes, many influenced by the Napoleonic code, which was first adopted in 1810. The Napoleonic code criminalized all abortion without exception, making it a felony, the most serious type of crime. Both the abortionist and the woman having the abortion could be condemned to long prison terms. Perhaps the punishment was the reason the law was rarely enforced for many of the same reasons U.S. laws were ineffective: courts and police believed women who had abortions were unfortunate victims, often desperate. During the nineteenth century, French women continued to have abortions, and the rates increased among the middle and upper classes. Another contrast with the British and American cases is that the French government has a long tradition of pronatalism, that is, promoting policies that will increase the birth rate. After World War I, with its great loss of life, and in the face of even more abortions, the government adopted a statute designed to make it difficult for women to limit their pregnancies. The laws of 1920 and 1923 criminalized both abortion and contraception; at the same time the laws reduced the penalties on the assumption that the courts would be more likely to convict if less draconian prison terms were involved. In 1939 a new law allowed for abortion to save the life of the mother, but it also required that doctors report all pregnancies to the police.

Women continued to have abortions despite these strict regulations. The rate increased in the 1960s. Thus, the issue of reform came to the policy agenda because of alarm about the rising incidence of illegal abortions. Family planning groups were working on a conditional reform proposal (abortions would be legal for health, fetal deformity, rape, and incest) when the women's movement organized and took up the issue. They demanded free abortion on demand and brought their demands to public attention by some innovative forms of direct action. They pioneered the "Abortion Manifesto," where hundreds of prominent women publicly declare that they have had illegal abortions and challenge the police to arrest them. The feminist organization *Choisir* (To Choose) formed to publicize a trial prosecuting a teenage woman and her mother charged under the criminal law (Halimi 1973). Feminist groups set up clinics (like Jane in the United States) to counsel and help women obtain abortions.

The modernizing government of President Valery Giscard d'Estaing and his Health Minister Simone Veil agreed that the only way to reduce illegal abortions (and reduce the pressure from the campaign) was to develop a periodic law allowing choice for women in the first 10 weeks of pregnancy. The Veil law passed in 1975 and was made permanent in 1979. In 1983, the government agreed to fund abortions through the national health insurance plan (McBride Stetson 1987, 53–79; Robinson 2001). Then, in 1988, women in France became the first to have access to RU-486, the so-called abortion pill.

Opposition to these reforms came primarily from conservative legislators and the Roman Catholic Church. A small pro-life organization called *Laissez les vivre* ("Let them live") was involved in the public debate; their pro-life constitutional amendments and bills got nowhere. It was not until the early 1990s that antiabortion groups took direct action to promote their agenda. From 1991 to 1993, they took aim at doctors, clinics, and hospitals who performed abortions by blocking entrances and harassing clients and employees. They received advice and support from the U.S. organization, Operation Rescue. The minister for women's issues, Véronique Neiertz, convinced the government to make such activity illegal, and her 1993 law now protects access to abortion clinics. This action reinforced the French abortion triad: women have control over the abortion decision in the first weeks of pregnancy; doctors can decline on the basis of conscience, but abortion is largely a regular medical practice, either via surgery or pills, and the state acts to protect the system against pro-life opponents.

Nordic Countries

In general, the Nordic countries—Norway, Denmark, Sweden, Finland, and Iceland—began to loosen the restrictions on doctors' powers to perform abortions as early as the 1930s. The rise of women's movements in the 1960s pushed governments to further liberalize, either by greatly expanding the number of conditions justifying abortion (Iceland) or by establishing abortion on demand (other countries). The majority of citizens support the current laws, which give the power in the abortion triad to women, but some antiabortion groups and the Christian Democratic parties remain opposed. In all of these countries, however, the official view, which received majority support, is that legal abortion is a necessary last resort; sex education and family planning are emphasized to prevent the need for abortions. In this section, we'll look at three of the countries in more detail (Rolston and Eggert 1994 is the source of most of this information).

In 1962, when Sherri Finkbine could not convince U.S. doctors to terminate her pregnancy on the grounds of severe fetal deformity, she found what she needed in Sweden. In the 1940s, the government had expanded the conditions for abortion to include medical risk, fetal deformity, and pregnancy by rape. Nevertheless, this reform did not answer many women's demands for abortion; illegal abortions continued to increase, and Swedish women started traveling to Eastern Europe, where abortion was legal under the communist governments. The women's rights movement provoked intense debate over what the law should be. In 1975, women's rights advocates were successful when the Social Democratic government enacted a law making abortion a woman's decision—to the twelfth week of pregnancy with no questions asked and to the eighteenth week with counseling. Later abortions are conditional. The Social Democratic party, which has governed Sweden for most of the past 75 years, remains a strong supporter of the law. The Christian Democrats oppose, but they have not attempted to change the law when they have been in power.

Sweden's neighbor, Norway, took more time to change its criminal abortion laws, and expanded the grounds to include socio-medical, eugenic, and ethical conditions in 1966. Administration of the law was fairly liberal, but the number of illegal abortions continued to increase. As in Sweden, the women's rights movement promoted a law based on women's right to self-determination. Despite opposition from Christian leaders and groups who defended the restrictive law, the Norwegian parliament passed a new law in 1978 that gives women the choice to terminate their pregnancies up to 12 weeks on request and free of charge. After 12 weeks, abortions must meet strict conditions.

Denmark follows the Nordic pattern rather closely. Abortion was criminalized until the 1930s when medical, ethical, and eugenic conditions were expanded. However, the law was restrictive because special medical committees had to approve requests from doctors and their patients. Women's rights groups led the campaign for women's self-determination and started making referrals to Eastern European countries. The Socialist party agreed with the demands and helped pass the 1973 law that allows abortion to the twelfth week of pregnancy on a woman's request. Denmark is a bit different from the other countries because there is an active pro-life movement. They have tried, unsuccessfully, to get the government to reverse the law. Debates over the ethics of stem cell research and new reproductive technologies have moved toward official declarations that human life begins at fertilization. So far, such statements include exceptions for abortion laws, but Danish abortion rights activists, like their American counterparts, express concern that the legal personhood for the fetus would, eventually, undermine women's choice in abortion.

Ireland and Germany

Ireland and Germany are exceptions to the abortion politics in the common-law and civil-law countries just described. As a former colony of Great Britain, Ireland has a common-law tradition and inherited the law that abortion was prohibited except to save the life of the mother. Yet instead of following the path of greater liberalization found in the other common-law countries, Ireland's abortion law is even more restrictive than it was under British law. In the case of Germany, a civil-law country like France and the Nordic countries, the government responded to demands from the women's movements in the 1970s to allow for women's self-determination. But this policy was thwarted by the Federal Constitutional Court, which has ruled such liberal laws as unconstitutional. In both countries the abortion triad favors the power of the state to prohibit and control both women and doctors.

Ireland has a "silent export": thousands of women who travel to England each year to get abortions under the British 1967 law (Hadley 1996). Although theoretically Irish law permits abortions to save the life of a pregnant woman, in practice the ban on performance of abortion is absolute. The major debates surround the rights of family-planning organizations to give information and refer women to British clinics. Antiabortion activists are powerful and well connected, because they reflect the teaching of the Roman Catholic Church, which is especially strong in Ireland. They meet little opposition to their demand that unborn life be protected completely. To ensure that these views would be the foundation of Irish government, they successfully promoted a 1983 amendment to the Constitution to protect unborn life: "The State acknowledges the right to life of the unborn and, with due regard to the equal right to life of the mother, guarantees in its laws to respect, as far as practicable, by its laws defend and vindicate that right." The Irish government issued regulations prohibiting groups from providing counseling on abortion or assistance in referrals abroad. In 1993, during negotiations over the treaty forming the European Union (EU), the antiabortion forces obtained a secret agreement exempting their abortion law from oversight by the EU and its laws.

The abortion policy debates in Ireland have been about rights to information and to travel abroad for abortions, not debates over liberalization of the national prohibitions. The people approved these rights by referendum in 1993, but they did not accept another proposal that would have allowed abortions for the mother's life and physical health. Rulings of the Supreme Court, however, seem to mean that abortions to save a life, including the threat of suicide, might not be prosecuted. Still, few doctors are willing to take the risk, and there are few advocates for any kind of reform, let alone guaranteeing women's choice on the matter. The women's movement is divided and, pragmatically, has tended to focus on issues they have a chance of winning, not abortion (Mahon 2001).

The abortion conflict in Germany involves arguments equivalent to those in other Western European countries, that is, women's movement claims to self-determination against the Christian values demanding protection of the fetus's right to life. What makes it different from other European countries, however, is the infusion of special historical circumstances into that debate. After World War II, Germany was divided into two parts. When the two parts reunited in 1990, they had two different abortion laws. The Federal Republic, also called West Germany, had adopted a constitution promoting democracy and human rights. When the parliament responded to the demands for women's self-determination by passing a liberal law in 1975, the Federal Constitutional Court declared that it violated constitutional guarantees of rights to life, including the life of the unborn. Only a restrictive conditional law—medical, fetal handicap, rape/incest conditions—would pass constitutional muster. The Democratic Republic of Germany, also called East Germany, with a government dominated by the Communist party, placed a high priority on women's rights and equality and enacted a law in 1972 that provides abortion on request up to 12 weeks. In the East, German women became used to abortion as a means of birth control while in the West, German woman often traveled to the Netherlands to receive abortions because of the strict law at home.

During the negotiations that preceded unification, the two Germanys sought to reconcile their laws through compromise (Kamenitsa 2001). The division over the abortion policy was so great that it defied agreement and the issue was delayed until after unification. The process involved the former states of the East join-ing the West under the Federal Republic's constitution. The two sides put together a complex compromise that became law, only to, once again, be declared in violation of the constitution by the Federal Constitutional Court. This time the court issued guidelines that the parliament put into a new law in 1995. Abortion in all cir-cumstances is a criminal offense, but women and their doctors will not be prosecuted if the following conditions are met: the woman is in a state of distress and conflict or pregnant by rape or incest and she receives counseling against proceeding with the abortion at least 3 days before the abortion is to be performed. Health insur-ance only covers abortions for poor women.

Mediterranean Countries: Italy, Spain, Portugal, and Greece

Western European countries bordering on the Mediterranean Sea share some aspects of abortion politics. In all these countries the decision whether to liberalize abortion law or not is a Left/Right issue, that is the parties of the Left, such as Socialists, Commu-nists, and Social Democrats, have typically favored more liberal laws. Parties of the Right, such as Conservatives and Christian Democrats, have opposed liberal laws. Another similarity is that the Catholic Church—Roman or Orthodox—which opposes abortion, is an important player in politics and has historic ties as a state religion. These countries have important differences as well. The place of the Catholic Church in political debate and the popularity of its positions vary from dominant in Portugal, influ-ential in Italy, to in decline in Spain and Greece.

Italy was the first of these countries to liberalize its criminal abortion law. The debate over reform was dramatic, and an active women's movement was joined by left-wing activists staging demonstrations and dominating the headlines for weeks in the mid-1970s (Calloni 2001). The result was conditional reform per-mitting women to apply for abortions within the first 90 days of pregnancy on conditions typical of those found in other countries with indications laws: mental and physical health, fetal deformity, rape, or incest. Added to these were social, family, and other circumstances to which a woman can attest to obtain the termination. Thus, on paper, the law became one of the most liberal in Europe because it was based on the woman's request. Efforts to overturn the law with a referendum failed in 1983 ,and a majority of the Italian voters confirmed the reform. In practice, however, abortions are often difficult to get, and most doctors invoke the conscience clause and refuse to perform the procedures. The Vatican from time to time warns Catholics they will face excommunication if they assist. At the same time, abortion—whether legal or illegal—has long been a way Italian women have practiced birth control. Today they have access to contraception, and when that fails, most have little trouble ending their pregnancies.

Women in Greece also seem to pay little attention to what the government or the church says about abortion. The criminal law was liberalized in the 1970s and then further changed in 1986 allowing abortion on request for the first 12 weeks of pregnancy. These changes had little effect because the old criminal law had never been enforced for doctors or women. A main argument for the law was to avoid embarrassment to the legal system from the flagrant violation of the old law. Today there is a high incidence of abortion, and only a small minority is opposed to the legalization of the procedure, despite the official opposition of the Orthodox Catholic Church.

In Spain, too, the Catholic Church was unable to prevent the new democracy from legalizing abortion in 1985 in the face of a high rate of illegal abortions. Two arguments favored reform: first, the criminal law was ineffective in preventing abortion and, second, the Socialist government placed modernization of the legal system as a high priority (Valiente 2001). The government wanted to bring Spain in line with its West European counterparts as quickly as possible; enacting liberal abortion laws was part of that process. Spain's law is actually quite restrictive by European standards; it permits abortion for medical, eugenic, and criminal conditions only. At the same time, the procedure is based in private clinics with little supervision from the state, permitting more liberal implementation.

The EU has issued standards for states to follow in protecting women's reproductive health. Portugal's high rate of illegal abortion, including maternal deaths, has placed its abortion policy in the spotlight. The law has been quite restrictive on paper and in practice. The government has regularly prosecuted not only doctors but also women themselves and has issued prison sentences. The Socialist party has for some time wanted to bring the law more in line with that in other member states of the EU. They have been reluctant to proceed in the face of a 1998 referendum that failed because opponents stayed away from the polls and prevented a valid decision. A similar result occurred in a 2007 referendum; however, there was a strong majority in favor of a more liberal law among those who did vote.

In March 2007, the parliament voted to make abortion legal in the first 10 weeks of pregnancy. With a change in the law in Portugal, abortion is now legal, at least in the first weeks of pregnancy, in all the countries in Western Europe, with the exception of Ireland. For most countries the abortion triad places women in charge with more or less reliance on their doctors. All of these countries are successful democracies and members of the EU. It is not surprising that there is a convergence in the policies and practices with respect to abortion. In the next section we turn to the other half of Europe, which has followed a different trajectory to arrive at nearly the same place.

Central and Eastern Europe

The nations of Central and Eastern Europe (CEE) include the Russian Federation and all the European countries that were under the influence of the Soviet Union during the socialist era from 1946 until around 1990 (including Albania, Bulgaria, Czechoslovakia (now Czech Republic and Slovakia), the German Democratic Republic, Hungary, Poland, Romania, and Yugoslavia and its successor states, along with Lithuania, Latvia, Estonia, and Ukraine). Their abortion politics and policies have been greatly influenced by their experience under Soviet domination. Most of them had restrictive laws until the 1950s when, after Stalin's death, the Soviet government quietly legalized abortion. The CEE countries followed suit, some following the Soviet 1955 law that permitted abortion on women's request in the first trimester while others passed conditional laws. Most of these laws were very liberal in practice. At the same time, there was little information about or access to contraception. Thus, there was a very high incidence of induced abortion in CEE during the socialist period.

The relation between abortion and contraception in the political cultures of the CEE countries was quite different from the views that developed in Western Europe and among family planning groups in the United States. Stenvol (2006) calls these differences the "problematization" of birth control. In the West, contraception is the preferred method of birth control, while abortion is a last resort—a necessary evil. In the East, the dominant issue frame considered modern contraception—intrauterine devices (IUDs), pills—to be dangerous, even unnatural. Abortion, on the other hand, was seen as more natural—even as a form of cleansing. This view coincided with the absence of contraceptive services in the health clinics of the socialist states.

Although these socialist laws may resemble laws in Western Europe and the United States, legal abortion in socialist countries was imbedded in a political and cultural context that was radically different from that of the West. Thus, it is not accurate to describe these laws as providing choice for women or advancing women's rights. In practice, Russian and CEE women had no choice in family planning; they had to resort to abortion to plan their childbearing, and they did—in large numbers. Women could expect to have many abortions over the course of their reproductive years, but it was the doctors who were in control. The abortion policy triad favored physicians who had the means to provide safe abortions; there were no private clinics and no rights to travel to other countries (McBride Stetson 1996).

There was one exception to the liberal use of abortion in the CEE countries—Romania. It followed the Soviet model until the 1960s when the regime of Nikolai Ceauşescu put an extremely restrictive birth control policy in place with the goal of achieving a dramatic boost in population growth rates. Contraception and abortion were prohibited, except for women over age 45 or to save their lives,. Declaring the fetus to be socialist property, the government monitored pregnant women until they gave birth. Abortion rates remained high, according to estimates, but all of them were illegal (Baban 1999, 200).

Around 1990, all of these countries underwent a transition from socialism to market-based economies and democratizing governments. For the most part, however, the new regimes kept their abortion laws from the socialist era; although in the case of Hungary and Romania, the laws became more liberal and allowed abortion on women's request in the first trimester. Other laws and practices changed, however. Contraceptives have become available, and there has been an increase in private medical practice, which has given women more choices. In some countries, antiabortion groups formed; many of these were connected to the Roman Catholic or Orthodox Catholic Churches. New family planning groups came together as well, influenced by international campaigns for reproductive health. Nevertheless, to date, some aspects of abortion politics have not changed. The frames of debates about abortion laws rarely include arguments for women's rights or choice; there is little discussion of the personhood of the fetus either. The dominant issue frame of abortion keeps it in the realm of necessary medical practice, and in most countries, abortion remains the preferred means of birth control. Thus, despite the dramatic changes in the transition from socialism to democracy, the ideas of preventing unwanted pregnancies or advancing women's rights, fetal rights, and individual privacy are not popular.

The exception to this general pattern in the CEE countries is Poland. Before 1990, Poland had a fairly restrictive conditional law, which came into effect in 1956 in the wake of the legalization in the Soviet Union. Officially, women could obtain abortions only on certain conditions, but they were freely available in practice. Yet the Roman Catholic groups opposed the law from the beginning, and many parliamentary deputies spoke out even before the transition. One of the first acts of the new conservative government was to restrict access to abortion, and in 1993, the parliament adopted a new law that allowed abortions only when three physicians certified the pregnancy was a serious threat to the life or health of the woman, if the pregnancy was the result of a crime reported to the police, or if the fetus would be severely deformed. In 1996, a more left-leaning government tried to liberalize the law, but the constitutional court overturned the changes. The 1993 law was reinstated and remains in place. Poland's policies tend to reflect the doctrine of the Roman Catholic Church. Although not illegal, contraceptives are difficult to get and described as "early abortifacients," a view similar to that of some of the pro-life Catholic groups in the United States (Githens 1996). When parliamentarians approved the 1996 reform, Pope John Paul II, the "Polish pope" declared, "A nation that kills its own children is a nation without a future" (quoted in Kulczycki 1999, 110). Even though Poland has the most restrictive law in Europe, next to Ireland, conservative and Roman Catholic groups continue to campaign to prohibit all abortion.

Latin America

Countries in Latin America, which include Brazil and the Spanish-speaking nations of the Caribbean, Central America, and South America, criminalized abortions when they put their modern penal codes in place in the late nineteenth and early twentieth centuries. For the most part, those restrictive laws are still on the books; indeed, some have become even more punitive. Some laws have a specific exception for the life and health of the mother; others do not prosecute for these conditions. A few overlook abortions if the pregnancy is the result of a criminal act such as rape or incest. Chile, El Salvador, and Nicaragua have laws that allow for no exceptions, even if the mother's life is seriously threatened by the pregnancy. Cuba—a socialist country—is the one exception to this general pattern. In 1965, 6 years after the Cuban revolution, the government issued a new law permitting abortion on request up to the tenth week of pregnancy. Cuban clinics allow menstrual regulation treatments, a procedure that extracts the contents of the uterus before the results of a pregnancy test are performed or available.

Along with widespread criminalization, the other notable feature of abortion politics and policy in Latin American countries is the high abortion rate. Millions of illegal abortions are performed, many by untrained clandestine abortionists in unsafe conditions or even by women themselves. Evidently, the restrictive laws are rarely enforced as there are relatively few prosecutions associated with these abortions. At the same time, there is a cost in the comparatively high rates of maternal deaths due to botched abortions. Two countries with very restrictive laws that do pay attention to prosecution are Chile and El Salvador (Htun 2003; Hitt 2006). In the latter case, *New York Times* journalist Jack Hitt reported that women are often arrested in their hospital beds, while recovering from infections and hemorrhages.

In some countries, leaders have recognized that the increases in abortions are in part due to the lack of contraception, especially for the poor. This has provoked politicians to take a more active stance on providing contraception to reduce the abortion toll. The Chilean government, for example, has responded to the relentless increases in illegal abortions by promoting extensive family planning services in public clinics, including access to emergency contraception. Mexico, despite the claims of its revolutionary ideology that its plans for social equality would make birth control unnecessary, has also accepted the need for family planning.

In Brazil, despite a restrictive law, abortion—both safe and unsafe—is widely practiced. Brazil also has a more hospitable climate for reform politics. Proposals for liberalizing the law that allows abortion only for rape or to save a woman's life have reached the level of presidential politics. This is an exception to the norm in Latin America. Despite the evidence of the effects of the prohibitions on maternal health, political leaders rarely bring the question of abortion to the policy agenda, except to propose a more restrictive law as occurred in Nicaragua in 2006.

Why has there been no liberalization of abortion laws in Latin America? One reason is the rocky political history in the 1960s and 1970s, decades when reform movements were developing in the Western democracies. Military regimes ruled many countries, repressing groups, especially women's rights activists, likely to demand change. The transition to democracy in the 1980s and 1990s has opened up new opportunities for participation. In recent years, women especially have become involved in politics, and governments have responded by modernizing laws toward more gender equality (Htun 2003). At the same time, they have not changed many laws relating to reproductive issues.

Latin American countries still lack the components that have led to law reforms in the United States and Europe. Domestic pro-choice movements do not exist; the groups that are most interested in promoting reform are external to the countries, such as Human Rights Watch, the Center for Reproductive Rights, and Women's Link Worldwide. They work with a small number of local feminists, family planning groups, and physicians, but they cannot mobilize enough public opinion and activism to gain attention of political parties and politicians. In addition, they face a very strong adversary: the Roman Catholic Church.

Just when the opportunities for participation improved, Pope John Paul II turned his attention to the Latin American countries in an effort to strengthen the Catholic Church's position there. Along with an emphasis on unity, hierarchy, and discipline in the national churches, he made opposition to divorce, birth control, and abortion a top priority. The church's stance empowered Catholic parties and politicians in many Latin American countries; it also increased the presence of antiabortion officials at any international discussion of population, reproductive health, and women's rights.

At the same time, the pro-life groups in the United States are very interested in maintaining the restrictive laws in Latin America. Human Life International uses Catholic doctrine to organize pro-life groups in many countries. The pro-life support of the Mexico City policy has had the effect of denying U.S. family planning funds to organizations that might otherwise promote reform. One of the main arguments in favor of this policy is that it would place the United States in a position of unduly interfering with the abortion laws—in this case restrictive ones—in sovereign countries.

Finally, reform efforts have little chance in the Latin American legislatures. Antiabortion politicians are strongly committed to their pro-life positions; many are closely associated with the Catholic hierarchy in their country. Those legislators who are not pro-life either have little interest in the abortion issue or actively avoid getting involved with what they may see as a dangerous conflict. The top politicians, even a feminist like Chile's President Michelle Bachelet, do not challenge the current laws. Public opinion is either ambivalent or disinterested providing few resources to any elected politician who takes up the issue. An exception is the April 2007 decriminalization of abortion in Mexico City by the city council, an action which received widespread support despite opposition from the Catholic hierarchy.

If there is to be a change in the abortion policy in most Latin American countries it is likely to follow the lead of the high court in Colombia. As part of a regional litigation strategy, Women's Link Worldwide attorneys challenged Colombia's restrictive abortion law as a violation of its international treaty obligations to ensure human rights, in this case, women's rights to life and health. The court ruled that abortion must be permitted for threats to a woman's health or life and in cases of rape, incest, and fetal deformity. Although the resulting policy remains restrictive compared with laws in Europe, the Colombian court's response suggests a promising avenue to change. At the same time, pro-life organizations outside the region consider such litigation in Latin American courts to be an attack on the rights of the pre-born and warn of a *Roe v. Wade* effect spreading in the region.

East and South Asia

The laws on the books in Asian countries vary from restrictive, as in Indonesia, to abortion on request, as in China. Regardless of the formal rules, however, abortion is generally a widespread means of birth control in Asian countries. The use of modern contraceptives, such as the hormone pill or the IUD, arrived much later than in Western countries. Many women remain ignorant of these methods or afraid of their effects, despite efforts of international and domestic family planning organizations. The abortion issue is not high on the public agendas in any country, and there is little public debate about changing the laws or the practices.

Since the 1950s, most governments have taken a direct interest in the size and composition of their populations. This is often a more straightforward and direct approach in authoritarian systems than in the more democratic ones. It is important to consider the practice of abortion in the context of such population policies. Rather than responding to demands for greater liberalization or restrictions from political groups or social movements, political leaders assess the abortion rates according to the way they contribute to demographic goals. In this brief review of abortion policy and politics in Japan, China, Korea, and India, we will see that strategies to shape fertility behavior may have unintended consequences.

Japan is an island with a large population. After its defeat in World War II, the government wanted to keep population growth under control and to be sure that families would not reproduce genetically inferior offspring. The legalization of abortion in 1948 included several eugenic conditions that allowed abortions, along with social and economic conditions and threats to a woman's health. In fact, it didn't much matter what the law said because doctors would perform abortions on a woman's request and did not require any proof of a legally required condition. Over the years, there have been a few debates over the abortion law. These have occupied a relatively small group of elites either from the right, where they are trying to reduce the high abortion rate, or from the left, where coalitions of feminists, family planning organizations, and socialists have overcome efforts to tighten up the law (Gelb 2003). In 1996, parliament revised the abortion law to remove the language about eugenics (abolishing forced sterilization of the handicapped, for example). This was more a response to groups with disabilities than any attempt at abortion reform, and it left the general policy intact.

The participation of Japanese politicians, especially women, in international conferences in the 1990s brought home the realization that Japan was behind the rest of the industrialized democracies because of the high rate of abortion and the low use of contraceptives (Norgren 2001). In fact, modern contraceptives weren't even legal. As a result of their efforts, these leaders were able to persuade the government to legalize the hormone pill in 1999. Since these reforms, the abortion rate has begun to decline, and the use of contraception has increased, although fewer than 10 percent of couples use pills or IUDs, relying instead on condoms and withdrawal (Sato and Iwasawa 2006). Public discussion of reproductive issues is infrequent, and there is scarce attention to sex education; many women remain ignorant of contraception and family planning until they find themselves seeking their first abortion.

One other feature of abortion politics in Japan caught public attention in the 1990s. Some Buddhist temples set aside space for parents to remember their aborted fetuses in a ritual called *mizuko kuyo*. The Western press described these as apologies to the fetus, a way of assuaging guilt of parents who have ended its life. However, others have reported that such practices are a blatant attempt by the temples to cash in on the lucrative abortion practice (Hardacre 1997). In fact, it is likely that the main political force for maintaining the status quo is the medical profession, which reaps big profits (at $1,000 per procedure) from legal abortion.

China has the largest population in the world—1.2 billion people. The country's politics have been turbulent in the past 60 years—ranging from a Communist social revolution to the rise of a market economy. Regardless of the frequent political and economic upheavals, the population has grown steadily. As a result, all Chinese leaders have adhered to a strict antigrowth policy since the 1970s In 1979, the government adopted the "one-child" approach, which sought to limit each couple to one child. To accomplish this goal, the government also instituted nationwide family planning programs that included information, education, and services for contraception and an abortion policy that allowed abortion on request up to 6 months of pregnancy when contraception failed. Economic incentives and disincentives completed the policy. Organized social pressures on women to abort their second or third pregnancies and even forced sterilization were reported. According to the UN, the one-child policy has been limited to the majority Han population in the urban areas.

Demographic studies show that the policy has slowed the fertility rates in China, and the government has extended it to at least 2010. But the policy has had an unintended consequence: it has upset the sex balance. A normal ratio of male to female births is 105/100. In China, since the 1970s, the ratio has been as high as 114/100. The phenomenon of the missing millions of girls has been attributed to female-selective abortion (FSA) and neglect, abandonment, or infanticide of female babies (Miller 2001). It works something like this: There is a cultural preference for male children. When a couple is pressured to limit their childbearing to one child, they prefer to give birth to a boy. If they can learn the sex of the fetus before birth, through amniocentesis or ultrasound, they will choose abortion if it is female. In communities where such technologies are not available, then parents resort to other strategies. In the current climate in China, few questions are asked of women seeking abortions, and they are free, safe, and easily accessible.

Other Asian countries also have the FSA phenomenon and the resulting imbalanced sex ratios. Korea has a restrictive abortion law, allowing abortion only for a few conditions: life and health of the mother, hereditary diseases of the parents, or pregnancy as a result of rape and incest. Despite the restrictive law, Korea adopted a successful population policy to reduce the birth rate from 6.3 births per woman in 1955 to 1.08 births per woman in 2005, below the 2.1 replacement level (the U.S. level is 2.1). Despite attention to family planning services, however, abortion has been the primary means for birth control among Korean women. The cultural and political pressure to have small families, coupled with widespread abortion, led to a sex imbalance that reached 115/100 in 1994 and is now around 108/100 (Byun 2006).

India has a comparatively flexible abortion statute, which it adopted in 1971. Abortion is permitted up to 20 weeks of gestation to preserve the life and health of the mother and for a risk of fetal deformity or handicap. The statute also accepts reasons of rape and contraceptive failure when the abortion is used to limit the number of children. India too has been troubled with the growth rate of its huge population and has established a policy to encourage family planning by bringing contraceptive services to the diverse country and even providing incentives for sterilization. The goal of the abortion law was to reduce the high incidence of illegal abortions and maternal death. The rate of illegal abortion remains high, however, especially among the poor.

To adapt to the new standard of smaller families, Indian women, like their counterparts in China, Korea, and Pakistan, looked for ways to ensure that they would give birth to as many boys as possible. The widespread availability of ultrasound technology gave rise to a lucrative business for doctors who promised to ensure that the next child would be a boy. If the ultrasound showed a woman was carrying a female fetus, the doctor could easily provide an abortion so the couple could try again for a boy. This practice of FSA brought the sex ratio as high as 112/100 in the early 1990s (Miller 2001).

After widespread international publicity about the millions of "missing girls" (aborted females) in these Asian countries, the governments moved to prohibit abortion for sex selection—in Korea in 1987, India in 1994, and China in 2003. These bans are difficult to enforce, although China and India have tried to regulate the use of ultrasound equipment for determining the sex of a fetus. The question of skewed sex ratios has been the topic of international debate. Feminists decry the cultural position of girls and women in these countries that is represented by the figures. They argue that it is part of a strict patriarchy that has stayed in place despite economic modernization. Human rights activists see the deliberate aborting of only females as a violation of human rights. Some sociologists warn that generations of boys and men will be unable to marry and be part of a viable family; and, at loose ends, they can cause violence, increased crime, and social unrest (Hudson and den Boer 2004). On the other side, there are claims that the demographic pattern is temporary; with fewer girls, the value of women will increase and in the long term births will reestablish the normal balance. Others say the imbalance is effective in reducing population growth (fewer women to give birth). Finally, some warn not to get too worked up over the reports because the data on abortions and births in these countries is notoriously unreliable (Miller 2001).

Africa and the Middle East

Abortion laws among the countries in the Middle East and Africa have little variation. They are almost universally restrictive, prohibiting abortion in all circumstances, but allowing the procedure to save a woman's life; such laws empower the state's role in the abortion triad rather than doctors or women. Only a few countries, mostly in Africa, allow exceptions for physical and mental health and only one or two for cases of fetal deformity or for social and economic reasons. At the same time, the incidence of unsafe abortions and maternal deaths ranges from moderate to very high (World Health Organization 2004). Prosecutions for illegal abortions are rare, and there is little public debate about abortion policy as the issue is rarely on the agenda of political leaders.

The situation in Egypt is representative of the politics of abortion in North Africa and the Middle East. Egypt has long prohibited abortion by law in all circumstances but does not prosecute when abortions are to save a woman's life. At the same time, there are few prosecutions for any abortions because the law has stringent evidence requirements. "The intent to commit the act is not sufficient to be convicted of the offence of abortion. The prosecution also has to prove the pregnancy of the woman, the interruption of pregnancy and the illegal means to interrupt the pregnancy. Given these requirements, it is difficult for the prosecution to procure the evidence necessary for a conviction of the crime of abortion" (United Nations 2001, Vol. I, 135).

There are exceptions to the generalizations about the region. Israel, Tunisia, and Algeria, have established broader grounds for abortion—physical and mental health and fetal impairment. The abortion issue has recently been on the public agenda in Iran where the legislature agreed to extend legal abortion to include cases of fetal deformity along with threats to the pregnant woman's life. However, the conservative Council of Guardians, dominated by Muslim clerics, rejected the reform in 2005.

Kenya is representative of the politics of abortion in sub-Saharan Africa. Kenya retains a law, dating back to the period of British rule, that prohibits abortion except to preserve the life and health of the mother. Legal abortions are difficult to obtain because complex procedures must be met. The rate of illegal abortions is high, but there are few prosecutions. The government's family planning policy dates from the 1960s and is one of the earliest on the continent. Nevertheless, the rate of contraceptive use is low. The rate of unsafe abortions contributes to Kenya's high rate of maternal death; the rate of abortions among adolescents in on the rise. All of these facts point to a problem with abortion policy in Kenya.

Despite the concerns of many family planning groups and other health professionals, the abortion issue is not on the national agenda (Kulczycki 1999). Antiabortion forces in the country are strong, especially the Roman Catholic bishops and conservatives. When public officials have mentioned the need for a policy change, there is an immediate negative reaction from the antiabortion groups. Cultural factors make it difficult to confront the problem of illegal abortion. Custom dictates, for example, that people marry early and that women have children through-out their reproductive years. Traditionalists consider abortion, like feminism, to be a foreign import; they claim that before the colonial period there were no abortions among the people of Kenya.

Other barriers to finding a solution to illegal abortion as well as other threats to women's health include a lack of contraception and prenatal care and health systems that cannot answer demands on them, especially among the poor. The government has become increasingly authoritarian since independence in the 1960s, which makes it difficult for advocates to get a hearing from the top leaders. Few doctors and family planning workers have taken up the abortion issue. The HIV/AIDS health chal-lenge has dominated social services since the 1990s; at the same time the Mexico City policy of the United States has limited the funds coming from foreign aid for reproductive health needs.

The exception to the general pattern in sub-Saharan Africa is South Africa. The end of the white-dominated rule of apartheid in the early 1990s opened the door for a reexamination of law and policy in South Africa. The newly empowered black citizens con-tributed to writing a new constitution and electing a democratic government. In the first election, the African National Congress campaigned on the pledge to liberalize the abortion law. They did so in 1996, changing the restrictive and racist conditional law to allow abortion on request in the first 12 weeks of pregnancy and up to 20 weeks on a set of broad grounds. Before the reform, there were high rates of unsafe abortions among poor black South Africans. Since the reform, more abortion services are available, but there are still problems in answering the demands. Still, the overall rate of unsafe abortions has declined.

The law is based on the idea of individual rights, especially women's rights. This reflects the significant attention in the 1996 constitution to women's equality and the establishment of influ-ential women's policy agencies that pushed a pro-choice agenda:

> Recognising that the Constitution protects the right of persons to make decisions concerning reproduction and to security in and control over their bodies;

Recognising that both women and men have the right to be informed of and to have access to safe, effective, affordable and acceptable methods of fertility regulation of their choice, and that women have the right of access to appropriate health care services to ensure safe pregnancy and childbirth;

Recognising that the decision to have children is fundamental to women's physical, psychological and social health and that universal access to reproductive health care services includes family planning and contraception, termination of pregnancy, as well as sexuality education and counseling programmes and services (Source: Preamble, Choice on Termination of Pregnancy Act 1996, www.info.gov.za/acts/1996).

The antiabortion forces have not given up the battle, and there was strong opposition to the initial liberalization of abortion policy in 1996. Many blacks oppose free abortion because they see it as a legacy of apartheid when white rulers tried to boost white birth rates and limit fertility of blacks. The pro-life opposition claims that this law violates the right to life guaranteed to the unborn in the constitution. The constitutional court has ruled, however, that this right does not extend to the fetus (United Nations 2001; Guttmacher et al 1998).

The United Nations

The World Health Organization has documented that the rate of unsafe abortions in developing countries is one of the most neglected world health problems. Estimates suggest that two of every five pregnancies worldwide are unplanned due to lack of information on contraception, lack of access to services, or failure of the method used (World Health Organization 2004). Many women in poor countries seek help from clandestine practitioners who are untrained and are likely to operate in unsafe conditions. The consequences can be frightening: "Severe complications, such as sepsis, hemorrhage, genital and abdominal trauma, perforated uterus and poisoning due to ingestion of harmful substances, may be fatal if left untreated . . . Unsafe abortion may lead to reproductive tract infections, chronic pelvic pain, pelvic inflammatory disease, and at times to infertility; genital trauma and infection may also warrant an immediate hysterectomy" (World Health Organization 2004, 4).

Transnational networks of women's nongovernmental organizations (NGOs) have taken the issues of unsafe abortion under the umbrella of demands for better reproductive health to the UN and other international organizations. Their goal is to frame debates and establish policies at the international level that will influence the abortion politics of member states (Petchesky 2003). Since the 1980s, coalitions of activists have attempted to link the right to abortion not only to women's rights and equality but also more generally to human rights. In international conferences these women's NGOs have encountered strong opposition from traditional and conservative groups, pro-life organizations, and, especially, the Roman Catholic Church.

The following are excerpts from three UN documents that take positions related to abortion:

1. *Convention for Elimination of Discrimination Against Women 1979* requires that "States Parties shall take all appropriate measures to eliminate discrimination against women in the field of health care in order to ensure, on a basis of equality of men and women, access to health care services, including those related to family planning" (Article 12).
2. The UN International Conference on Population and Development (ICPD) met in Cairo, Egypt in 1994 and agreed that "In no case should abortion be promoted as a method of family planning. All governments and relevant intergovernmental and non-governmental organizations are urged to strengthen their commitment to women's health, to deal with the health aspect of unsafe abortion as a major public health concern and to reduce the recourse to abortion through expanded and improved family planning services . . . In circumstances where abortion is not against the law, such abortion should be safe. In all cases women should have access to quality services for management and complications arising from abortion."
3. The Plan of Action for UN Fourth Conference on Women in Beijing, China, in 1995 declared that: "the human rights of women include their right to have control over and decide freely and responsibly on matters related to their sexuality, including sexual and reproductive health,

free of coercion, discrimination and violence." The report went on to assert: "The ability of women to control their own fertility forms an important basis for the enjoyment of other rights. Shared responsibility between women and men in matters related to sexual and reproductive behavior is also essential to improving women's health." On the question of unsafe abortion the plan declared, "Since unsafe abortion is a major threat to the health and life of women, research to understand and better address the determinants and consequences of induced abortion, including its effects on subsequent fertility, reproductive and mental health and contraceptive practice, should be promoted, as well as research on treatment of complications of abortions and post-abortion care" (Source: www.un.org/womenwatch/daw/beijing/index.html).

The transnational pro-life movement has met the women's rights coalition head-on at every UN venue where the issues of abortion may come up. Those opposed to abortion challenge terms such as "reproductive health," "reproductive rights," "family planning," and "women's rights as human rights." They warn that these terms are a way to make the right to abortion enforceable through treaty obligations and in international forums. Nowhere in the agreements has the UN adopted the position that abortion is a woman's right or choice and the 1994 ICPD document even explicitly proclaimed that abortion is not an acceptable form of family planning. Nevertheless, representatives of the George W. Bush administration to the UN conferences have repeatedly asked that the international bodies reject abortion in their documents. While the UN has not taken a pro-choice position, it has not taken the pro-life position either. The result is that the interpretation of the meaning of these documents and their significance depends on the views of leaders in the nearly 200 states that belong to the UN.

References

Baban, Adriana. "Romania." In *From Abortion to Contraception: A Resource to Public Policies and Reproductive Behavior in Central and Eastern Europe from 1917 to the Present,* edited by Henry P. David with assistance of Joanna Skilogianis, 191–222. Westport, CT: Greenwood Press, 1999.

Byun, Wha-soon. "The Imbalance of Sex Ratio and Reproductive Rights in Korea." International Political Science Association, Fukuoka, Japan. 2006. www.ipsa.org (accessed December, 31, 2006).

Calloni, Marina. "Debates and Controversies on Abortion in Italy." In *Abortion Politics, Women's Movements and the Democratic State: A Comparative Study in State Feminism,* edited by D. McBride Stetson, 181–204. Oxford: Oxford University Press, 2001.

Cohan, Alvin. "Abortion as a Marginal Issue: The Use of Peripheral Mechanisms in Britain and the United States." In *The New Politics of Abortion,* edited by J. Lovenduski and J. Outshoorn, 27–49. London: Sage, 1986.

Gelb, Joyce. *Gender Policies in Japan and the United States: Comparing Women's Movements, Rights, and Politics.* New York: Palgrave Macmillan, 2003.

Githens, Marianne. "Reproductive Rights and the Struggle with Change in Eastern Europe." In *Abortion Politics: Public Policy in a Cross Cultural Perspective,* edited by M. Githens and D. McBride Stetson, 55–70. New York: Routledge, 1996.

Guttmacher, Sally, Farzana Kapadia, Jim Te Water Nanda, and Helen De Pinho. "Abortion Reform in South Africa: A Case Study of the 1996 Choice on Termination of Pregnancy Act." *International Family Planning Perspectives* 1998 (24): 191–194.

Hadley, Janet. *Abortion: Between Freedom and Necessity.* Philadelphia, PA: Temple University Press, 1996.

Halimi, Gisèle. *The Right to Choose.* Brisbane, Australia: University of Queensland Press, 1973.

Hardacre, Helen. *Marketing the Menacing Fetus in Japan.* Berkeley: University of California Press, 1997.

Haussman, Melissa. *Abortion Politics in North America.* Boulder, CO: Lynne Rienner, 2005.

Hindell, Keith, and Madeleine Simms. *Abortion Law Reformed.* London: Peter Owen, 1970.

Hitt, Jack. "Pro-Life Nation." *The New York Times Magazine.* April 9, 2006. 41–47, 62, 72, 74.

Htun, Mala. *Sex and the State: Abortion, Divorce, and the Family under Latin American Dictatorships and Democracies.* Cambridge: Cambridge University Press, 2003.

Hudson, Valerie, and Andrea M. den Boer. 2004. *Bare Branches: The Security Implications of Asia's Surplus Male Population.* Cambridge: Cambridge University Press.

Kamenitsa, Lynn. "Abortion Debates in Germany." In *Abortion Politics, Women's Movements and the Democratic State: A Comparative Study in State Feminism,* edited by D. McBride Stetson, 111–134. Oxford: Oxford University Press, 2001.

Kulczycki, Andrzej. *The Abortion Debate in the World Arena.* New York: Routledge, 1999.

Mahon, Evelyn. "Abortion Debates in Ireland: An Ongoing Issue." In *Abortion Politics, Women's Movements and the Democratic State: A Comparative Study in State Feminism,* edited by D. McBride Stetson, 157–180. Oxford: Oxford University Press, 2001.

McBride Stetson, Dorothy. *Women's Rights in France.* Westport, CT: Greenwood Press, 1987.

McBride Stetson, Dorothy. "Abortion Policy Triads and Women's Rights in Russia, the United States and France." In *Abortion Politics: Public Policy in Cross Cultural Perspective,* edited by M. Githens and D. McBride Stetson, 97–118. New York: Routledge, 1996.

McBride Stetson, Dorothy. "Women's Movements' Defence of Legal Abortion in Great Britain." In *Abortion Politics, Women's Movements and the Democratic State: A Comparative Study in State Feminism,* edited by D. McBride Stetson, 135–156. Oxford: Oxford University Press, 2001.

Miller, Barbara. "Female-Selective Abortion in Asia: Patterns, Policies and Debates." *American Anthropologist* 103 (2001): 1083–1095.

Norgren, Tiana. *Abortion Before Birth Control: The Politics of Reproduction in Postwar Japan.* Princeton, NJ: Princeton University Press, 2001.

Petchesky, Rosalind Pollack. *Global Prescriptions: Gendering Health and Human Rights.* London: Zed Books, 2003.

Potts, Malcolm, Peter Diggory, and John Peel. *Abortion.* Cambridge, England: Cambridge University Press, 1977.

Robinson, Jean. "Gendering the Abortion Debate: The French Case." In *Abortion Politics, Women's Movements and the Democratic State: A Comparative Study in State Feminism,* edited by D. McBride Stetson, 87–110. Oxford: Oxford University Press, 2001.

Rolston, Bill, and Anna Eggert, eds. *Abortion in the New Europe: A Comparative Handbook.* Westport, CT: Greenwood Press, 1994.

Sato, Ryuzaburo, and Miko Iwasawa. "Contraceptive Use and Induced Abortion in Japan: How Is It so Unique among Developed Countries? *The Japanese Journal of Population* March 2006: 33–55.

Sheldon, Sally. *Beyond Control: Medical Power and Abortion Law.* London: Pluto Press, 1997.

Stenvol, Dag. "Contraception, Abortion, and State Socialism." International Political Science Association, Fukuoka, Japan, 2006. www.ipsa.org (accessed December 29, 2006).

United Nations. *Abortion Policies: A Global Review* Volumes I, II, III. New York: United Nations, 2001.

Valiente, Celia. 2001. "Gendering Abortion Debates: State Feminism in Spain." In *Abortion Politics, Women's Movements and the Democratic State: A Comparative Study in State Feminism,* edited by D. McBride Stetson, 229–246. Oxford: Oxford University Press, 2001.

World Health Organization. *Unsafe Abortion: Global and Regional Estimates of the Incidence of Unsafe Abortion and Associated Mortality in 2000.* Geneva, Switzerland: World Health Organization, 2004.

4

Chronology

The events in this chronology impart an impression of the origins, development, and outcomes of policy debates in three eras: the nineteenth century, which led to criminalization of abortion in the United States and other countries; the movement for reform of those criminal abortion policies in the first 70 years of the twentieth century; and the contemporary pro-choice versus pro-life standoff since 1973.

1803   The British parliament passes Lord Ellenborough's Act, an omnibus crime statute that makes abortion before quickening a criminal act and thus overturns the long-standing common-law practice of not prosecuting abortions performed before quickening.

1810   The Napoleonic law code criminalizes abortion making it a felony with no exceptions. This becomes a standard for civil-law countries in Europe.

1821   The Connecticut legislature passes the first abortion statute in the United States, which makes performing abortion by poison after quickening a crime. Missouri (1825) and Illinois (1827) pass similar statutes, beginning the process of criminalization.

1828   The New York state legislature passes a law that makes performing abortion by any means after quickening a crime.

1830	The decade that follows shows a noticeable increase in the number and rate of abortions, especially among middle-class married women.
1840	New abortion statutes spread among the states until by this date ten of the twenty-six states have some restrictions.
1845	J. Marion Sims, a gynecologist in New York, develops the modern speculum for vaginal medical examinations.
1847	The American Medical Association (AMA) forms and becomes the first professional association of doctors.
1857	Dr. Horatio Storer, an obstetrician and gynecologist, urges medical doctors to use their connections with politicians to make abortion illegal.
1859	The AMA declares that abortion at any stage of pregnancy kills a human being and resolves to campaign to criminalize abortion in all states.
1861	The British parliament enacts the Offenses Against the Person Act, which prohibits abortion—with no exceptions—and prosecutes both the abortionist and the woman undergoing the procedure. This act becomes law in the countries of the British Commonwealth, including Australia, Canada, India, Ireland, and New Zealand.
1869	Pope Pius IX officially puts the Roman Catholic Church in opposition to contraception and abortion in the papal bull (constitutional proclamation) *Apostolicae Sedis Moderationi*.
1870s	Dilation and curettage, or D&C, is developed as a method of early abortions, first in Germany and later in the United States.
1873	Congress enacts the Comstock Act, which makes it a federal crime to import or sell obscene materials,

including information about and devices for contraception and abortion, through interstate commerce.

1884   Pope Pius IX declares that an embryo has a soul from conception and that abortion for any reason, even to save the mother's life, is against Roman Catholic Church doctrine.

1900   At this time all states have criminalized abortion throughout pregnancy; some statutes permit exceptions only to save the life of the mother and some hold the woman as well as the abortionist liable for prosecution.

1915   The surgical procedures Joseph Lister developed in the 1860s finally come into common practice in both the operating room and the delivery room. As a result, abortion mortality and childbirth mortality begin to decline. At some point later, the two downward curves intersect, and abortion became less dangerous to the woman than childbirth.

1916   Margaret Sanger opens the first birth control clinic in the United States. Within a few years she is jailed for violating the Comstock Act.

1920   After the Bolshevik Revolution of 1917, Russia becomes the first country to legalize abortion on woman's request as a health measure to stem the health costs of illegal abortions. In 1936, Stalin recriminalizes abortion to promote population growth.

1921   The American Birth Control League forms after the reorganization of its parent organization, the National Birth Control League, which was founded in 1916.

1936   A study by Frederick J. Taussig shows that the illegal abortion rate in the United States has skyrocketed to 500,000 per year.

        A federal circuit court's decision in *U.S. v. One Package* (86 F.2d 737 [2nd Cir. 1936]) rules that the Comstock

1936
(*cont.*)
Act does not prevent the import and distribution of contraceptives and abortion devices for physicians to use in their medical practice. Unless state laws prevent it, contraceptives such as diaphragms are now available from doctors.

1937
The AMA recognizes birth control as integral to medical practice.

Margaret Sanger resigns from the American Birth Control League.

1939
Dr. Aleck Bourne is acquitted of criminal abortion in English courts when he explains that he has helped preserve the mental and physical health of a pregnant fourteen-year-old who had been raped. This establishes the *Bourne* defense, which liberalizes abortion practice in Great Britain, Canada, and other countries in the Commonwealth to allow the procedure to save the life and health of the mother.

1942
Dr. Alan Guttmacher calls for extensive liberalization of criminal abortion laws at the New York meeting of the American Birth Control League. At the same meeting, the members vote to change the organization's name to Planned Parenthood Federation of America.

1950s
To better regulate the practice of legal abortions in response to policy crackdowns and publicity, many hospitals create committees that must approve the procedures before doctors can perform them.

1953
Alfred Kinsey's controversial report, *Sexual Behavior in the Human Female,* appears. He reports that 22 percent of married women have had an abortion and that 90 percent of pregnancies outside marriage end in abortion.

1955
The Soviet Union quietly legalizes abortion, declaring it a woman's right.

Planned Parenthood sponsors a conference, "Abortion in America," led by Mary Calderone. The conference report is published in 1958.

1957   British physician Dr. Ian Donald develops technological applications for using ultrasound to view a developing fetus during pregnancy. It becomes widely available during the 1970s.

1958   The use of the vacuum aspiration technique for early abortions is pioneered in China.

1959   The American Law Institute (ALI) drafts a model abortion reform statute that would allow doctors to perform abortions for the health of the mother, if the fetus is deformed, or if the pregnancy was the result of rape or incest. These reforms are examples of "indications" abortion laws.

In his book *Babies by Choice or Chance,* Dr. Alan Guttmacher calls for more liberal abortion laws across the country.

1960   The U.S. Food and Drug Administration (FDA) approves the use of the hormone pill to prevent conception.

Dr. Alan Guttmacher and other physicians in New York form the Association for the Study of Abortion, one of the first organizations promoting reform of criminal abortion laws.

1962   Pat Maginnis of California forms the feminist Citizens' Committee for Humane Abortion Laws, which seeks to repeal criminal abortion laws.

Sherry Finkbine travels to Sweden to obtain a legal abortion after being denied by her hospital in Arizona. She fears she will give birth to a severely deformed child because she took thalidomide during her pregnancy without knowing it might cause birth defects.

1962
(*cont.*)

Her previously arranged abortion was denied after publicity about her situation. This marks the beginning of major public debate on abortion law reform.

1963

The U.S. government establishes the National Institute of Child Health and Human Development. Part of its mandate is to support and oversee research in reproductive science and contraceptive development.

1964

A rubella epidemic breaks out in the United States. The damage rubella can do to a fetus in early pregnancy is widely understood, and many women, primarily those with money and/or influence, demand and get legal abortions. But tens of thousands are prevented by restrictive laws.

Bill Baird opens a birth control clinic on Long Island and begins to give women referrals for abortion, becoming one of the first referral services in the country.

1965

The Supreme Court issues its ruling in *Griswold v. Connecticut* that the Constitution creates a zone of privacy where government may not intrude and that decisions by married couples about whether and when to have a child are inside that zone. States may not prohibit married couples from access to contraceptive information and services.

CBS Reports, the respected television news series, broadcasts "Turning Points in the Debate on Abortion and Birth Control," which includes interviews with clergy, doctors, lawyers, and population control advocates.

The *New York Times* endorses abortion law reform in an editorial.

1966

Roman Catholic priest (later bishop) James McHugh forms the National Right to Life Committee (NRLC); the NRLC becomes a national coordinating organization in 1971.

The National Organization for Women (NOW) forms as the first civil rights organization for women.

Laurence Lader's book *Abortion* is published; it details the extent of both legal and illegal abortion in the United States and the effects on women.

1967   The vacuum aspiration technique for performing abortions in the first weeks of pregnancy, first used in China, is presented to U.S. physicians in the journal *Obstetrics and Gynecology*. It quickly becomes the preferred method for first-trimester abortions, replacing the D&C.

At its second annual convention, NOW calls for the repeal of criminal abortion laws.

The AMA endorses the ALI model reform statute.

Colorado becomes the first state to pass the ALI model reform statute, followed by North Carolina and California.

The Virginia Society for Human Life forms, becoming the first state pro-life organization; state pro-life organizations are subsequently formed in Minnesota, Colorado, and Illinois.

After a 30-year campaign, the British Abortion Law Reform Association finds success when the British parliament enacts the Abortion Act, the first liberalization among European democracies. The act decriminalizes abortions performed when two doctors agree that pregnancy would risk the life and physical or mental health of the pregnant woman or any of her children, or if there is risk of fetal deformity.

1968   The American College of Obstetricians and Gynecologists endorses the ALI model reform statute.

The American Public Health Association becomes the first professional organization to support repeal of criminal abortion laws.

1968
(*cont.*)

Pope Paul VI issues *Humanae Vitae* (Human Life), a papal encyclical that reaffirms the opposition of the Roman Catholic Church to contraception and abortion.

The American Civil Liberties Union calls for repeal of all criminal abortion laws saying they obstruct women's reproductive rights and freedoms.

1969

The First National Conference on Abortion Laws convenes in Chicago. Lawrence Lader and Lonny Myers take this opportunity to form the National Association for the Repeal of Abortion Laws (NARAL).

Jane, the abortion counseling service of women's liberation, provides abortions outside the law for women in Chicago.

Attorneys Sarah Weddington and Linda Coffee ask Norma McCorvey to be the plaintiff Jane Roe in a case challenging the constitutionality of the nineteenth-century criminal abortion statute in Texas.

The Centers for Disease Control and Prevention begins their annual report of the number of legal abortions and the characteristics of the women who obtain them.

1970

The Hawaiian legislature repeals its criminal abortion statute, becoming the first state to legalize all abortions in the first 20 weeks of pregnancy. New York repeals its abortion law and permits abortion up to 24 weeks of pregnancy, followed by Alaska. The state of Washington repeals its law through a referendum.

Congress enacts the Family Planning Services and Population Research Act, which authorizes grants to organizations and public clinics for family planning.

The AMA extends support to doctors who perform abortions for social and economic conditions of women with problem pregnancies.

1971   A national poll shows that a majority of Americans support liberalization of abortion laws.

            Congress repeals most of the provisions of the 1873 Comstock Act.

1972   By this year, fourteen states have passed abortion reform statutes modeled after the ALI conditional reform.

            The American Bar Association goes on record in favor of legal abortion through the twentieth week of pregnancy.

            Governor Nelson Rockefeller of New York vetoes the state legislature's effort to rescind the 1970 abortion law that repealed criminal abortion.

            The Report of the Commission on Population Growth and the American Future calls for liberalizing abortion laws and providing federal support for family planning.

            In *Eisenstadt v. Baird* (405 U.S. 438), the Supreme Court declares that individuals have a right to privacy in contraception regardless of marital status. The effect is to legalize contraception completely in the United States. Justice William Brennan says: "If the right of privacy means anything, it is the right of the individual, married or single, to be free from unwarranted governmental intrusion into matters so fundamentally affecting a person as the decision whether to bear or beget a child." (453). The inclusion of "bear" along with "beget" portends the decision in *Roe* the next year.

1973   January 22. The Supreme Court rules that states may not prohibit abortion before the third trimester in *Roe v. Wade* and may not set up cumbersome procedures in *Doe v. Bolton*. The ruling declares the decision between a woman and her doctor regarding abortion to be in the zone of privacy.

1973
(*cont.*)
Senator James Buckley (R-NY) and six senators introduce the first constitutional amendment to supersede *Roe v. Wade*.

Referendums to permit abortion without condition up to 20 weeks of pregnancy fail by large margins in Michigan and South Dakota, a setback for the repeal advocates.

The NRLC is formally incorporated with the express purpose of overturning the *Roe v. Wade* decision. The NRLC holds the first national right-to-life convention.

The Religious Coalition for Abortion Rights and Catholics for a Free Choice are founded to support the right to family planning and abortion.

1974
Pro-life activists organize the March for Life in Washington, DC, on the anniversary of *Roe v. Wade*. This march becomes an annual event.

NARAL reorganizes with a new name: the National Abortion Rights Action League.

The West German national government enacts a liberal abortion law: the periodic model, which allows women to seek abortion in the first 3 months of pregnancy with mandatory counseling.

1975
The Subcommittee on Constitutional Amendments of the Senate Judiciary Committee holds extensive hearings on human life amendments that would reverse *Roe v. Wade*. The committee votes not to report any of the amendments to the full committee.

The National Women's Health Network forms to promote empowerment of women in relation to reproductive health.

The West German Constitutional Court rules that the German constitution protects the unborn child at all stages of pregnancy, which makes the 1974 liberal reform unconstitutional. The government subsequently passes an indications law saying abortions could be legal if for medical, genetic, ethical (after rape), or social hardship.

1976　　The Republican Party platform recognizes that there is an ongoing debate on abortion but supports the Human Life Amendment.

The Supreme Court rules that administrative regulations, including a requirement for spousal consent, unconstitutionally limit women's privacy in making decisions about abortion in *Planned Parenthood v. Danforth* (428 U.S. 552).

Congress attaches the Hyde Amendment to the health appropriations bill; the amendment limits use of Medicaid funds to abortions that save the life of the mother.

Laurence Lader leaves NARAL and forms Abortion Rights Mobilization. This move allows him to set his own agenda and not be limited by an organization he believes is not radical enough. His campaigns include attacks on the Catholic Church and action supporting the legalization of RU-486.

1977　　The Supreme Court rules that the state governments' denial of Medicaid funds for abortions is legal and constitutional in *Beal v. Doe* (432 U.S 438) and *Maher v. Roe* (432 U.S. 464).

In *Carey v. Population Services International* (432 U.S. 438), the Supreme Court holds that prohibitions on contraceptive advertisements and sales for minors are unconstitutional.

1979　　In *Bellotti v. Baird* (428 U.S. 132) the Supreme Court rules 9 to 0 that states may require minors to obtain parental consent to get an abortion as long as there is

1979
(*cont.*)
an alternative judicial procedure if consent is denied or the minor does not want to seek parental consent.

Abortion performed during first 10 weeks of pregnancy for a woman in a state of distress, passed in 1975 as a temporary measure, becomes formal law in France. The law requires the woman to undergo counseling and wait a week.

The Supreme Court rules that states must set precise standards for determining the viability of fetuses for statutes prohibiting third trimester abortions in *Colautti v. Franklin* (439 U.S. 379).

The United Nations adopts the Convention for the Elimination of All Forms of Discrimination Against Women, which requires signatories to promote a broad range of equal rights for women and men, including access to family planning. To date, the U.S. Senate has not ratified this treaty.

1980
The Republican Party platform endorses the Human Life Amendment and advocates that antiabortion justices be appointed at all levels of the federal courts.

The Supreme Court rules that the federal government may deny Medicaid funds for abortions in *Harris v. McRae* (448 U.S. 297).

Joe Scheidler forms the Pro-Life Action League, an organization devoted to direct action against abortion clinics and other providers. In 1985 he writes a manual for activists: *Closed: 99 Ways to Stop Abortion.*

1981
Ronald Reagan, the first president to adopt the pro-life position on abortion, takes office. His right-to-life essay "Abortion and the Conscience of the Nation" appears in 1983.

The Adolescent Family Life Act requires active involvement of religious groups in family planning and mandates adoption over abortion and abstinence over contraceptive education.

The U.S. Department of Health and Human Services issues regulations prohibiting family planning clinics supported by federal Title X funds from providing any information about abortion.

Justice Sandra Day O'Connor, nominated by President Reagan, is confirmed as the first woman justice on the Supreme Court.

The Senate Judiciary Committee holds hearings on the Helms Bill to prohibit abortion and on the Human Life Amendment. Although the committee recommends both be enacted, Senator Robert Packwood (R-OR) successfully filibusters on the Senate floor until they are withdrawn.

1983   The Human Life Amendment is debated in the full Senate and rejected 49–50.

In *City of Akron v. Akron Center for Reproductive Health* (462 U.S. 416), the Supreme Court invalidates a city ordinance requiring that abortions be performed in hospitals, with parental and/or informed consent, and after a 24-hour waiting period. The Court rules that these administrative hurdles unduly interfere with women's rights to obtain abortions. Justice O'Connor joins anti-*Roe* minority on the Court and writes that *Roe*'s trimester framework is on a "collision course with itself."

The National Black Women's Health Project, dedicated to informing African-American women about all health matters including reproductive health, is founded.

Irish voters add an antiabortion amendment to the Irish Constitution by a two to one margin. "The state acknowledges the right to life of the unborn, and,

1983   with due regard to the equal right to life of the
(*cont.*)   mother, guarantees in its laws to respect, and as far as
            practicable by its laws to defend and vindicate that
            right" (Article 40.3.3).

1984   Dr. Bernard Nathanson narrates a 30-minute film
            entitled "The Silent Scream" purporting to show an
            ultrasound of a fetus during an abortion. He directs
            the viewer to see the fetus appear to cry out. The film
            is shown around the country by pro-life activists.

            At the United Nations (UN) Conference on Popula-
            tion held in Mexico City, the Reagan administration
            announces that no foreign aid funds will be given to
            organizations or individuals that provide abortions,
            counsel abortions, or promote legalization of abortion
            anywhere in the world. This becomes known as the
            Mexico City policy or the Global Gag Rule.

1985   The Reagan administration presents a brief in *Thorn-
            burgh v. American College of Obstetricians & Gynecolo-
            gists* asking the Supreme Court to overturn *Roe v.
            Wade.*

            NARAL launches "Abortion Rights, Silent No More"
            in response to "The Silent Scream."

1986   President Reagan nominates Antonin Scalia to the
            Supreme Court, and he is confirmed overwhelmingly
            by the Senate. Justice Scalia becomes a reliable ally for
            the pro-life litigation strategy.

            The Supreme Court, in a 5 to 4 decision, invalidates a
            Pennsylvania law with administrative regulations in
            *Thornburgh v. American College of Obstetricians & Gyne-
            cologists* (476 U.S. 747); it rejects the request by the
            Reagan administration to overturn *Roe v. Wade.*

            NOW and other feminist organizations organize the
            first national March for Women's Lives bringing more
            than 100,000 advocates of the right to choose to Wash-
            ington, DC.

1987   President Reagan proposes restrictions for clinics funded under Title X's family planning programs, similar to the Mexico City policy, which forbids clinics from counseling clients about abortion.

The Senate holds hearings on President Reagan's nomination of Robert Bork to the Supreme Court. Bork is an outspoken critic of the constitutional right to privacy for contraception and abortion. The Senate votes not to confirm the nomination. President Reagan then nominates Anthony Kennedy, who wins confirmation easily.

1988   Operation Rescue, organized by Randall Terry, comes to prominence at the Democratic Convention in Atlanta. In 1991, the group stages weeks-long protests at an abortion clinic in Wichita, Kansas, an event that becomes a template for pro-life direct action against abortion practice.

The government of France approves use of RU-486, now known as mifepristone, as a nonsurgical alternative to early abortion. U.S. activists seek to bring the drug to the United States.

Becky Bell, age 17, dies after obtaining an illegal abortion. She left her home rather than comply with the parental notification law. Her case becomes a rallying point for pro-choice activists seeking to limit parental involvement laws.

The Supreme Court of Canada rules that the criminal abortion law is unconstitutional. This ruling leaves Canada with no national abortion regulations.

1989   In *Webster v. Reproductive Health Services* (492 U.S. 490) the Supreme Court upholds (5–4) several administrative hurdles, and a group of justices invite cases that directly challenge *Roe v. Wade* and legal abortion.

1990   The Supreme Court rules in *Ohio v. Akron Center for Reproductive Health* (497 U.S. 502) and in *Hodgson v.*

1990
(*cont.*)

State of Minnesota (497 U.S. 417) that states may require notification of one or both parents before a teenager may have an abortion, as long as she has the option of a judicial bypass.

1991

After stormy hearings in the Senate Judiciary Committee regarding Anita Hill's allegations of sexual harassment, the Senate confirms Clarence Thomas to replace Thurgood Marshall as the only African-American justice on the Supreme Court. Thomas quickly joins the anti-*Roe* group on the Court.

In *Rust v. Sullivan* (500 U.S. 173), a 5–4 decision upholds President George H. W. Bush's policy called the "gag" rule. The result is that the government can prohibit federal funds going to family planning programs from being used to discuss, counsel, give information about, or perform abortions.

1992

In *Planned Parenthood of South Eastern Pennsylvania v. Casey* (505 U.S. 833), the Supreme Court upholds the central holding in *Roe v. Wade* that a woman has liberty to choose abortion before the fetus is viable, and the state can regulate from conception. The case establishes the undue burden standard that state regulations are acceptable unless they constitute an obstacle to woman's exercise of her liberty. The decision goes on to declare that requiring spousal notification is an undue burden on women's liberty.

After the unification of West and East Germany, the new parliament endures a long debate to find a compromise between the strict West German abortion law and the liberal East German one. The compromise keeps abortion in the penal code but abortions will not be prosecuted if performed in the first 12 weeks of pregnancy after mandatory counseling and a waiting period. In 1993, the German Federal Constitutional Court declares this law unconstitutional asserting that the fetus has an absolute right to life against the actions of the pregnant woman. Abortion for medical and eugenic reasons will not be prosecuted if rigorous conditions are met.

1993   Immediately after taking office, President Bill Clinton rescinds the Mexico City policy, the domestic gag rule regarding family planning funds, and reinstates abortions for military personnel in military hospitals.

Congress permits the use of fetal tissue from abortions in National Institutes of Heatlh–funded research under strict regulations.

Dr. David Gunn, a physician who practices abortion in Georgia, Alabama, and Florida, is shot three times when entering a clinic in Pensacola, Florida. The shooter, Michael Griffin, serves a life sentence for the murder.

Poland's postcommunist government enacts a restrictive abortion law allowing legal abortion only for dangers to a woman's life and health, if pregnancy is the result of rape or incest, and for proven fetal abnormality. This law wins praise from Pope John Paul II.

1994   NARAL changes its name to National Abortion and Reproductive Rights Action League and pledges to work to guarantee all women full reproductive choices, not limited to abortion.

NOW's case against Joseph Scheidler charges that he is running a national conspiracy to blockade abortion clinics and demands damages under the federal anti-racketeering statute called the RICO (Racketeer Influenced and Corrupt Organization) Act. The Supreme Court rules in *NOW v. Scheidler* (510 U.S. 249) that violations do not have to have an economic component to be covered under the federal statute. This ruling sends the case back to the circuit court for rehearing and is not finally settled until 2006.

Congress enacts the Freedom of Access to Clinic Entrances (FACE) Act, which makes it a federal crime

1994 (*cont.*)	to use physical force to disrupt the business of abortion clinics.
	India outlaws the practice of prenatal screening for the purpose of sex selection, but the prohibition is rarely enforced.
	The UN Conference on Population and Development meets in Cairo, Egypt, and agrees that abortion should not be promoted as a method of family planning. Governments are urged to increase their commitment to reduce the number of unsafe abortions and improve women's health.
	In *Madsen v. Women's Health Center* (512 U.S. 753) an appeal by antiabortion protesters in Florida, the U.S. Supreme Court upholds as constitutional a buffer zone around health care clinics that is intended to protect access to the clinic.
	Dr. John Britton and Lt. Col. Jim Barrett are killed in front of a Pensacola Clinic. Two abortion clinic workers, Shannon Lowney and Leanne Nichols are murdered in Brookline, Massachusetts.
1995	The UN's Fourth Conference on Women meets in Beijing, China, and adopts an extensive plan of action that defines women's human rights to include reproductive rights and choice in family planning. Pro-life groups criticize the document as promoting abortion as a right.
	Congress reinstates the ban on abortions in military hospitals.
1996	The South African legislature enacts the Choice in Termination of Pregnancy Act, which permits abortion without condition to the twelfth week of pregnancy. South Africa is the only nation in Africa that permits abortion on a woman's request.

President Clinton vetoes the Partial Birth Abortion Ban Act passed by Congress because it fails to include an exception for the mother's health.

The FDA's Reproductive Health Advisory Committee recommends approval of mifepristone for use in non-surgical abortions in the United States. However, final approval does not happen for 4 years.

1997   Congress again passes the Partial Birth Abortion Ban Act, and President Clinton again vetoes it because it does not contain an exception for women's health.

1998   In upstate New York, an antiabortion extremist assassinates abortion doctor Bernard Slepian, who is standing at a window in his house with his family around him.

The FDA approves the first dedicated product for emergency contraception for use in the United States.

1999   Democrats for Life forms; the mainstream Democratic Party refuses affiliation.

2000   The FDA approves the use of mifepristone, also known as RU-486 or the abortion pill.

The Supreme Court invalidates state bans on partial-birth abortions in *Stenberg v. Carhart* (530 U.S. 914) because the statutes are unconstitutionally vague and do not include an exception for a woman's health.

2001   Immediately after taking the oath of office, President George W. Bush reinstates the Mexico City policy.

2002   Secretary of Health and Human Services Tommy Thompson issues a regulation making fetuses eligible for health care under the Children's Health Insurance Program. Pro-choice activists claim the action is a way to establish legal personhood for the fetus.

2002   Congress passes the Born Alive Victims Protection
(*cont.*) Act, which requires doctors to take all possible steps
        to save the lives of fetuses that survive abortions.

2003   NARAL changes its name to NARAL Pro-choice
        America, pledging to educate citizens and politicians
        about reproductive rights and to work to elect pro-
        choice candidates to office.

        NOW is denied the right to sue abortion clinic pro-
        testers under federal racketeering statues in *Scheidler
        v. NOW* (537 U.S. 393).

        The state of Florida executes Paul Hill for the 1994
        murders of Dr. John Britton and his escort James Bar-
        rett outside an abortion clinic in Pensacola, Florida.
        Connected to the Army of God, Hill claims before his
        death that he has no remorse for his actions and will
        meet his reward in heaven.

        President Bush signs the federal Partial Birth Abor-
        tion Ban Act, which places an absolute prohibition on
        the procedure with no exceptions. Congress reports
        its "finding" that the procedure is never necessary to
        protect a woman's health. Similar bills were passed in
        1996 and 1998 and vetoed by President Clinton.

2004   Pro-choice activists organize the March for Women's
        Lives in Washington, DC, one of the largest demon-
        strations in U.S. history.

        President Bush signs the Unborn Victims of Violence
        Act, also called "Laci and Connor's Law," which
        makes injury to a fetus by an attack on a pregnant
        woman a separate crime in federal jurisdictions.

2005   The Republican Mike Rounds, governor of South
        Dakota, signs the Women's Health and Human Life
        Protection Act, which prohibits abortions except to
        save the life of the mother. Some pro-life activists
        hope this will be the challenge that overturns *Roe v.*

Wade. Pro-choice activists begin campaigning to rescind the law.

The Senate confirms John Roberts to replace William Rehnquist as chief justice of the Supreme Court. In early 2006, Samuel Alito takes the seat formerly held by retiring Justice O'Connor. There is widespread agreement that Justice Kennedy is likely to become the "swing" vote between the pro-*Roe* and anti-*Roe* justices.

Susan Wood, director of the Office of Women's Health in the FDA, resigns over the FDA's failure to approve over-the-counter sales of emergency contraception. She claims the agency head is motivated by ideology and ignores advice by science committees.

Representative Louise Slaughter (D-NY) and Senator Harry Reid (D-NE) introduce the Prevention First Act in Congress. The act, which is on the agenda again in 2006 and 2007, will provide funds and regulations to promote the use of contraception and reduce the incidence of unintended pregnancies.

2006 Voters approve a referendum to rescind the restrictive criminal abortion law in South Dakota.

Congress rejects the Child Custody Protection Act, which would make it a federal crime to accompany a minor across state lines to avoid parental notification requirements.

After news of fatal infections among women taking the abortion pill, pro-life activists promote "Holly's Law," which would suspend the approval of RU-486. They claim that the FDA approval process was too hasty, and the drug is dangerous to women.

The FDA approves the sale of emergency contraception over the counter (without prescription) to women over 17.

2006
(*cont.*)

The Supreme Court rules again in *Scheidler v. NOW* (04-1244) that the RICO Act does not apply to antiabortion groups' obstruction of clinic access, because it would establish the precedent that civic action by organizations could be prosecuted. This ruling overturns an early ruling in 1994 that the NOW could sue for damages under the RICO Act.

In *Ayotte v. Planned Parenthood of Northern New England, et al* (546 U.S. 320), the U.S. Supreme Court unanimously sustains its precedent that abortion laws must protect a woman's health and safety. The Supreme Court asks the lower court to consider whether the New Hampshire legislature would have wanted this law to have a medical emergency exception. If not, the Court says the law should be struck down in its entirety.

Representative Henry Hyde (R-IL), architect of the Hyde Amendment, retires from Congress at the end of the year.

President Bush vetoes an act to fund embryonic stem cell research, based on his view that such research kills human beings. On the same day he signs the Fetal Farming Protection Act, which prohibits use of tissue from embryos conceived for the purpose of their tissues.

President Bush appoints Dr. Eric Keroack as head of the Office of Population Affairs. Before the appointment he was director of a network of faith-based "crisis pregnancy centers" that promote abstinence and oppose birth control as demeaning to women. This appointment produces widespread opposition among pro-choice advocates.

2007

The parliament of Portugal votes 161–69 to legalize abortion in the first 10 weeks of pregnancy. The President signed the act; all Western European countries except Ireland have legal abortion.

The Democratic Party regains the majority in the House of Representatives and the Senate. Some pro-choice activists launch a new campaign to repeal the ban on funding abortions: "Hyde: 30 Years is Enough!"

Dr. Eric Keroack resigns as head of the Office of Population Affairs in the midst of charges of Medicaid fraud in Massachusetts where he had operated pregnancy crisis centers.

The Mexico City city council legalizes abortion on request in the first trimester of pregnancy. This law is the first legalization in Latin America since Cuba. The Roman Catholic Church and feminists wage competing demonstrations over the issue.

The Supreme Court rules that the Federal Partial Birth Abortion Ban Act is constitutional in *Gonzales v. Carhart*. This is the first time that the Court has approved abortion restrictions that do not include exceptions for women's health.

5

Biographical Sketches

The major players in the abortion debates since the 1960s are here, along with ones from the nineteenth century (Stoner) and early twentieth century (Sanger). Most of the individuals portrayed through these brief biographies are still active in the abortion conflict. But the dates after each name show that some of the pioneers in the pro-choice and pro-life movements have retired or are aging, and some have passed away recently. Does this mean the movements will change? A new generation will have to carry on the crusades. For most, the *Roe v. Wade* decision will not be a personal memory but a historical fact. It remains to be seen how abortion politics will change as a result.

Bill Baird (1932–)

Born in Brooklyn to a family of limited means, Bill Baird is a permanent part of the history of reproductive law in the United States. As a young man he went to work for a company that manufactured contraceptive foam. It was the 1950s, and there were many restrictions on the information, sale, and distribution pertaining to birth control methods. He took his "plan van" to poor neighborhoods in New York and gave talks and demonstrations challenging these laws. He developed tactics to push law enforcement to arrest him and then take his case to court and the press.

In the mid-1960s, Baird established a birth control clinic and gave referrals to doctors who would perform abortions. In 1967, after the Supreme Court decision legalizing contraceptives for married couples, students at Boston University invited Baird to give a talk on birth control. There he directly challenged the Massachusetts law and was arrested. It took 5 years for his case—*Eisenstadt v. Baird*—to reach the Supreme Court. The justices ruled that states could not deny equal protection to unmarried people in getting contraceptives and went on to declare the right to "bear and beget" a child a fundamental right. Baird continued his feisty stance toward restrictions on reproductive rights, including challenging parental consent laws in *Belotti v. Baird* in 1979.

Baird's relationships with the rest of the pro-choice movement have been mixed. Some admire his "shock tactics" as necessary to get public attention. Others think he is too radical and an embarrassment. He defends his role and contribution through his business, the Pro-Choice League, and through articles and speeches at the group's website (www.prochoiceleague.com).

Robert H. Bork (1927–)

Robert H. Bork has been an important figure in the abortion debates of the last 30 years in two ways. As a legal scholar, his writings about judicial philosophy have influenced pro-life activists and conservative judges alike. As a nominee to the Supreme Court in 1987, he became the center of a televised debate about his views and their relationship to the right to privacy established by *Griswold v. Connecticut* and *Roe v. Wade.*

Bork earned his undergraduate and law degrees at the University of Chicago and served as a professor of law at Yale University. In the 1970s, he was solicitor general of the United States and was appointed to the U.S. Circuit Court in Washington, DC, in 1982. To Bork, the U.S. Constitution should be read as the framers intended, in other words strictly and with its original meaning. He is sharply critical of the Supreme Court's rulings that the Constitution ensures a right to privacy when there is no mention of that right in the text. In Bork's view, such rulings by unelected officials undermine democracy; judges should adjudicate and "not legislate from the bench," a phrase that has become a code word for judges who support abortion rights.

During the 1987 confirmation hearings, Bork took the opportunity to describe his philosophy fully, which opened him to strenuous opposition, even attacks from some senators. In the end, his nomination was rejected by 58 to 42 votes. The experience led to the coining of the term "to bork," which means to defeat judicial appointees through an attack on character, philosophy, and history rather than their qualifications and experience. As a result, nominees have avoided being "borked" by remaining silent on any contentious issue, especially the status of *Roe v. Wade*.

Bork has continued to write about his views, including *Slouching Toward Gomorrah: Modern Liberalism and American Decline* in 1996. This book reflects the pro-life belief that the social movements of the 1960s and 1970s, especially feminism and sexual liberation, have undermined American culture and even Western Civilization.

John Bayard Britton (1925–1994)

Dr. John Britton was 69 when Paul Hill made him what the *New York Times* called "an uncertain martyr." After graduating from the University of Virginia Medical School in 1949, he became a family care physician in Fernandina Beach, Florida. By all accounts his medical career was a bit rocky as he got in trouble with the medical establishment from time to time. His patients saw him as compassionate as well as a bit eccentric.

He was not a model pro-choice physician, therefore, when he volunteered at a Pensacola abortion clinic to replace Dr. David Gunn, who had been killed by an antiabortion protester. Britton seemed to be ambivalent about abortion and would turn away women so they could think about their decisions. Nevertheless, he stated that women should be able to have legal abortions and defied the abortion protesters and the danger they posed. Some reported that perhaps Britton took on the risky abortion job because he needed the money. In any event he put on his ill-fitting bullet-proof vest and flew to the job once a week.

On July 29, 1994, Paul Hill, with a newly purchased shotgun, waited for Britton's arrival with his escort, James Barrett, and June Barrett, the escort's wife. He shot Dr. Britton in the head and killed him, killed Barrett, and wounded Barrett's wife. Extremist pro-life groups praised the killing, but most organizations distanced themselves from the growing violence in the 1990s against doctors working in abortion clinics.

Judie Brown (1944–)

Judie Brown has devoted nearly 40 years to the pro-life movement. In 1969, with her husband, Paul Brown, she passed out literature opposing a liberal abortion law up for referendum in the state of Washington. In 1976, as a member of Ohio's Right to Life Committee, she moved her activism to the national stage, first participating in the 1976 March for Life and later on the staff of the National Right to Life Committee (NRLC). While there she used direct mail to increase the membership of the organization but parted with the leadership when she discovered that developing grassroots membership was not a high priority for the NRLC.

In 1979 she formed a new organization—the American Life League—which claims to have hundreds of thousands of members nationwide. Brown wanted an organization that would work to overcome what she saw as an anti-life ethic. She adheres closely to the position of the Roman Catholic Church and opposes abortion, modern contraception, stem cell research, and euthanasia. Brown uses the American Life League website as a forum for commentary on issues of interest, including promotion of a Right to Life Act that would give legal personhood to embryos and fetuses. She proposes a complete ban on all abortions with no exceptions declaring that medical opinion shows that abortion is never needed to save a woman's life.

Mary Steichen Calderone (1904–1998)

Dr. Mary Calderone was to the study of human sexuality what Margaret Sanger was to birth control—the one who nearly single-handedly changed the nation's approach to the topic. Her early life didn't suggest that she would have such an influence one day. The daughter of the noted photographer Edward Steichen, Mary frittered away her days at Vassar and eventually left in the early 1920s to become an actress. Fifteen years later, much changed by life, she graduated from medical school, a divorced mother challenging a male-dominated field. She married again in 1941 and spent her career in school and public health positions.

In 1953 Calderone was offered the position of medical director at Planned Parenthood; one of her first activities was to sponsor a 1955 conference that publicly discussed the question of reform of criminal abortion laws for the first time. Although she had a role in forming the reform movement, Calderone left Planned Parenthood at the age of 60 to form a new organization to focus on sexuality and sex education: the Sex Information and Education Council of the United States (SIECUS). There she promoted sex education that was frank, nonjudgmental, and comprehensive. She believed women had the right to express love, especially in marriage, without the fear of unwanted pregnancy. Calderone supported legal abortion but preferred to focus on preventing pregnancy. SIECUS has had a role in developing the idea that sexuality is a positive force and that sex education should not enforce any particular standard. With these views, both Calderone and SIECUS provoked strenuous opposition from pro-life activists.

Gloria Feldt (1942–)

Gloria Feldt served as president of the Planned Parenthood Federation of America (PPFA) for nine years. Feldt brought a strong feminist perspective to her leadership as well as a commitment to engaging pro-life adversaries in political and policy arenas. A native of Texas, Feldt had gotten pregnant and married at the age of 15 and moved to Odessa where her husband found work. By the age of twenty she had three children; she connects her situation in those days directly to the lack of education and access to effective contraception. Availability of the birth control pill in 1962 made it possible for her to start college. It took her 12 years to graduate.

Feldt started with Planned Parenthood in 1974 as a regional executive director, then moved to Arizona, eventually becoming national president in 1996. Her ambitious agenda included revitalizing the local affiliates and their services and developing a 25-year plan for PPFA. She is best known for her leadership in promoting family planning as a human right and contraception as a necessity for women not an option. She also became head of the Planned Parenthood Political Action Committee and worked to support pro-choice candidates. Feldt helped promote contraceptive equity policies in state legislatures. She was an organizing leader of the 2004 March for Women's Lives and helped draft the Prevention First Act—not yet passed—to establish a federal policy for preventing unwanted pregnancies. Active in international networks, Feldt was part of the U.S. delegation to the Cairo Plus Five meeting in 1999, a follow-up to the United Nations 1994 Population and Development Conference. She resigned as PPFA president in January 2006. She is author of two books: *Behind Every Choice is a Story* (2003) and *The War on Choice: The Right-wing Attack on Women's Rights and How to Fight Back* (2004).

Sherri Chessen Finkbine (1930–)

In 1962, Sherri Finkbine was 29 years old, married, the mother of four children, hostess of the local children's TV show *Romper Room,* and pregnant with her fifth child. She was devastated to learn that during her pregnancy she had taken pills containing thalidomide, a tranquilizer, which her husband Bob brought from Europe. The Finkbines had read the news stories that linked the drug to serious fetal deformity, and they were afraid their child would be a victim. Their doctor arranged with the local hospital for a therapeutic abortion based on the threat of the pregnancy to Sherri's mental health. However, hospital officials worried that publicity surrounding the case would invite prosecution and denied the procedure. The Finkbines eventually traveled to Sweden and requested an abortion under its conditional law. Sherri had to see a psychiatrist and receive permission from the Royal Medical Board. Finally approved, the abortion went forward.

The press followed the story from Arizona all the way to Sweden. The Vatican denounced the whole thing as a crime, and Sherri lost her job at the TV station, but the Finkbines' ordeal had a major effect on the public's view of abortion in the United States. People began to see the kind of personal problems that can give rise to the termination of a pregnancy. This view replaced the traditional image of abortion as a matter of criminal prosecution of doctors. With this story, the tide began to turn in the effort to gain a hearing on criminal abortion laws and provided the public support needed to mobilize the pro-choice movement.

The Finkbines had two more children but divorced in 1974. In 1991, Sherri married a physician who had practiced at the

Phoenix hospital that had denied her abortion. In 1992, HBO produced a film about the case called *A Private Matter.*

Wanda Franz (1944?–)

Wanda Franz became president of the nation's largest pro-life organization, the National Right to Life Committee (NRLC) in 1991. In her position she presents the pro-life perspective on topics of the day through the NRLC website, in speeches, and on radio and television. Franz holds a PhD in developmental psychology and spent her career on the faculty of West Virginia University, teaching and writing articles and books on child development. She became active in the early days of the pro-life movement and was president of the West Virginia Right to Life committee for fifteen years.

Franz served in the Reagan and George H. W. Bush administrations as consultant to the Office of Population Affairs from 1983 to 1991 and as an expert adviser on adolescent sex education. She wrote the introduction to Ronald Reagan's book *Abortion & the Conscience of the Nation.* After becoming president of NRLC she played a prominent role at the United Nations Cairo Conference on Population and Development in 1994. She is now an emeritus professor at West Virginia University, having retired in 2003.

Kim Gandy (1954–)

Kim Gandy has been president of the National Organization for Women (NOW) since 2001, having been reelected to a second term in 2005. But she has been at the center of the abortion debates on Capitol Hill for nearly twenty years. Born and educated in Louisiana, she received her bachelor's degree in mathematics from Louisiana Tech and joined NOW in 1973. Her first successful campaign was to overturn Louisiana's marital property law, which gave complete control over a couple's property to the husband. Law school followed, and she soon was working her way up the NOW hierarchy.

As executive vice president in charge of legislation and litigation, Gandy was a key figure in all the pro-choice campaigns of the 1990s, including the battle against the partial-birth abortion ban. She took the lead in NOW's suit against abortion protesters (*NOW v. Scheidler*) and served on the committee that drafted the Freedom of Access to Clinic Entrances Act. As NOW's president, she chairs the NOW Foundation and the NOW political action committee, which publishes a list of pro-choice candidates in each election. She is also the chief spokesperson for NOW and typically takes a spirited and firm feminist position on the issues of the day, such as access to emergency contraception, appointments to the Supreme Court, the South Dakota abortion ban, and partial-birth abortion litigation.

Alan Guttmacher (1898–1974)

During his residency, after graduating from Johns Hopkins Medical School, Alan Guttmacher had a life-changing experience when he came face to face with dying women who had had illegal abortions. He embarked on a distinguished career as an obstetrician, including serving as chief of obstetrics at Sinai Hospital in Baltimore, Maryland, but he never stopped working to increase women's information and options for family planning. He became active in the American Birth Control League, the forerunner of the Planned Parenthood Federation of America (PPFA). At a PPFA meeting in 1942, he made one of the first calls for the liberalization of abortion laws.

At first, Guttmacher's proposals involved a limited extension of the criminal laws to allow therapeutic abortions when women's health was at risk. Then, as the debate developed and more groups got involved, he favored increasing the number of grounds for legal abortions. In his 1959 book, *Babies by Choice or Chance,* Guttmacher called for more liberal and uniform abortion laws across the country, but he also noted that reform would take place only when there was citizen support. He was present at the 1959 American Law Institute meeting that proposed reform to include health, fetal deformity, and rape and incest conditions and became national president of Planned Parenthood in 1962. In 1964, he founded the Association for the Study of Abortion, which began to publicize the issue, and he made it clear that he opposed abortion on demand.

Guttmacher lived to see the legalization of both contraception and abortion. In the end, he called the decision in *Roe v. Wade* "wise and courageous." While he was president, PPFA began to develop an institute to do research on family planning and educate the public. As a memorial, the institute was named after Guttmacher; it remains a major source of information about sexual and reproduction health issues.

Martin Haskell (1946–)

Dr. Martin Haskell, a physician from Cincinnati, Ohio, operates three abortion clinics. He is well aware of the difficulties of terminating pregnancies that have advanced to the second trimester. Until the late 1980s, the only procedures available for such abortions required up to three days in the hospital. He was willing to perform them but was frustrated as more and more hospitals turned patients and their doctors away. In his effort to respond to the needs of his patients, he developed a procedure he called intact dilation and extraction (or evacuation), also called intact D&E or D&X, which did not require a hospital stay.

In 1992, he presented a paper describing the procedure at a risk-management seminar sponsored by the National Abortion Federation, the association of abortion providers. He was likely unaware of the storm of pro-life activism the paper would provoke. When printed and in circulation, the paper soon came to the attention of the National Conference of Catholic Bishops and the National Right to Life Committee (NRLC). Its graphic description of the procedure in which the fetus is killed while in the birth canal seemed to these pro-life groups to be something different from an abortion. The committee commissioned a set of drawings, which are still available on its website, to show that this procedure killed a child outside the womb, in the process of being born. The NRLC labeled the procedure "partial-birth abortion" and Representative Charles Canady (R-FL) introduced a bill banning the procedure in Congress in 1995.

Harrison Hickman (1953–)

Harrison Hickman, a pollster and consultant to Democratic candidates and NARAL, was born, raised, and educated in North Carolina, received an M.A. from the University of Nebraska, and studied statistics at the University of Michigan. In the 1980s, Hickman developed a successful strategy for defeating pro-life proposals in conservative southern states. In his own politics he combined support for Democratic issues such as civil rights and equality with a strong attachment to personal autonomy and a respect for the deeply held anti-government beliefs of the conservative South.

In 1984, he was called upon to work with pro-choice groups facing an antiabortion constitutional amendment campaign in Arkansas. Personally he opposed abortion but at the same time believed it should be legal because of his belief in individual rights. At the start, the polls showed strong support for the antiabortion amendment as well as negligible acceptance for legal abortion for reasons of women's rights, sexual freedom, or freedom of religion. For the Arkansas campaign he devised a strategy that would link the opposition to the proposed amendment with the widespread antigovernment beliefs of the voters. Government rules limiting access to abortion were linked to government intrusion in the family, as well as to gun control and busing. The committee leading the pro-choice campaign was renamed the "Stop Big Government" committee. The strategy turned the outcome around when the amendment lost by a tiny margin. In *Bearing Right,* William Saletan offers this strategy as a way for abortion rights activists to counter the strength of pro-life action frames in abortion debates.

Paul T. Hill (1954–2003)

In 2003, the state of Florida executed Paul Hill by lethal injection for the killing of Dr. John Britton and James Barrett outside a Pensacola abortion clinic in 1994. Hill went to his death without remorse for his action. He had long believed and professed that killing those who perform abortions is a just way to defend the unborn, just like defending one's own children. He expected to receive God's reward in heaven, he said in his posthumous manifesto "Mix My Blood with the Blood of the Unborn."

Hill was born in Miami and found religion after a somewhat misspent youth. He became a Presbyterian minister and had a congregation in South Carolina. Becoming increasingly active in antiabortion activism, he left his ministry; some report he was excommunicated for his radical views while others say he left voluntarily because of what he considered the meek position of his church on the abortion issue. He was in touch with the militant

Army of God; eventually he moved to Pensacola where he founded his own small militant group, Defensive Action, and became a fixture outside the Ladies Center. When Michael Griffin shot clinic physician Dr. David Gunn, Hill defended the killing as justified and appeared on any TV show that would have him to state his case.

When Dr. Britton replaced Dr. Gunn at the clinic, Hill purchased a shotgun and waited for him to arrive, shooting the doctor and his escort, James Barrett, and wounding Barrett's wife. He put down the gun and walked away and was arrested within minutes. Although there were some court challenges to Hill's death sentence, he seemed to welcome it and looked forward to being a martyr. Before he died he established a website to present his story and to make the case for his place in heaven, but mainstream pro-life organizations and activists have distanced themselves from Hill and have rejected his methods.

Henry Hyde (1924–)

Among the pro-life advocates in Congress, Henry J. Hyde, Republican Representative from Illinois, will no doubt be the most remembered. Shortly after he was elected to the House in 1974, Hyde sponsored an amendment to an appropriations bill to deny the use of federal Medicaid funds to finance abortions for poor women except when necessary to save their lives. The amendment passed with little debate that first year and has been reauthorized in Congress ever since. Called the Hyde Amendment, it has withstood lobbying, appeals to public opinion, and litigation from pro-choice organizations challenging the constitutionality of the ban on federal funds for abortion.

Hyde was born into an Irish-Catholic family and attended Catholic schools, including Georgetown and Loyola, where he earned his law degree. He left the Democratic Party in the 1950s because it was too liberal and joined the Republicans. After the success of the Hyde Amendment, he became a major spokesperson for the pro-life position as the party made opposition to abortion an integral part of its platform and voted to support the Human Life Amendment. In 1981, Hyde sponsored the Human Life Bill authored by Senator Jesse Helms (R-SC) in the House of Representatives, which would have codified his belief that human life begins at conception. This proposal, in line with Roman

Catholic doctrine, demonstrated his views that religious values should be an integral part of policy debates, especially with respect to abortion. Hyde retired from the House of Representatives in 2006 and remains a sought-after speaker among pro-life groups.

Frances Kissling (1943–)

Frances Kissling was raised a Catholic, attended Catholic schools, and even spent six months in a convent. Nevertheless, she grew up to be not only one of the most provocative critics of the Roman Catholic Church but also one committed to provoking a rebellion from the inside. From her position as president of Catholics for a Free Choice (CFFC), she campaigns to overturn the church's staunch pro-life doctrine. To Kissling, the church's opposition to abortion is an effort to maintain control over women. If they really cared about the unborn, she argues, they would do more to prevent abortions by supporting contraception to prevent unwanted pregnancies. Let women be free moral agents, she asks.

Kissling participated in social activism in the 1960s, which led to working in abortion clinics in the 1970s. She was a cofounder of the National Abortion Federation, and served as its director until 1980. In 1982 she became president of CFFC. She has close ties with several pro-choice groups, such as the Alan Guttmacher Institute, the Sex Information and Education Council of the United States, and the International Women's Health Coalition. Her activism has won her many allies, but she remains extremely controversial. Syndicated columnist Ellen Goodman has called her the thoughtful and eloquent "philosopher of the pro-choice movement," whereas George Neumayr of the *American Spectator* called her a "repulsive heretic." Kissling retired as President of CFFC on March 1, 2007, and then became a fellow at the Radcliffe Institute for Advanced Studies at Harvard University.

Lawrence Lader (1919–2006)

Lawrence Lader was born in New York City and graduated from Harvard University. After service in the army in World War II, he began a career as a writer, first as a foreign correspondent and later as a freelancer for popular magazines. When he decided to write his first book, he chose to write a biography of Margaret Sanger, the pioneer for birth control. From interviews with her, he became convinced that it was important for women to have control over their childbearing; without it they could not lead independent lives. Sanger told him about the effects of illegal abortions on women's health, and he realized there was little information on the subject. His 1966 book *Abortion* began: "Abortion is the dread secret of our society."

The book came out one year after the *Griswold v. Connecticut* case that established legal contraception for married couples as a protected right to privacy. Lader advocated for laws that would make the decision to have an abortion another right of privacy. He joined with Betty Friedan and Bernard Nathanson to start NARAL to campaign for law repeal and succeeded when New York eliminated abortion restrictions in 1970. Friedan named him the "father of the abortion rights movement," and Justice Harry Blackmun cited Lader's book nine times in *Roe v. Wade*.

In 1976, Lader left NARAL to form Abortion Rights Mobilization and concentrated his attacks on the Roman Catholic Church, at one point suing unsuccessfully to remove its tax-exempt status because of its pro-life political activities. He also sponsored the development of RU-486 in the United States and was named "feminist of the year" by the Feminist Majority for his leadership in getting the abortion pill into the U.S.

Ellen McCormack (1926–)

Ellen McCormack ran for the Democratic Party's presidential nomination in 1976 on a single issue: support for a Human Life Amendment. A Roman Catholic mother of four, she was a leader of New York right-to-life activists when she entered primaries in twenty states. As a result of support from her organization, she became the first woman to qualify for federal matching campaign funds under newly passed reform guidelines. In 1980, she opposed Ronald Reagan in the general election as the candidate of the New York–based Right to Life Party, receiving 32,327 votes in three states. Her entry into the primaries in 1976 brought publicity to the pro-life movement and warned the other candidates that opposition to legal abortion was becoming an electoral issue.

Norma McCorvey (1947–)

In 1969, Norma McCorvey was living in Texas and pregnant with her third child. She was poor, unemployed, and had only a tenth-grade education; both her children had been adopted by others. She wanted an abortion but could not afford to travel to California where it was legal. So she told the doctor that she had been raped because someone suggested this might persuade the doctor. When rejected for the procedure, she eventually came in contact with attorneys Sarah Weddington and Linda Coffee, who were looking for a plaintiff in their challenge to the constitutionality of Texas's restrictive law. Thus, McCorvey became Jane Roe against Henry Wade, District Attorney of Dallas County. The lawyers protected her anonymity, but did not help her get the abortion she had wanted. After she gave birth, she put her third child up for adoption.

In 1980, McCorvey identified herself as the Roe of *Roe v. Wade*. She became involved in the pro-choice movement and eventually worked for an abortion clinic. Her 1994 book *I Am Roe* detailed her version of the case. In 1995 she was attracted to the work of Operation Rescue and became part of the pro-life movement, converting to Catholicism in 1998. Her second book, *Won by Love*, tells the story of her conversion. She petitioned the Supreme Court to overturn the 1973 ruling, claiming that it was harmful to women; her petition was denied. McCorvey's supporters charge that she was a pawn for the feminist lawyers and the pro-choice movement lawyers in their campaign to legalize abortion.

Paul Marx (1920?–)

Father Paul Marx was one of seventeen children born to a strict Catholic family in Minnesota. He found his calling to the priesthood and became a Benedictine monk in 1947. With the rise of debate about population, birth control, and abortion, he began to speak out on the topic guided by Roman Catholic doctrine. To promote his work he organized pro-life institutes in several states even before the pro-life movement got underway in the 1970s. Seeing his message as important to the world, he formed Human Life International (HLI), located near Washington, DC, in 1980. From this base he embarked on a worldwide mission to promote natural family planning and other aspects of Catholic perspective through traveling, speaking, and working with national pro-life organizations. HLI was especially active in opposing efforts to establish family planning and legal abortion in Latin America.

With the blessing of Pope John Paul II, Marx's message was that modern artificial contraception led to the destruction of nations. To Marx, contraception is not only an abortifacient, but it also leads to massive increases in abortion and decreases in birthrates. There is a decline in marriage as well as increases in single-parent families, abusive sex, venereal disease, and euthanasia. Fertility declines and populations begin to decline, which spells collapse. Marx challenged anyone to show him a nation where widespread use of contraception and legal abortion had not resulted in a decline in family morality. He instructed his audiences in means of natural family planning, which he claimed brought families together and did not lead to infidelity and promiscuous sex. Marx wrote of his work in *Faithful for Life* and *The Death Peddlers*, which are available from Human Life International. He retired in 1999 and returned to his abbey in Minnesota.

Kate Michelman (1942–)

Kate Michelman served as president of NARAL for 20 years (1985–2004), and her tenure left a major imprint on the abortion debates. At one point *Washingtonian Magazine* named her as one of the 100 most powerful women in Washington. She has been a tireless spokesperson for the pro-choice ideal that women retain a constitutional right to choose abortion and that the pro-life platform must be defeated. Michelman has been an adviser to many high-level politicians including, notably, Bill Clinton and Hilary Rodham Clinton.

From her post at NARAL, she led the pro-choice movement organizations through many ups and downs. When she took the position, the movement had been pushed to a defensive position, struggling to protect legal abortion itself because of erosion of support in the Supreme Court. She stepped into the fray leading the successful campaign to reject Robert Bork's Supreme Court nomination and testifying against Clarence Thomas as well. She campaigned vigorously for Bill Clinton and brought resources of NARAL to support his removal of the Mexico City policy and the veto of bans on partial-birth abortion.

She has long given credit for her vigorous stamina in the pro-choice cause to her own life. Her husband abandoned her and her three young daughters in the late 1960s. Left with little support, she found out shortly after her husband left that she was pregnant. The pregnancy nearly drove her to suicide, and she qualified for a therapeutic abortion under pre-*Roe* policies. The memory of the humiliation and powerlessness she felt when she had to get approval from an all-male hospital committee and the husband who deserted her never left and sustained her activism. She remains a prominent spokesperson for abortion rights.

Bernard Nathanson (1926–)

Dr. Bernard Nathanson has become famous in the abortion debates because he completely changed his views from proabortion to antiabortion. As an obstetrics/gynecology physician, he joined Lawrence Lader and feminist Betty Friedan, among others, to found NARAL in the late 1960s and served as chair of its medical committee. In 1971, soon after New York legalized abortion, he opened a large abortion clinic, which performed thousands of abortions for New York women as well as women from out of state.

In the mid-1970s the use of ultrasound technology allowed Nathanson to study what he called "fetology," and he came to believe abortion was a form of infanticide. He told the story of his change of heart in *Aborting America,* which was published in 1979. Nathanson claimed that, as an insider, he knew the pro-choice movement was built on lies, fabricated statistics, and cynical slogans. He confessed his past as a thoughtless abortionist, including aborting his own child.

Nathanson came to national prominence with the production and distribution of his film, *The Silent Scream,* in 1984. It showed the ultrasound of an abortion and its effects on the fetus; Nathanson's narration was designed to show that abortion was a form of infanticide. His next film, *The Edge of Reason,* contained a similar graphic portrayal of late-term abortion. The films became controversial; Planned Parenthood charged that Nathanson's films were based on ideology, not on medical science. Nevertheless, Nathanson continues to be a prominent pro-life speaker, describing his confession and conversion to the cause of the unborn. In 1996, he completed his conversion and became a Roman Catholic; he wrote about this change in *Hand of God*.

Margaret Sanger (1879–1966)

Margaret Sanger is famous today as the founder of the birth control movement in America. Her 1938 autobiography tells the story of her awakening to the plight of desperate poor women who were enslaved by repeated pregnancies. Trained as a nurse, Sanger worked among the immigrant families in New York City slums in the early twentieth century, attending more than one woman who was dying from an attempt at self-abortion. She vowed to arm women with knowledge about contraception but soon ran afoul of the federal prohibitions in the Comstock Act of 1873. She had to flee the country at one point and was eventually jailed.

Sanger founded the American Birth Control League, which became the Planned Parenthood Federation of America. She also led the campaign to legalize contraception; her most significant victory in that regard was the 1936 federal court decision in the *U.S. v. One Package* case, which allowed doctors to receive contraception for medical uses. She lived just long enough to see the complete legalization of contraception in the states in 1965.

Although Sanger made conflicting statements on the subject of abortion, it is clear that she focused on birth control as a way to prevent the serious risks of illegal abortion. Yet she also understood the women's desire for the procedure when contraception failed. Sanger remains a symbolic and controversial figure in the abortion debate. Pro-life advocates accuse her of being an atheist who advocated racial purity through her association with the eugenics movement and an advocate of abortion as a means of birth control. Pro-choice feminists consider her a pioneer for women's rights to self-determination and a feminist who liberated women's sexuality.

Joseph M. Scheidler (1927–)

Joseph Scheidler is the national director of the Pro-Life Action League (PLAL) and the defendant in the National Organization for Women's (NOW) case against obstruction of abortion clinics. Scheidler is a strong Catholic; he studied for the priesthood for a time, then married and had seven children. As a strong conservative Catholic he has always opposed abortion. Like other Catholics, the decision that the fetus was not a person in *Roe v. Wade* stunned him and pushed him to work full time to prevent abortions. He organized PLAL and developed a strategy for direct action against clinics. His goal was to try to reduce the number of abortions and, as he has stated, save lives. He outlined his methods in *Closed: 99 Ways to Stop Abortion*. Patrick Buchanan has called him the "green beret of the pro-life movement."

In the 1980s and 1990s, Scheidler traveled extensively, taking his message of saving lives directly to abortion clinics or "abortion mills" as he calls them. To him, abortion is always immoral, never permitted—it's simple. Every woman who can be persuaded not to go ahead with a termination is another life saved, and Scheidler is proficient in sidewalk counseling. NOW claims that his tactics include violence and intimidation and are illegal. The feminists have engaged Scheidler in a 12-year court battle over his activism. They claimed that the nationwide campaign against abortion clinics and their clients constituted a violation of the federal anti-racketeering statute. Both sides had temporary victories, but Scheidler won the war when the Supreme Court ruled that this racketeering statute only applied to economic racketeering and not to civil action and protest.

Patricia Schroeder (1940–)

For more nearly 25 years, from 1973 to 1997, Representative Patricia Schroeder (D-CO) was a reliable ally in Congress for feminists and the pro-choice movement. She graduated with honors from the University of Minnesota and Harvard Law School when quotas limiting the number of women students were still in place. She moved with her husband to Denver, Colorado, and worked for the National Labor Relations Board and Planned Parenthood. She ran for Congress and became one of only sixteen women (out of 435 members) in 1973. She joined Congress at a time when the women's rights movement was in ascendance, bringing a full equality agenda to Congress. The women's rights movement found a courageous advocate in Schroeder who, as she built her seniority and status, brought their message to the committees and the debating floor. She led the Congressional Caucus for Women's Issues from 1979 to 1995.

Schroeder ran for president in 1988, but withdrew from the race after facing strong opposition to her candidacy. She retained her passionate commitment to women's rights, especially the right to self-determination with respect to pregnancy and child-bearing. She advocated a comprehensive policy approach to women's reproductive health. Her legislative successes include sponsorship of the Freedom of Access to Clinic Entrances Act and the Violence Against Women Act. When the partial-birth abortion issue swept through the Congress, she battled against the tide by charging that the ban was just a smoke screen for the real pro-life goal—the criminalization of all abortion procedures. Schroeder retired from Congress at the end of 1996 and became president of the American Publishers Association.

Eleanor Smeal (1939–)

A graduate of Duke University and the University of Florida, Eleanor Smeal has become one of the most important feminist activists in the United States. She served as president of the National Organization for Women (NOW) from 1977 to 1982 and 1985 to 1987. During these years she led the finally unsuccessful campaign for ratification of the equal rights amendment and then turned to the goal of defending *Roe v. Wade* and access to legal abortion for American women. She organized and led the first National March for Women's Lives in 1986 and developed the legal strategy to counter Operation Rescue and clinic violence of the late 1980s and early 1990s. After leaving the presidency of NOW, Smeal founded the Feminist Majority Foundation (FMF).

Her goal in organizing FMF was to empower women to act politically in their own interests. The issue of reproductive rights is a major focus. In 1989 she produced two videos—*Abortion for Survival* and *Abortion Denied: Shattering Women's Lives*—to raise awareness of the effects of punitive and restrictive abortion laws in the United States. as well as other countries. Smeal used the organization's resources to lead the successful campaign for the Freedom of Access to Clinic Entrances Act, which makes it a federal crime to use physical force to obstruct access to abortion clinics. She also waged the 12-year campaign for approval of mifepristone (RU-486), the "abortion pill."

Christopher Smith (1953–)

Representative Christopher Smith (R-NJ) heads the bipartisan Pro-life Caucus in the House of Representatives where he has represented New Jersey since 1981. His view on the issue is absolute: to him all abortion is murder; there are no exceptions for health, rape, incest, or fetal deformity. Smith also considers abortion a threat to women whose lives are destroyed by their experiences in what he calls "torture and killing centers." He has led the pro-life legislative agenda against abortions in military hospitals, in favor of the Mexico City gag rules, and to ban partial-birth abortions. He even successfully derailed a bipartisan bankruptcy reform bill over language that prohibited clinic protesters from using bankruptcy to avoid paying damages awarded in court judgments (as Randall Terry had done in 1998). He is the architect of the Unborn Child Pain Awareness Act.

The abortion issue shaped his early political career. In 1976, he ran as a Democrat while serving as executive director of the New Jersey Right to Life Committee. But he soon switched to the Republican Party when the Democrats supported *Roe v. Wade*. He takes a moral stand on most policy issues and is prominent in promoting human rights issues. Although he has a perfect pro-life voting record, he does not always toe the line on other issues associated with the right wing of the Republican Party. In this way he has formed alliances with feminists to curb sex trafficking and pornography. When Republicans nationwide were being defeated in the 2006 elections, Smith won his with 66 percent of the vote.

Ann E. W. Stone (1952–)

Ann Stone got involved in Republican Party politics in the 1970s through her association with Richard Viguerie and others who were trying to build Republicans into a majority party. The abortion issue became divisive after the pro-life Republicans achieved dominance in party organization and elections, beginning with the election of Ronald Reagan in 1980. The party faced the loss of many moderates and other Republicans that supported legal abortion. To counter that, the leadership encouraged the formation of groups within the party that would give an organizational presence for both pro-life and pro-choice views.

In 1990, Stone organized Republicans for Choice, which has consistently opposed strong pro-life planks in the party's platforms. She uses the organization and its website as a forum for criticizing the party leaders' unwillingness to allow a place for pro-choice politicians and policies. Stone links the right to privacy in abortion to other issues of limited government that appeal to Republican voters. At the same time, she urges pro-choice voters not to assume that a candidate's party is a way to determine his or her position on women's right to privacy. Some Democrats are anti-choice, she argues, and some moderate Republicans favor *Roe v. Wade*. To Stone, the party would be better off if it were not identified with the pro-life movement because most voters are interested in other issues.

Ann Stone continues to work in the direct-mail business and serves as a founding board member and vice president of the National Women's History Museum organization.

Horatio Robinson Storer (1830–1922)

Dr. Horatio Storer, a native of Boston, Massachusetts, attended Harvard College and earned his medical degree at Harvard Medical School. He opened a practice in 1855 in the relatively new field of gynecology and only 2 years later launched a campaign among physicians to criminalize abortion. He worked on two fronts: he built a network of physicians in other states, and he worked to gain support of the Massachusetts medical associations. Both tactics were successful; he convinced the American Medical Association (AMA) to endorse his campaign.

The AMA appointed a committee to make a recommendation on the issue, and Storer drafted the report. He noted the rapidly increasing incidence of abortion and linked it to a dangerous demoralization of American society. He blamed the problem on unscrupulous people seeking to benefit from the demand for abortion and to the ignorance, mainly of women, that abortions end human lives. In 1859, the AMA adopted Storer's report and resolved to work to make abortion a crime in every state except to save the life of the mother. Storer saw his goal achieved fully by 1900.

Although he is not famous anymore, Storer is a controversial figure in abortion and women's health circles. The pro-life advocates see him as the grandfather of their movement and the man who saved women from exploitation by quack abortionists. The National Right to Life Committee named its foundation after him. Pro-choice feminists have uncovered his contributions to establishing male-dominated medical treatment of women and have exposed his theory that women's emotional problems were related to their reproductive systems. To cure them, he removed their ovaries, an operation he performed many times in his career.

Randall Terry (1959–)

It was the 1980s when Randall Terry began his crusade against abortion. He had grown up in New York, graduated from the Elim Bible Institute, married, and become a leader in his evangelical church. Concerned about the moral decay of American society, he participated in the 1984 March for Life in Washington, DC. Shortly after that he and his wife started Project Life, which involved the two taking turns standing outside abortion clinics in Binghamton, New York, and trying to persuade women not to go in. This led to rescue missions to occupy and block entrances to abortion clinics. In 1987, Terry organized Operation Rescue and recruited activists to join direct action campaigns, first in Cherry Hill, New Jersey, and later in cities in the South and Midwest.

Terry claims to have been arrested more than forty times and became a co-defendant in the National Organization for Women's (NOW) lawsuit against clinic protesters, *NOW v. Scheidler*, which sought to use the federal antiracketeering law to sue groups obstructing clinics for damages. Terry left Operation Rescue in the mid-1990s and eventually settled the case with NOW out of court. Soon after, however, he declared bankruptcy and avoided paying any fines or damages. Some pro-choice activists blame Terry and his crusade for clinic violence. His message tapped into the fervent religious feelings of his followers and urged extreme action to stop what he called the killing of babies. Allegations continue that those who murdered abortion doctors in the 1990s were carrying out what they thought Terry wanted.

After the Operation Rescue days, Terry fell from grace with his religious followers when he left his wife and married another woman. He moved to Florida and has campaigned for the state legislature, so far unsuccessfully.

Richard Viguerie (1933–)

Richard Viguerie takes credit for building the conservative movement in America in the 1960s and 1970s. A key component of that movement was the pro-life activism that rose in the 1970s. Viguerie calls himself a pioneer in the use of direct mail. He lent his business, American Target Advertising, and his expertise to the new antiabortion groups to send millions of letters, especially in states with a large number of Christian evangelicals, to spread information about the abortion issue and to raise funds. As a strategist and consultant he was present at the formation of such pro-life groups as the Moral Majority. By the mid 1970s, the conservative movement could claim so much voter support that it can be credited for the shift in the Republican Party from a moderate to a pro-life party.

Thus, Viguerie deserves credit for turning a small number of Roman Catholic politicians who were dismayed at the Supreme Court decision in *Roe v. Wade* into a strong and successful political movement against legal abortion. The coalition he built brought about the Reagan years, anti-*Roe* appointments to the federal courts, and passage of the Partial-Birth Abortion Ban Act. He recounts the tale of these and other successes in his 2004 book: *America's Right Turn: How Conservatives Used New and Alternative Media to Take Power.* He is a native of Texas and a Catholic, and he has devoted his life to his cause. He remains a harsh judge of those who don't toe the pro-life line. In 2004, Viguerie criticized President George W. Bush for not speaking out strongly enough against abortion or using it as a major campaign issue.

Sarah Weddington (1945–)

Sarah Weddington had been out of University of Texas law school only 6 years when she became the youngest person to win a case before the Supreme Court. The opportunity came when a small group of feminist activists involved in the early days of the movement for abortion rights in Austin, Texas, asked her opinion about the legal status of their plan to begin a referral service for women seeking abortions in Mexico. Her research into this question revealed a strategy for challenging the constitutionality of Texas's nineteenth-century law, which prohibited all abortions except to save the life of the mother. Along with her colleague, Linda Coffee, Weddington located Norma McCorvey, who would become their plaintiff "Roe." The winning case was *Roe v. Wade*, which abolished criminal abortion laws in the United States in January 1973.

Weddington has been a pioneer for women's rights in many ways. She served in the Texas legislature 1973–1975, the first woman to be elected from Austin. She then joined the federal government as the first woman to be general counsel at the U.S. Department of Agriculture. When Midge Constanza resigned from her position as special assistant to President Jimmy Carter for women's issues, Weddington took the post until 1981. Since then she has traveled widely debating women's rights and working to promote women's leadership. Her book describing her experiences in the great *Roe v. Wade* case, *A Question of Choice*, was published in 1992.

6

Data and Documents

Introduction

Facts pertaining to the abortion conflict found here include some historical documents, such as early laws and proposals, excerpts from the major Supreme Court rulings that establish constitutional law, and proposed and enacted federal statutes, such as the Freedom of Access to Clinics Entrances, Partial-Birth Abortion Ban, Laci and Connor's law, and Prevention First. Data selected for this chapter show the current laws in the states pertaining to regulations and funding and the trends in abortion rates and ratios showing who gets abortions. Finally, some representative samples of public opinion polls document the ambivalence among American voters over this difficult issue.

Historical Documents

Blackstone's Commentaries

By definition, English common law is "unwritten" law in that it is contained in all the precedents of the English courts. However, William Blackstone wrote four volumes describing the common law as it was practiced in the eighteenth century, and these have been updated and reprinted from time to time. Here is what he had to say about abortion and, indirectly, partial-birth abortion long before the twenty-first-century debate.

Under murder: the person being killed must be *"a reasonable creature in being, and under the king's peace,"* at the time of the killing. . . . To kill a child in the mother's womb is now no murder, but great misprision; but if the child be born alive, and dieth by reason of a potion or bruises it received in the womb, it seems by the better opinion, to be murder in such as administered or gave them. [sic]

So if a mortal wound be given to a child while in the act of being born, for instance, upon the head as soon as the head appears, and before the child has breathed, it may be murder, if the child is afterward born alive and dies hereof. It must be proved, however, that the entire child has been born into the world of the living state; and the fact of its breathing is not a conclusive proof thereof. But the fact of its being still connected with the mother by the umbilical cord will not prevent the killing from being murder.

(Source: *Commentaries on The Laws of England:* in four books by William Gladstone. Vol IV. New York: Harper Bros., 1872 p. 198.)

Lord Ellenborough's Act of 1803. 32 *Geo III* c. 58, sec 2.

The British parliament placed criminal abortions in statute form in 1803 setting a standard for the U.S. states to follow.

II. 'And whereas it may sometimes happen that Poison or some other noxious and destructive Substance or Thing may be given, or other Means used, with Intent to procure Miscarriage or Abortion where the Woman may not be quick with Child at the Time, or it may not be proved that she was Quick with Child;' be it therefore further enacted, That if any Person or Persons, from and after the said first Day of *July* in the said Year of our Lord One thousand eight hundred and three, shall wilfully [sic] and maliciously administer to, or cause to be administered to, or taken by any Woman, any Medicines, Drug, or other Substance or Thing whatsoever, or shall use or employ, or cause or procure to be used or employed, any Instrument or other Means whatsoever, with Intent thereby to cause or procure the Miscarriage of any Woman not being, or not being proved to be, quick with Child at the Time of administering such Things or using such Means, that then and in every such Case the Person or Persons so offending, their Counsellors, Aiders, and Abettors, knowing of and privy to such Offence, shall be and are hereby declared to be guilty of Felony, and shall be liable to be fined, imprisoned, set in and upon the Pillory, publickly or privately whipped, or to suffer one or more of the said Punishments, or to be transported beyond the Seas for any Term not exceeding fourteen Years, at the Discretion of the Court before which such Offender shall be tried and convicted.

(Source: AOL. The Abortion Law Homepage. http://members.aol .com/abtrbng/lea.htm.)

American Medical Association Resolution 1859

Adoption of the following resolution marked the formal campaign to criminalize abortion in the United States.

Resolved, That while physicians have long been united in condemning the act of producing abortion, at every period of gestation, except as necessary for preserving the life of either mother or child, it has become the duty of this Association, in view of the prevalence and increasing frequency of the crime, publicly to enter an earnest and solemn protest against such unwarrantable destruction of human life.

Resolved, That in pursuance of the grand and noble calling we profess, the saving of human lives, and of the sacred responsibilities thereby devolving upon us, the Association present this subject to the attention of the several legislative assemblies of the Union, with the prayer that the laws by which the crime of procuring abortion is attempted to be controlled may be revised, and that such other action may be taken in the premises as they in their wisdom may deem necessary.

Resolved, That the Association request the zealous co-operation of the various State Medical Societies in pressing this subject upon the legislatures of their respective states.

(Source: Dyer, Frederick. "Horatio Robinson Storer M.D. and the Physicians Crusade Against Abortion." *Life and Learning IX*, 1998. www .uffl.org/vol%209/dyer9.pdf.)

Comstock Act of 1873

Congress outlawed information and materials related to contraception and abortion through the Comstock Act. It banned these in interstate commerce and from importation and transport through the mails.

Be it enacted by the Senate and House of Representatives of the United States of America in Congress assembled, That whoever, within the District of Columbia, or any of the Territories of the United Sates, or any other place within the exclusive jurisdiction of the United Sates, shall sell or lend, or give away, or in any manner exhibit, or shall offer to sell, or to lend, or to give away, in any manner to exhibit, or shall otherwise publish or offer to publish in any manner, or shall have in his possession, for any such purpose or purposes, any obscene book, pamphlet, paper, writing, advertisement, circular, print, picture, drawing or other representation, figure, or image on or of paper or other material, or any cast, instrument, or other article of any immoral nature, or any drug or medicine, or any article whatever, for the prevention of conception, or for causing unlawful abortion, or shall advertise the same for sale, or shall write or print, or cause to be written or printed, any card, circular, book, pamphlet, advertisement, or notice of any kind, setting when, where, how, or of whom, or by what means, any of the articles in this section hereinbefore mentioned, can be purchased or obtained, or shall manufacture, draw, or print, or in any wise make any of such articles, shall be deemed guilty of a misdemeanor, and on conviction thereof in any court of the United States . . . shall be imprisoned at hard labor in the penitentiary for not less than six months nor more than five years for each offense, or fined not less than one hundred dollars nor more than two thousand dollars, with costs of the court.

(Source: U.S. Statutes. Chapt. CCLVII. March 3, 1873.)

American Law Institute Model Penal Code: Abortion. Adopted 1959.

This American Law Institute model for conditional legal abortion became the first proposal for reform of criminal abortion laws in the 1960s. Many doctors and abortion activists promoted this proposal before Roe v. Wade *was decided. Several states adopted similar laws including Georgia. The Georgia law was declared unconstitutional in* Doe. v. Bolton, *the companion case to* Roe v. Wade.

Section 230.3. Abortion.

(1) Unjustified Abortion. A person who purposely and unjustifiably terminates the pregnancy of another otherwise than by a live birth commits a felony of the third degree or, where the pregnancy has continued beyond the twenty-sixth week, a felony of the second degree.

(2) Justifiable Abortion. A licensed physician is justified in terminating a pregnancy if he believes there is substantial risk that continuance of the pregnancy would gravely impair the physical or mental health of the mother or that the child would be born with grave physical or mental defect, or that the pregnancy resulted from rape, incest, or other felonious intercourse. All illicit intercourse with a girl below the age of 16 shall be deemed felonious for purposes of this subsection. Justifiable abortions shall be performed only in a licensed hospital except in case of emergency when hospital facilities are unavailable. [Additional exceptions from the requirement of hospitalization may be

incorporated here to take account of situations in sparsely settled areas where hospitals are not generally accessible.]

(3) Physicians' Certificates; Presumption from Non-Compliance. No abortion shall be performed unless two physicians, one of whom may be the person performing the abortion, shall have certified in writing the circumstances which they believe to justify the abortion. Such certificate shall be submitted before the abortion to the hospital where it is to be performed and, in the case of abortion following felonious intercourse, to the prosecuting attorney or the police. Failure to comply with any of the requirements of this Subsection gives rise to a presumption that the abortion was unjustified.

(Source: Reprinted from *Doe v. Bolton* Appendix B to the opinion. [410 U.S. 179, 205 1973].)

Humanae Vitae

ENCYCLICAL OF POPE PAUL VI ON THE REGULATION OF BIRTH
JULY 25, 1968. Excerpts relating to birth control.

With this 1968 encyclical, Pope Paul VI clarified the church's opposition to contraception and abortion at a key point in the abortion reform debate.

Responsible Parenthood

10. Married love, therefore, requires of husband and wife the full awareness of their obligations in the matter of responsible parenthood, which today, rightly enough, is much insisted upon, but which at the same time should be rightly understood. Thus, we do well to consider responsible parenthood in the light of its varied legitimate and interrelated aspects.

With regard to the biological processes, responsible parenthood means an awareness of, and respect for, their proper functions. In the procreative faculty the human mind discerns biological laws that apply to the human person.

With regard to man's innate drives and emotions, responsible parenthood means that man's reason and will must exert control over them.

With regard to physical, economic, psychological and social conditions, responsible parenthood is exercised by those who prudently and generously decide to have more children, and by those who, for serious reasons and with due respect to moral precepts, decide not to have additional children for either a certain or an indefinite period of time.

Responsible parenthood, as we use the term here, has one further essential aspect of paramount importance. It concerns the objective moral order which was established by God, and of which a right conscience is the true interpreter. In a word, the exercise of responsible parenthood requires that husband and wife, keeping a right order of priorities, recognize their own duties toward God, themselves, their families and human society.

From this it follows that they are not free to act as they choose in the service of transmitting life, as if it were wholly up to them to decide what is the right course to follow. On the contrary, they are bound to ensure that what they do corresponds to the will of God the Creator. The very nature of marriage and its use makes His will clear, while the constant teaching of the Church spells it out.

Observing the Natural Law

11. The sexual activity, in which husband and wife are intimately and chastely united with one another, through which human life is transmitted, is, as the recent Council recalled, "noble and worthy."' It does not, moreover, cease to be legitimate even when, for reasons independent of their will, it is foreseen to be infertile. For its natural adaptation to the expression and strengthening of the union of husband and wife is not thereby suppressed. The fact is, as experience shows, that new life is not the result of each and every act of sexual intercourse. God has wisely ordered laws of nature and the incidence of fertility in such a way that successive births are already naturally spaced through the inherent operation of these laws. The Church, nevertheless, in urging men to the observance of the precepts of the natural law, which it interprets by its constant doctrine, teaches that each and every marital act must of necessity retain its intrinsic relationship to the procreation of human life.

Union and Procreation

12. This particular doctrine, often expounded by the magisterium of the Church, is based on the inseparable connection, established by God, which man on his own initiative may not break, between the unitive significance and the procreative significance which are both inherent to the marriage act.

The reason is that the fundamental nature of the marriage act, while uniting husband and wife in the closest intimacy, also renders them capable of generating new life—and this as a result of laws written into the actual nature of man and of woman. And if each of these essential qualities, the unitive and the procreative, is preserved, the use of marriage fully retains its sense of true mutual love and its ordination to the supreme responsibility of parenthood to which man is called. We believe that our contemporaries are particularly capable of seeing that this teaching is in harmony with human reason.

Faithfulness to God's Design

13. Men rightly observe that a conjugal act imposed on one's partner without regard to his or her condition or personal and reasonable

wishes in the matter, is no true act of love, and therefore offends the moral order in its particular application to the intimate relationship of husband and wife. If they further reflect, they must also recognize that an act of mutual love which impairs the capacity to transmit life which God the Creator, through specific laws, has built into it, frustrates His design which constitutes the norm of marriage, and contradicts the will of the Author of life. Hence to use this divine gift while depriving it, even if only partially, of its meaning and purpose, is equally repugnant to the nature of man and of woman, and is consequently in opposition to the plan of God and His holy will. But to experience the gift of married love while respecting the laws of conception is to acknowledge that one is not the master of the sources of life but rather the minister of the design established by the Creator. Just as man does not have unlimited dominion over his body in general, so also, and with more particular reason, he has no such dominion over his specifically sexual faculties, for these are concerned by their very nature with the generation of life, of which God is the source. "Human life is sacred—all men must recognize that fact," Our predecessor Pope John XXIII recalled. "From its very inception it reveals the creating hand of God."

Unlawful Birth Control Methods

14. Therefore We base Our words on the first principles of a human and Christian doctrine of marriage when We are obliged once more to declare that the direct interruption of the generative process already begun and, above all, all direct abortion, even for therapeutic reasons, are to be absolutely excluded as lawful means of regulating the number of children. Equally to be condemned, as the magisterium of the Church has affirmed on many occasions, is direct sterilization, whether of the man or of the woman, whether permanent or temporary.

Similarly excluded is any action which either before, at the moment of, or after sexual intercourse, is specifically intended to prevent procreation—whether as an end or as a means.

Neither is it valid to argue, as a justification for sexual intercourse which is deliberately contraceptive, that a lesser evil is to be preferred to a greater one, or that such intercourse would merge with procreative acts of past and future to form a single entity, and so be qualified by exactly the same moral goodness as these. Though it is true that sometimes it is lawful to tolerate a lesser moral evil in order to avoid a greater evil or in order to promote a greater good, it is never lawful, even for the gravest reasons, to do evil that good may come of it—in other words, to intend directly something which of its very nature contradicts the moral order, and which must therefore be judged unworthy of man, even though the intention is to protect or promote the welfare of an individual, of a family or of society in general. Consequently, it is a serious error to think that a whole married life of otherwise normal relations can justify sexual intercourse which is deliberately contraceptive and so intrinsically wrong.

(Source: Vatican/Holy See. www.vatican.va/holy_father/paul_vi/encyclicals/documents/hf_p-vi_enc_25071968_humanae-vitae_en.html.)

The Essential Supreme Court Cases: Excerpts

Griswold v. Connecticut 381 U.S. 479 (1965)

The Supreme Court votes to overturn Connecticut's contraception prohibition statute on the grounds that marital sex is in a protected zone of privacy.

MR. JUSTICE DOUGLAS delivered the opinion of the Court.

Appellant Griswold is Executive Director of the Planned Parenthood League of Connecticut. Appellant Buxton is a licensed physician and a professor at the Yale Medical School who served as Medical Director for the League at its Center in New Haven—a center open and operating from November 1 to November 10, 1961, when appellants were arrested.

They gave information, instruction, and medical advice to married persons as to the means of preventing conception. They examined the wife and prescribed the best contraceptive device or material for her use. Fees were usually charged, although some couples were serviced free.

The statutes whose constitutionality is involved in this appeal are 53-32 and 54-196 of the General Statutes of Connecticut (1958 rev.). The former provides:

"Any person who uses any drug, medicinal article or instrument for the purpose of preventing conception shall be fined not less than fifty dollars or imprisoned not less than sixty days nor more than one year or be both fined and imprisoned."

Section 54-196 provides:

"Any person who assists, abets, counsels, causes, hires or commands another to commit any offense may be prosecuted and punished as if he were the principal offender."

. . .

The foregoing cases suggest that specific guarantees in the Bill of Rights have penumbras, formed by emanations from those guarantees that help give them life and substance. See Poe v. Ullman, 367 U.S. 497, 516 -522 (dissenting opinion). Various guarantees create zones of privacy. The right of association contained in the penumbra of the First Amendment is one, as we have seen. The Third Amendment in its prohibition against the quartering of soldiers "in any house" in time of peace without the consent of the owner is another facet of that privacy. The Fourth Amendment explicitly affirms the "right of the people to be secure in their persons, houses, papers, and effects, against unreasonable searches and seizures." The Fifth Amendment in its Self-Incrimination Clause enables the citizen to create a zone of privacy which government may not force him to surrender to his detriment. The Ninth Amendment provides: "The enumeration in the Constitution, of certain rights, shall not be construed to deny or disparage others retained by the people."

The Fourth and Fifth Amendments were described in Boyd v. United States, 116 U.S. 616, 630 , as protection against all governmental invasions "of the sanctity of a man's home and the privacies of life." We recently referred in Mapp v. Ohio, 367 U.S. 643, 656 , to the Fourth Amendment as creating a "right to privacy, no less important than any other right carefully and particularly reserved to the people." See Beaney, The Constitutional Right to Privacy, 1962 Sup. Ct. Rev. 212; Griswold, The Right to be Let Alone, 55 Nw. U. L. Rev. 216 (1960).

. . .

The present case, then, concerns a relationship lying within the zone of privacy created by several fundamental constitutional guarantees. And it concerns a law which, in forbidding the use of contraceptives rather than regulating their manufacture or sale, seeks to achieve its goals by means having a maximum destructive impact upon that relationship. Such a law cannot stand in light of the familiar principle, so often applied by this Court, that a "governmental purpose to control or prevent activities constitutionally subject to state regulation may not be achieved by means which sweep unnecessarily broadly and thereby invade the area of protected freedoms." NAACP v. Alabama, 377 U.S. 288, 307. Would we allow the police to search the sacred precincts of marital bedrooms for telltale signs of the use of contraceptives? The very idea is repulsive to the notions of privacy surrounding the marriage relationship.

We deal with a right of privacy older than the Bill of Rights—older than our political parties, older than our school system. Marriage is a coming together for better or for worse, hopefully enduring, and intimate to the degree of being sacred. It is an association that promotes a way of life, not causes; a harmony in living, not political faiths; a bilateral loyalty, not commercial or social projects. Yet it is an association for as noble a purpose as any involved in our prior decisions.

Eisenstadt v. Baird 405 U.S. 438 (1972)

The Supreme Court strikes down the Massachusetts criminal contraceptive law and extends the Griswold right to marital privacy to all individuals married or single, declaring the right to bear and beget a child a fundamental right of individuals.

MR. JUSTICE BRENNAN delivered the opinion of the Court.

Appellee William Baird was convicted at a bench trial in the Massachusetts Superior Court under Massachusetts General Laws Ann., c. 272, 21, first, for exhibiting contraceptive articles in the course of delivering a lecture on contraception to a group of students at Boston University and, second, for giving a young woman a package of Emko vaginal foam at the close of his address.

. . .

Massachusetts General Laws Ann., c. 272, 21, under which Baird was convicted, provides a maximum five-year term of imprisonment for "whoever . . . gives away . . . any drug, medicine, instrument or article whatever [405 U.S. 438, 441] for the prevention of conception," except as authorized in 21A. Under 21A, "[a] registered physician may administer to or prescribe for any married person drugs or articles intended for the prevention of pregnancy or conception. [And a] registered pharmacist actually engaged in the business of pharmacy may furnish such drugs or articles to any married person presenting a prescription from a registered physician." As interpreted by the State Supreme Judicial Court, these provisions make it a felony for anyone, other than a registered physician or pharmacist acting in accordance with the terms of 21A, to dispense any article with the intention that it be used for the prevention of conception. The statutory scheme distinguishes among three distinct classes of distributees—first, married persons may obtain contraceptives to prevent pregnancy, but only from doctors or druggists on prescription; second, single persons may not obtain contraceptives from anyone to prevent pregnancy; and, third, married or single persons may obtain contraceptives from anyone to prevent, not pregnancy, but the spread of disease. This construction of state law is, of course, binding on us. E. g., Groppi v. Wisconsin, 400 U.S. 505, 507 (1971).

. . .

If under Griswold the distribution of contraceptives to married persons cannot be prohibited, a ban on distribution to unmarried persons would be equally impermissible. It is true that in Griswold the right of privacy in question inhered in the marital relationship. Yet the marital couple is not an independent entity with a mind and heart of its own, but an association of two individuals each with a separate intellectual and emotional makeup. If the right of privacy means anything, it is the right of the individual, married or single, to be free from unwarranted governmental intrusion into matters so fundamentally affecting a person as the decision whether to bear or beget a child. See Stanley v. Georgia, 394 U.S. 557 (1969). See also Skinner v. Oklahoma, 316 U.S. 535 (1942); Jacobson v. Massachusetts, 197 U.S. 11, 29 (1905).

On the other hand, if Griswold is no bar to a prohibition on the distribution of contraceptives, the State could not, consistently with the

Equal Protection Clause, outlaw distribution to unmarried but not to married persons. In each case the evil, as perceived by the State, would be identical, and the underinclusion would be invidious. Mr. Justice Jackson, concurring in Railway Express Agency v. New York, 336 U.S. 106, 112 -113 (1949), made the point:

"The framers of the Constitution knew, and we should not forget today, that there is no more effective practical guaranty against arbitrary and unreasonable government than to require that the principles of law which officials would impose upon a minority must be imposed generally. Conversely, nothing opens the door to arbitrary action so effectively as to allow those officials to pick and choose only a few to whom they will apply legislation and thus to escape the political retribution that might be visited upon them if larger numbers were affected. Courts can take no better measure to assure that laws will be just than to require that laws be equal in operation."

Although Mr. Justice Jackson's comments had reference to administrative regulations, the principle he affirmed has equal application to the legislation here. We hold that by providing dissimilar treatment for married and unmarried persons who are similarly situated, Massachusetts General Laws Ann., c. 272, 21 and 21A, violate the Equal Protection Clause.

Roe v. Wade 410 U.S. 113 (1973)

The Supreme Court extends the right to privacy to women seeking abortion and refuses to declare the fetus a person under the Constitution. The case decriminalizes abortion in the United States.

MR. JUSTICE BLACKMUN delivered the opinion of the Court

The Texas statutes that concern us here are Arts. 1191–1194 and 1196 of the State's Penal Code. These make it a crime to "procure an abortion," as therein defined, or to attempt one, except with respect to "an abortion procured or attempted by medical advice for the purpose of saving the life of the mother." Similar statutes are in existence in a majority of the States.

The Constitution does not explicitly mention any right of privacy. In a line of decisions, however, going back perhaps as far as Union Pacific R. Co. v. Botsford, 141 U.S. 250, 251 (1891), the Court has recognized that a right of personal privacy, or a guarantee of certain areas or zones of privacy, does exist under the Constitution. In varying contexts, the Court or individual Justices have, indeed, found at least the roots of that right in the First Amendment, Stanley v. Georgia, 394 U.S. 557, 564 (1969); in the Fourth and Fifth Amendments, Terry v. Ohio, 392 U.S. 1, 8 -9 (1968), Katz v. United States, 389 U.S. 347, 350 (1967), Boyd v. United States, 116 U.S. 616 (1886), see Olmstead v. United States, 277 U.S. 438, 478 (1928) (Brandeis, J., dissenting); in the penumbras of the Bill of

Rights, Griswold v. Connecticut, 381 U.S., at 484-485; in the Ninth Amendment, id., at 486 (Goldberg, J., concurring); or in the concept of liberty guaranteed by the first section of the Fourteenth Amendment, see Meyer v. Nebraska, 262 U.S. 390, 399 (1923). These decisions make it clear that only personal rights that can be deemed "fundamental" or "implicit in the concept of ordered liberty," Palko v. Connecticut, 302 U.S. 319, 325 (1937), are included in this guarantee of personal privacy. They also make it clear that the right has some extension to activities relating to marriage, Loving v. Virginia, 388 U.S. 1, 12 (1967); procreation, Skinner v. Oklahoma, 316 U.S. 535, 541-542 (1942); contraception, Eisenstadt v. Baird, 405 U.S., at 453-454; id., at 460, 463-465 (WHITE, J., concurring in result); family relationships, Prince v. Massachusetts, 321 U.S. 158, 166 (1944); and child rearing and education, Pierce v. Society of Sisters, 268 U.S. 510, 535 (1925), Meyer v. Nebraska, supra.

This right of privacy, whether it be founded in the Fourteenth Amendment's concept of personal liberty and restrictions upon state action, as we feel it is, or, as the District Court determined, in the Ninth Amendment's reservation of rights to the people, is broad enough to encompass a woman's decision whether or not to terminate her pregnancy. The detriment that the State would impose upon the pregnant woman by denying this choice altogether is apparent. Specific and direct harm medically diagnosable even in early pregnancy may be involved. Maternity, or additional offspring, may force upon the woman a distressful life and future. Psychological harm may be imminent. Mental and physical health may be taxed by child care. There is also the distress, for all concerned associated with the unwanted child, and there is the problem of bringing a child into a family already unable, psychologically and otherwise, to care for it. In other cases, as in this one, the additional difficulties and continuing stigma of unwed motherhood may be involved. All these are factors the woman and her responsible physician necessarily will consider in consultation.

On the basis of elements such as these, appellant and some amici argue that the woman's right is absolute and that she is entitled to terminate her pregnancy at whatever time, in whatever way, and for whatever reason she alone chooses. With this we do not agree. Appellant's arguments that Texas either has no valid interest at all in regulating the abortion decision, or no interest strong enough to support any limitation upon the woman's sole determination, are unpersuasive. The Court's decisions recognizing a right of privacy also acknowledge that some state regulation in areas protected by that right is appropriate. As noted above, a State may properly assert important interests in safeguarding health, in maintaining medical standards, and in protecting potential life. At some point in pregnancy, these respective interests become sufficiently compelling to sustain regulation of the factors that govern the abortion decision. The privacy right involved, therefore, cannot be said to be absolute.

In fact, it is not clear to us that the claim asserted by some amici that one has an unlimited right to do with one's body as one pleases bears a close relationship to the right of privacy previously articulated in the Court's decisions. The Court has refused to recognize an unlimited right of this kind in the past. Jacobson v. Massachusetts, 197 U.S. 11 (1905) (vaccination); Buck v. Bell, 274 U.S. 200 (1927) (sterilization).

We, therefore, conclude that the right of personal privacy includes the abortion decision, but that this right is not unqualified and must be considered against important state interests in regulation.

. . .

The appellee and certain amici argue that the fetus is a "person" within the language and meaning of the Fourteenth Amendment. In support of this, they outline at length and in detail the well-known facts of fetal development. If this suggestion of personhood is established, the appellant's case, of course, collapses, for the fetus' right to life would then be guaranteed specifically by the Amendment. The appellant conceded as much on reargument. On the other hand, the appellee conceded on reargument that no case could be cited that holds that a fetus is a person within the meaning of the Fourteenth Amendment.

The Constitution does not define "person" in so many words. Section 1 of the Fourteenth Amendment contains three references to "person." The first, in defining "citizens," speaks of "persons born or naturalized in the United States." The word also appears both in the Due Process Clause and in the Equal Protection Clause. "Person" is used in other places in the Constitution: in the listing of qualifications for Representatives and Senators, Art. I, 2, cl. 2, and 3, cl. 3; in the Apportionment Clause, Art. I, 2, cl. 3; 53 in the Migration and Importation provision, Art. I, 9, cl. 1; in the Emolument Clause, Art. I, 9, cl. 8; in the Electors provisions, Art. II, 1, cl. 2, and the superseded cl. 3; in the provision outlining qualifications for the office of President, Art. II, 1, cl. 5; in the Extradition provisions, Art. IV, 2, cl. 2, and the superseded Fugitive Slave Clause 3; and in the Fifth, Twelfth, and Twenty-second Amendments, as well as in 2 and 3 of the Fourteenth Amendment. But in nearly all these instances, the use of the word is such that it has application only postnatally. None indicates, with any assurance, that it has any possible pre-natal application.

All this, together with our observation, supra, that throughout the major portion of the 19th century prevailing legal abortion practices were far freer than they are today, persuades us that the word "person," as used in the Fourteenth Amendment, does not include the unborn.

Doe v. Bolton 410 U.S. 179 (1973)

In the companion case to Roe v. Wade, *the court defined the extent of the medical judgment or health exception for abortion restrictions.*

MR. JUSTICE BLACKMUN delivered the opinion of the Court.

In this appeal, the criminal abortion statutes recently enacted in Georgia are challenged on constitutional grounds.

. . .

As the appellants acknowledge, the 1968 statutes are patterned upon the American Law Institute's Model Penal Code, 230.3 (Proposed Official Draft, 1962), reproduced as Appendix B, post, p. 205. The ALI proposal has served as the model for recent legislation in approximately one-fourth of our States. The new Georgia provisions replaced statutory law that had been in effect for more than 90 years. Georgia Laws 1876, No. 130, 2, at 113. The predecessor statute paralleled the Texas legislation considered in Roe v. Wade, supra, and made all abortions criminal except those necessary "to preserve the life" of the pregnant woman. The new statutes have not been tested on constitutional grounds in the Georgia state courts.

Section 26-1201, with a referenced exception, makes abortion a crime, and 26-1203 provides that a person convicted of that crime shall be punished by imprisonment for not less than one nor more than 10 years. Section 26-1202 (a) states the exception and removes from 1201's definition of criminal abortion, and thus makes noncriminal, an abortion "performed by a physician duly licensed" in Georgia when, "based upon his best clinical judgment . . . an abortion is necessary because:

"(1) A continuation of the pregnancy would endanger the life of the pregnant woman or would seriously and permanently injure her health; or

"(2) The fetus would very likely be born with a grave, permanent, and irremediable mental or physical defect; or

"(3) The pregnancy resulted from forcible or statutory rape."

. . .

Appellants argue that 26-1202 (a) of the Georgia statutes, as it has been left by the District Court's decision, is unconstitutionally vague. This argument centers on the proposition that, with the District Court's having struck down the statutorily specified reasons, it still remains a crime for a physician to perform an abortion except when, as 26-1202 (a) reads, it is "based upon his best clinical judgment that an abortion is necessary." The appellants contend that the word "necessary" does not warn the physician of what conduct is proscribed; that the statute is wholly without objective standards and is subject to diverse interpretation; and that doctors will choose to err on the side of caution and will be arbitrary.

The net result of the District Court's decision is that the abortion determination, so far as the physician is concerned, is made in the exercise of his professional, that is, his "best clinical," judgment in the light of all the attendant circumstances. He is not now restricted to the three situations originally specified. Instead, he may range farther afield wherever his medical judgment, properly and professionally exercised, so dictates and directs him.

The vagueness argument is set at rest by the decision in United States v. Vuitch, 402 U.S. 62, 71-72 (1971), where the issue was raised with respect to a District of Columbia statute making abortions criminal "unless the same were done as necessary for the preservation of the mother's life or health and under the direction of a competent licensed practitioner of medicine." That statute has been construed to bear upon psychological as [410 U.S. 179, 192] well as physical well-being. This being so, the Court concluded that the term "health" presented no problem of vagueness. "Indeed, whether a particular operation is necessary for a patient's physical or mental health is a judgment that physicians are obviously called upon to make routinely whenever surgery is considered." Id., at 72. This conclusion is equally applicable here. Whether, in the words of the Georgia statute, "an abortion is necessary" is a professional judgment that the Georgia physician will be called upon to make routinely.

We agree with the District Court, 319 F. Supp., at 1058, that the medical judgment may be exercised in the light of all factors—physical, emotional, psychological, familial, and the woman's age—relevant to the wellbeing of the patient. All these factors may relate to health. This allows the attending physician the room he needs to make his best medical judgment. And it is room that operates for the benefit, not the disadvantage, of the pregnant woman.

Planned Parenthood of Southeastern Pa. v. Casey, 505 U.S. 833 (1992)

In this compromise decision, the Supreme Court affirms the central holding in Roe v. Wade, *protects women's liberty from undue burdens and affirms the states' power to protect fetal life. These principles stand as controlling precedent for subsequent cases regarding regulations of abortion coming before the federal courts.*

JUSTICE O'CONNOR, JUSTICE KENNEDY, and JUSTICE SOUTER announced the judgment of the Court and delivered the opinion of the Court

. . .

Men and women of good conscience can disagree, and we suppose some always shall disagree, about the profound moral and spiritual implications of terminating a pregnancy, even in its earliest stage. Some of us as individuals find abortion offensive to our most basic principles of morality, but that cannot control our decision. Our obligation is to define the liberty of all, not to mandate our own moral code. The underlying constitutional issue is whether the State can resolve these philosophic questions in such a definitive way that a woman lacks all choice in the matter, except perhaps in those rare circumstances in which the pregnancy is itself a danger to her own life or health, or is the result of rape or incest.

It is conventional constitutional doctrine that, where reasonable people disagree, the government can adopt one position or the other . . . . That theorem, however, assumes a state of affairs in which the choice does not intrude upon a protected liberty. Thus, while some people might disagree about whether or not the flag should be saluted, or disagree about the proposition that it may not be defiled, we have ruled that a State may not compel or enforce one view or the other. See West Virginia Bd. of Ed. v. Barnette, 319 U.S. 624 (1943); Texas v. Johnson, 491 U.S. 397 (1989).

Our law affords constitutional protection to personal decisions relating to marriage, procreation, contraception, family relationships, child rearing, and education. Carey v. Population Services International, 431 U.S., at 685. Our cases recognize the right of the individual, married or single, to be free from unwarranted governmental intrusion into matters so fundamentally affecting a person as the decision whether to bear or beget a child. Eisenstadt v. Baird, supra, 405 U.S., at 453 (emphasis in original). Our precedents "have respected the private realm of family life which the state cannot enter." Prince v. Massachusetts, 321 U.S. 158, 166 (1944). These matters, involving the most intimate and personal choices a person may make in a lifetime, choices central to personal dignity and autonomy, are central to the liberty protected by the Fourteenth Amendment. At the heart of liberty is the right to define one's own concept of existence, of meaning, of the universe, and of the mystery of human life. Beliefs about these matters could not define the attributes of personhood were they formed under compulsion of the State.

These considerations begin our analysis of the woman's interest in terminating her pregnancy, but cannot end it, for this reason: though the abortion decision may originate within the zone of conscience and belief, it is more than a philosophic exercise. Abortion is a unique act. It is an act fraught with consequences for others: for the woman who must live with the implications of her decision; for the persons who perform and assist in the procedure; for the spouse, family, and society which must confront the knowledge that these procedures exist, procedures some deem nothing short of an act of violence against innocent human life; and, depending on one's beliefs, for the life or potential life that is aborted. Though abortion is conduct, it does not follow that the State is entitled to proscribe it in all instances. That is because the liberty of the woman is at stake in a sense unique to the human condition, and so, unique to the law. The mother who carries a child to full term is subject to anxieties, to physical constraints, to pain that only she must bear. That these sacrifices have from the beginning of the human race been endured by woman with a pride that ennobles her in the eyes of others and gives to the infant a bond of love cannot alone be grounds for the State to insist she make the sacrifice. Her suffering is too intimate and personal for the State to insist, without more, upon its own vision of the woman's role, however dominant that vision has been in the course of our history and our culture. The destiny of the woman must be shaped to a large extent on her own conception of her spiritual imperatives and her place in society.

It should be recognized, moreover, that in some critical respects, the abortion decision is of the same character as the decision to use contraception, to which Griswold v. Connecticut, Eisenstadt v. Baird, and Carey v. Population Services International afford constitutional protection. We have no doubt as to the correctness of those decisions. They support the reasoning in Roe relating to the woman's liberty, because they involve personal decisions concerning not only the meaning of procreation but also human responsibility and respect for it. As with abortion, reasonable people will have differences of opinion about these matters. One view is based on such reverence for the wonder of creation that any pregnancy ought to be welcomed and carried to full term, no matter how difficult it will be to provide for the child and ensure its wellbeing. Another is that the inability to provide for the nurture and care of the infant is a cruelty to the child and an anguish to the parent. These are intimate views with infinite variations, and their deep, personal character underlay our decisions in Griswold, Eisenstadt, and Carey. The same concerns are present when the woman confronts the reality that, perhaps despite her attempts to avoid it, she has become pregnant.

It was this dimension of personal liberty that Roe sought to protect, and its holding invoked the reasoning and the tradition of the precedents we have discussed, granting protection to substantive liberties of the person. Roe was, of course, an extension of those cases and, as the decision itself indicated, the separate States could act in some degree to further their own legitimate interests in protecting prenatal life. The extent to which the legislatures of the States might act to outweigh the interests of the woman in choosing to terminate her pregnancy was a subject of debate both in Roe itself and in decisions following it.

. . .

From what we have said so far, it follows that it is a constitutional liberty of the woman to have some freedom to terminate her pregnancy. We conclude that the basic decision in Roe was based on a constitutional analysis which we cannot now repudiate. The woman's liberty is not so unlimited, however, that, from the outset, the State cannot show its concern for the life of the unborn and, at a later point in fetal development, the State's interest in life has sufficient force so that the right of the woman to terminate the pregnancy can be restricted.

That brings us, of course, to the point where much criticism has been directed at Roe, a criticism that always inheres when the Court draws a specific rule from what in the Constitution is but a general standard. We conclude, however, that the urgent claims of the woman to retain the ultimate control over her destiny and her body, claims implicit in the meaning of liberty, require us to perform that function. Liberty must not be extinguished for want of a line that is clear. And it falls to us to give some real substance to the woman's liberty to determine whether to carry her pregnancy to full term.

We conclude the line should be drawn at viability, so that, before that time, the woman has a right to choose to terminate her pregnancy. We adhere to this principle for two reasons. First, as we have said, is the doctrine of stare decisis. Any judicial act of line-drawing may seem somewhat arbitrary, but Roe was a reasoned statement, elaborated with great care. We have twice reaffirmed it in the face of great opposition. See Thornburgh v. American College of Obstetricians and Gynecologists, 476 U.S., at 759; Akron I, 462 U.S., at 419-420. Although we must overrule those parts of Thornburgh and Akron I which, in our view, are inconsistent with Roe's statement that the State has a legitimate interest in promoting the life or potential life of the unborn, see infra, at 40-41, the central premise of those cases represents an unbroken commitment by this Court to the essential holding of Roe. It is that premise which we reaffirm today.

The second reason is that the concept of viability, as we noted in Roe, is the time at which there is a realistic possibility of maintaining and nourishing a life outside the womb, so that the independent existence of the second life can, in reason and all fairness, be the object of state protection that now overrides the rights of the woman. See Roe v. Wade, 410 U.S., at 163. Consistent with other constitutional norms, legislatures may draw lines which appear arbitrary without the necessity of offering a justification. But courts may not. We must justify the lines we draw. And there is no line other than viability which is more workable. To be sure, as we have said, there may be some medical developments that affect the precise point of viability, see supra, at 17-18, but this is an imprecision within tolerable limits, given that the medical community and all those who must apply its discoveries will continue to explore the matter. The viability line also has, as a practical matter, an element of fairness. In some broad sense, it might be said that a woman who fails to act before viability has consented to the State's intervention on behalf of the developing child.

The woman's right to terminate her pregnancy before viability is the most central principle of Roe v. Wade. It is a rule of law and a component of liberty we cannot renounce.

On the other side of the equation is the interest of the State in the protection of potential life. The Roe Court recognized the State's "important and legitimate interest in protecting the potentiality of human life." Roe, supra, at 162. The weight to be given this state interest, not the strength of the woman's interest, was the difficult question faced in Roe. We do not need to say whether each of us, had we been Members of the Court when the valuation of the state interest came before it as an original matter, would have concluded, as the Roe Court did, that its weight is insufficient to justify a ban on abortions prior to viability even when it is subject to certain exceptions. The matter is not before us in the first instance, and, coming as it does after nearly 20 years of litigation in Roe's wake we are satisfied that the immediate question is not the soundness of Roe's resolution of the issue, but the precedential force that must be accorded to its holding. And we have concluded that the essential holding of Roe should be reaffirmed.

Yet it must be remembered that Roe v. Wade speaks with clarity in establishing not only the woman's liberty but also the State's "important and legitimate interest in potential life." Roe, supra, at 163. That portion of the decision in Roe has been given too little acknowledgment and implementation by the Court in its subsequent cases. Those cases decided that any regulation touching upon the abortion decision must survive strict scrutiny, to be sustained only if drawn in narrow terms to further a compelling state interest. See, e.g., Akron I, supra, at 427. Not all of the cases decided under that formulation can be reconciled with the holding in Roe itself that the State has legitimate interests in the health of the woman and in protecting the potential life within her. In resolving this tension, we choose to rely upon Roe, as against the later cases.

Roe established a trimester framework to govern abortion regulations. Under this elaborate but rigid construct, almost no regulation at all is permitted during the first trimester of pregnancy; regulations designed to protect the woman's health, but not to further the State's interest in potential life, are permitted during the second trimester; and, during the third trimester, when the fetus is viable, prohibitions are permitted provided the life or health of the mother is not at stake. Roe, supra, at 163-166. Most of our cases since Roe have involved the application of rules derived from the trimester framework. See, e.g., Thornburgh v. American College of Obstetricians and Gynecologists, supra; Akron I, supra.

The trimester framework no doubt was erected to ensure that the woman's right to choose not become so subordinate to the State's interest in promoting fetal life that her choice exists in theory, but not in fact. We do not agree, however, that the trimester approach is necessary to accomplish this objective. A framework of this rigidity was unnecessary, and, in its later interpretation, sometimes contradicted the State's permissible exercise of its powers.

Though the woman has a right to choose to terminate or continue her pregnancy before viability, it does not at all follow that the State is prohibited from taking steps to ensure that this choice is thoughtful and informed. Even in the earliest stages of pregnancy, the State may enact rules and regulations designed to encourage her to know that there are philosophic and social arguments of great weight that can be brought to bear in favor of continuing the pregnancy to full term, and that there are procedures and institutions to allow adoption of unwanted children as well as a certain degree of state assistance if the mother chooses to raise the child herself. "[T]he Constitution does not forbid a State or city, pursuant to democratic processes, from expressing a preference for normal childbirth." Webster v. Reproductive Health Services, 492 U.S., at 511 (opinion of [505 U.S. 833, 873] the Court) (quoting Poelker v. Doe, 432 U.S. 519, 521 (1977)). It follows that States are free to enact laws to provide a reasonable framework for a woman to make a decision that has such profound and lasting meaning. This, too, we find consistent with Roe's central premises, and indeed the inevitable consequence of our holding that the State has an interest in protecting the life of the unborn.

We reject the trimester framework, which we do not consider to be part of the essential holding of Roe. See Webster v. Reproductive Health Services, supra, at 518 (opinion of REHNQUIST, C.J.); id., at 529 (O'CONNOR, J., concurring in part and concurring in judgment) (describing the trimester framework as "problematic"). Measures aimed at ensuring that a woman's choice contemplates the consequences for the fetus do not necessarily interfere with the right recognized in Roe, although those measures have been found to be inconsistent with the rigid trimester framework announced in that case. A logical reading of the central holding in Roe itself, and a necessary reconciliation of the liberty of the woman and the interest of the State in promoting prenatal life, require, in our view, that we abandon the trimester framework as a rigid prohibition on all pre-viability regulation aimed at the protection of fetal life. The trimester framework suffers from these basic flaws: in its formulation, it misconceives the nature of the pregnant woman's interest; and in practice, it undervalues the State's interest in potential life, as recognized in Roe.

As our jurisprudence relating to all liberties save perhaps abortion has recognized, not every law which makes a right more difficult to exercise is, ipso facto, an infringement of that right. An example clarifies the point. We have held that not every ballot access limitation amounts to an infringement of the right to vote. Rather, the States are granted substantial flexibility in establishing the framework within which voters choose the candidates for whom they wish to vote. Anderson v. Celebrezze, 460 U.S. 780, 788 (1983); Norman v. Reed, 502 U.S. 279 (1992).

The abortion right is similar. Numerous forms of state regulation might have the incidental effect of increasing the cost or decreasing the availability of medical care, whether for abortion or any other medical procedure. The fact that a law which serves a valid purpose, one not designed to strike at the right itself, has the incidental effect of making it more difficult or more expensive to procure an abortion cannot be enough to invalidate it. Only where state regulation imposes an undue burden on a woman's ability to make this decision does the power of the State reach into the heart of the liberty protected by the Due Process Clause.

Excerpts from Important Proposed and Enacted Statutes

Human Life Amendment: Three Versions

In the 1970s, in response to the Supreme Court ruling that the Constitution prohibited states from outlawing abortion, pro-life advocates proposed amendments to the Constitution to override the decision. None of them passed the Congress.

1. Rep. Angelo D. Roncallo (R-NY) 5/30/74 93 H. J. Res. 1041

"SECTION 1. Abortion is hereby prohibited within the United States and all territory subject to the jurisdiction thereof. As used in this article, abortion means the intentional destruction of unborn human life, which life begins at the moment of fertilization.

"SECTION 2. Congress and the several States shall have concurrent power to enforce this article by appropriate legislation."

2. Sen. William L. Scott (R-VA) 6/6/75 94 S. J. Res. 91

"The power to regulate the circumstances under which pregnancy may be terminated is reserved to the States."

3. Sen. Jesse Helms (R-NC) 12/16/81 97 S. J. Res. 137

"SECTION 1. The right to life is the paramount and most fundamental right of a person.

SECTION 2. With respect to the right to life guaranteed to persons by the fifth and fourteenth articles of amendment to the Constitution, the word 'person' applies to all human beings, irrespective of age, health, function, or condition of dependency, including their unborn offspring at every stage of their biological development including fertilization.

SECTION 3. No unborn person shall be deprived of life by any person: Provided, however, That nothing in this article shall prohibit a law allowing justification to be shown for only those medical procedures required to prevent the death of either the pregnant woman or

182 Data and Documents

her unborn offspring, as long as such law requires every reasonable effort be made to preserve the life of each.

SECTION 4. Congress and the several States shall have the power to enforce this article by appropriate legislation."

(Source: National Committee for the Human Life Amendment. www .nchla.org/docdisplay.asp?ID=74.)

Freedom of Choice Act of 1993

In anticipation of an anti-Roe majority on the Supreme Court in the early 1990s, the pro-choice movement organized a campaign to put the guarantees of Roe into law through Congressional action. The act did not pass. Following is the text of the proposed legislation as reported in the Senate.

A BILL To protect the reproductive rights of women, and for other purposes.

(a) FINDINGS—Congress finds the following:

(1) The 1973 Supreme Court decision in Roe v. Wade established constitutionally based limits on the power of States to restrict the right of a woman to choose to terminate a pregnancy. Under the strict scrutiny standard enunciated in Roe v. Wade, States were required to demonstrate that laws restricting the right of a woman to choose to terminate a pregnancy were the least restrictive means available to achieve a compelling State interest. Since 1989, the Supreme Court has no longer applied the strict scrutiny standard in reviewing challenges to the constitutionality of State laws restricting such rights.

(2) As a result of the Supreme Court's recent modification of the strict scrutiny standard enunciated in Roe v. Wade, certain States have restricted the right of women to choose to terminate a pregnancy or to utilize some forms of contraception, and these restrictions operate cumulatively to—

(A)(i) increase the number of illegal or medically less safe abortions, often resulting in physical impairment, loss of reproductive capacity or death to the women involved;

(ii) burden interstate commerce by forcing women to travel from States in which legal barriers render contraception or abortion unavailable or unsafe to other States or foreign nations;

(iii) interfere with freedom of travel between and among the various States;

(iv) burden the medical and economic resources of States that continue to provide women with access to safe and legal abortion ; and

(v) interfere with the ability of medical professionals to provide health services;

(B) obstruct access to and use of contraceptive and other medical techniques that are part of interstate and international commerce;

(C) discriminate between women who are able to afford interstate and international travel and women who are not, a disproportionate number of whom belong to racial or ethnic minorities; and

(D) infringe upon women's ability to exercise full enjoyment of rights secured to them by Federal and State law, both statutory and constitutional.

(3) Although Congress may not by legislation create constitutional rights, it may, where authorized by its enumerated powers and not prohibited by a constitutional provision, enact legislation to create and secure statutory rights in areas of legitimate national concern.

(4) Congress has the affirmative power both under section 8 of article I of the Constitution of the United States and under section 5 of the Fourteenth Amendment of the Constitution to enact legislation to prohibit State interference with interstate commerce, liberty or equal protection of the laws.

(b) PURPOSE—It is the purpose of this Act to establish, as a statutory matter, limitations upon the power of States to restrict the freedom of a woman to terminate a pregnancy in order to achieve the same limitations as provided, as a constitutional matter, under the strict scrutiny standard of review enunciated in Roe v. Wade and applied in subsequent cases from 1973 to 1988.

SEC. 3. FREEDOM TO CHOOSE.

(a) IN GENERAL—A State—

(1) may not restrict the freedom of a woman to choose whether or not to terminate a pregnancy before fetal viability;

(2) may restrict the freedom of a woman to choose whether or not to terminate a pregnancy after fetal viability unless such a termination is necessary to preserve the life or health of the woman; and

(3) may impose requirements on the performance of abortion procedures if such requirements are medically necessary to protect the health of women undergoing such procedures.

(b) RULES OF CONSTRUCTION—Nothing in this Act shall be construed to—

(1) prevent a State from protecting unwilling individuals or private health care institutions from having to participate in the performance of abortions to which they are conscientiously opposed;

(2) prevent a State from declining to pay for the performance of abortions; or

(3) prevent a State from requiring a minor to involve a parent, guardian, or other responsible adult before terminating a pregnancy.

(Source: 103d Congress; 1st Session; S. 25; [Report No. 103-42].)

Freedom of Access to Clinics Entrances Act (FACE) of 1994

After a dramatic increase in violence at abortion clinics, Congress enacted the following bill making forceful obstruction a federal offense.

(a) Prohibited activities. —Whoever—

(1) by force or threat of force or by physical obstruction, intentionally injures, intimidates or interferes with or attempts to injure, intimidate or interfere with any person because that person is or has been, or in order to intimidate such person or any other person or any class of persons from, obtaining or providing reproductive health services;

(2) by force or threat of force or by physical obstruction, intentionally injures, intimidates or interferes with or attempts to injure, intimidate or interfere with any person lawfully exercising or seeking to exercise the First Amendment right of religious freedom at a place of religious worship; or

(3) intentionally damages or destroys the property of a facility, or attempts to do so, because such facility provides reproductive health services, or intentionally damages or destroys the property of a place of religious worship, shall be subject to the penalties provided in subsection (b) and the civil remedies provided in subsection (c), except that a parent or legal guardian of a minor shall not be subject to any penalties or civil remedies under this section for such activities insofar as they are directed exclusively at that minor.

(b) Penalties. —Whoever violates this section shall—

(1) in the case of a first offense, be fined in accordance with this title, or imprisoned not more than one year, or both; and

(2) in the case of a second or subsequent offense after a prior conviction under this section, be fined in accordance with this title, or imprisoned not more than 3 years, or both; except that for an offense involving exclusively a nonviolent physical obstruction, the fine shall be not more than $10,000 and the length of imprisonment shall be not more than six months, or both, for the first offense; and the fine shall, notwithstanding section 3571, be not more than $25,000 and the length of imprisonment shall be not more than 18 months, or both, for a subsequent offense; and except that if bodily injury results, the length of imprisonment shall be not more than 10 years, and if death results, it shall be for any term of years or for life.

(c) Civil remedies. —

(1) Right of action. —

(A) In general. —Any person aggrieved by reason of the conduct prohibited by subsection (a) may commence a civil action for the relief set forth in subparagraph (B), except that such an action may be brought under subsection (a)(1) only by a person involved in providing or seeking to provide, or obtaining or seeking to obtain, services in a facility that provides reproductive health services, and such an action may be brought under subsection (a)(2) only by a person lawfully exercising or seeking to exercise the First Amendment right of religious freedom at a place of religious worship or by the entity that owns or operates such place of religious worship.

(B) Relief. —In any action under subparagraph (A), the court may award appropriate relief, including temporary, preliminary or permanent injunctive relief and compensatory and punitive damages, as well as the costs of suit and reasonable fees for attorneys and expert witnesses. With respect to compensatory damages, the plaintiff may elect, at any time prior to the rendering of final judgment, to recover, in lieu of actual damages, an award of statutory damages in the amount of $5,000 per violation.

(Source: 18 U.S.C. § 248.)

Partial-Birth Abortion Ban Act 2003

After two attempts during President Bill Clinton's administration, pro-life activists were successful in 2003 when President George W. Bush signed the federal ban on partial-birth abortions. In 2007, the Supreme Court upheld the constitutionality of this law.

The Congress finds and declares the following:

(1) A moral, medical, and ethical consensus exists that the practice of performing a partial-birth abortion—an abortion in which a physician deliberately and intentionally vaginally delivers a living, unborn child's body until either the entire baby's head is outside the body of the mother, or any part of the baby's trunk past the navel is outside the body of the mother and only the head remains inside the womb, for the purpose of performing an overt act (usually the puncturing of the back of the child's skull and removing the baby's brains) that the person knows will kill the partially delivered infant, performs this act, and then completes delivery of the dead infant—is a gruesome and inhumane procedure that is never medically necessary and should be prohibited.

(2) Rather than being an abortion procedure that is embraced by the medical community, particularly among physicians who routinely perform other abortion procedures, partial-birth abortion remains a disfavored procedure that is not only unnecessary to preserve the health of the mother, but in fact poses serious risks to the long-term health of women and in some circumstances, their lives. As a result, at least 27 States banned the procedure as did the United States Congress which voted to ban the procedure during the 104th, 105th, and 106th Congresses.

(3) In Stenberg v. Carhart, 530 U.S. 914, 932 (2000), the United States Supreme Court opined "that significant medical authority supports the proposition that in some circumstances, [partial birth abortion]

would be the safest procedure" for pregnant women who wish to undergo an abortion. Thus, the Court struck down the State of Nebraska's ban on partial-birth abortion procedures, concluding that it placed an "undue burden" on women seeking abortions because it failed to include an exception for partial-birth abortions deemed necessary to preserve the "health" of the mother.

. . .

13) There exists substantial record evidence upon which Congress has reached its conclusion that a ban on partial-birth abortion is not required to contain a "health" exception, because the facts indicate that a partial-birth abortion is never necessary to preserve the health of a woman, poses serious risks to a woman's health, and lies outside the standard of medical care. Congress was informed by extensive hearings held during the 104th, 105th, 107th, and 108th Congresses and passed a ban on partial-birth abortion in the 104th, 105th, and 106th Congresses. These findings reflect the very informed judgment of the Congress that a partial-birth abortion is never necessary to preserve the health of a woman, poses serious risks to a woman's health, and lies outside the standard of medical care, and should, therefore, be banned.

. . .

SEC. 3. PROHIBITION ON PARTIAL-BIRTH ABORTIONS.
a) In General. —Title 18, United States Code, is amended by inserting after chapter 73 the following:
"CHAPTER 74—PARTIAL-BIRTH ABORTIONS
"Sec. 1531. Partial-birth abortions prohibited." (a) Any physician who, in or affecting interstate or foreign commerce, knowingly performs a partial-birth abortion and thereby kills a human fetus shall be fined under this title or imprisoned not more than 2 years, or both. This subsection does not apply to a partial-birth abortion that is necessary to save the life of a mother whose life is endangered by a physical disorder, physical illness, or physical injury, including a life-endangering physical condition caused by or arising from the pregnancy itself.

(Source: 18 USC 1531; Public Law 108-105 108th Congress.)

The Unborn Victims of Violence Act of 2004

In 2004, Congress enacted a law making the attack on a pregnant woman that injures the fetus she is carrying a separate crime; this law is also called "Laci and Connor's law."

(a) In General.—Title 18, United States Code, is amended by inserting after chapter 90 the following:
(a)(1) Whoever engages in conduct that violates any of the provisions of law listed in subsection (b) and thereby causes the death of, or bodily injury (as defined in section 1365) to, a child, who is in utero at

the time the conduct takes place, is guilty of a separate offense under this section.

(2)(A) Except as otherwise provided in this paragraph, the punishment for that separate offense is the same as the punishment provided under Federal law for that conduct had that injury or death occurred to the unborn child's mother.

(B) An offense under this section does not require proof that—(i) the person engaging in the conduct had knowledge or should have had knowledge that the victim of the underlying offense was pregnant; or (ii) the defendant intended to cause the death of, or bodily injury to, the unborn child.

(C) If the person engaging in the conduct thereby intentionally kills or attempts to kill the unborn child, that person shall instead of being punished under subparagraph (A), be punished as provided under sections 1111, 1112, and 1113 of this title for intentionally killing or attempting to kill a human being.

(D) Notwithstanding any other provision of law, the death penalty shall not be imposed for an offense under this section.

. . .

(c) Nothing in this section shall be construed to permit the prosecution—(1) of any person for conduct relating to an abortion for which the consent of the pregnant woman, or a person authorized by law to act on her behalf, has been obtained or for which such consent is implied by law; (2) of any person for any medical treatment of the pregnant woman or her unborn child; or (3) of any woman with respect to her unborn child.

(d) As used in this section, the term 'unborn child' means a child in utero, and the term 'child in utero' or 'child, who is in utero' means a member of the species homo sapiens, at any stage of development, who is carried in the womb.

(Source: Public Law 108-212 118 STAT. 568. 18 USC 1841 108th Congress.)

Unborn Child Pain Awareness Act of 2005

The following is a bill introduced in the 109th Congress by pro-life legislators but that did not pass. It was introduced in the Senate as S 51.

Congress makes the following findings:

(1) At least 20 weeks after fertilization, an unborn child has the physical structures necessary to experience pain.

(2) There is substantial evidence that by 20 weeks after fertilization, unborn children draw away from certain stimuli in a manner which in an infant or an adult would be interpreted as a response to pain.

(3) Anesthesia is routinely administered to unborn children who have developed 20 weeks or more past fertilization who undergo prenatal surgery.

(4) There is substantial evidence that the abortion methods most commonly used 20 weeks after fertilization cause substantial pain to an unborn child, whether by dismemberment, poisoning, penetrating or crushing the skull, or other methods. Examples of abortion methods used 20 weeks after fertilization include, but are not limited to the following:

(A) The Dilation and Evacuation (D&E) method of abortion is commonly performed in the second trimester of pregnancy. In a dilation and evacuation abortion, the unborn child's body parts are grasped at random with a long-toothed clamp. The fetal body parts are then torn off of the body and pulled out of the vaginal canal. The remaining body parts are grasped and pulled out until only the head remains. The head is then grasped and crushed in order to remove it from the vaginal canal.

(B) Partial-Birth Abortion is an abortion in which the abortion practitioner delivers an unborn child's body until only the head remains inside the womb, punctures the back of the child's skull with a sharp instrument, and sucks the child's brains out before completing the delivery of the dead infant.

(5) Expert testimony confirms that by 20 weeks after fertilization an unborn child may experience substantial pain even if the woman herself has received local analgesic or general anesthesia.

(6) Medical science is capable of reducing such pain through the administration of anesthesia or other pain-reducing drugs directly to the unborn child.

The Public Health Service Act (42 U.S.C. 201 et seq.) is amended by adding at the end the following:

`SEC. 2902. REQUIREMENT OF INFORMED CONSENT.

(1) IN GENERAL —Before any part of an abortion involving a pain-capable unborn child begins, the abortion provider or his or her agent shall provide the pregnant woman involved, by telephone or in person, with the information described in paragraph (2).

(2) REQUIRED INFORMATION-

(A) ORAL STATEMENT-

(i) IN GENERAL —An abortion provider or the provider's agent to whom paragraph (1) applies shall make the following oral statement to the pregnant woman (or in the case of a deaf or non-English speaking woman, provide the statement in a manner that she can easily understand):

You are considering having an abortion of an unborn child who will have developed, at the time of the abortion, approximately XX weeks after fertilization. The Congress of the United States has determined that at this stage of development, an unborn child has the physical structures necessary to experience pain. There is substantial evidence that by this point, unborn children draw away from surgical instruments in a manner which in an infant or an adult would be interpreted as a response to pain. Congress finds that there is substantial evidence that

the process of being killed in an abortion will cause the unborn child pain, even though you receive a pain-reducing drug or drugs. Under the Federal Unborn Child Pain Awareness Act of 2005, you have the option of choosing to have anesthesia or other pain-reducing drug or drugs administered directly to the pain-capable unborn child if you so desire. The purpose of administering such drug or drugs would be to reduce or eliminate the capacity of the unborn child to experience pain during the abortion procedure. In some cases, there may be some additional risk to you associated with administering such a drug.

(ii) DESCRIPTION OF RISKS —After making the statement required under clause (i), the abortion provider may provide the woman involved with his or her best medical judgment on the risks of administering such anesthesia or analgesic, if any, and the costs associated therewith.

(iii) ADMINISTRATION OF ANESTHESIA —If the abortion provider is not qualified or willing to administer the anesthesia or other pain-reducing drug in response to the request of a pregnant woman after making the statement required under clause (i), the provider shall—(I) arrange for a qualified specialist to administer such anesthesia or drug; or (II) advise the pregnant woman—(aa) where she may obtain such anesthesia or other pain-reducing drugs for the unborn child in the course of an abortion; or (bb) that the abortion provider is unable to perform the abortion if the woman elects to receive anesthesia or other pain-reducing drugs for her unborn child.

(Source: H.R. 356; 109th Congress; S.R. 21 109th Congress.)

Prevention First Act

The supporters of the Prevention First bill want the government to increase and maintain funding for contraceptive information and services; it is framed as a way to prevent unwanted pregnancy. Following is the text of the bill as introduced in the House as H.R.819 in 2007 (110th Congress).

The Congress finds as follows:

(1) Healthy People 2010 sets forth a reduction of unintended pregnancies as an important health objective for the Nation to achieve over the first decade of the new century, a goal first articulated in the 1979 Surgeon General's Report, Healthy People, and reiterated in Healthy People 2000: National Health Promotion and Disease Prevention Objectives.

(2) Although the Centers for Disease Control and Prevention (referred to in this section as the 'CDC') included family planning in its published list of the Ten Great Public Health Achievements in the 20th Century, the United States still has one of the highest rates of unintended pregnancies among industrialized nations.

(3) Each year, 3,000,000 pregnancies, nearly half of all pregnancies, in the United States are unintended, and nearly half of unintended pregnancies end in abortion.

(4) In 2004, 34,400,000 women, half of all women of reproductive age, were in need of contraceptive services and supplies to help prevent unintended pregnancy, and nearly half of those were in need of public support for such care.

(5) The United States has the highest rate of infection with sexually transmitted diseases of any industrialized country. In 2005, there were approximately 19,000,000 new cases of sexually transmitted diseases, almost half of them occurring in young people ages 15 to 24. According to the CDC, these sexually transmitted diseases impose a tremendous economic burden with direct medical costs as high as $14,100,000,000 per year.

(6) Increasing access to family planning services will improve women's health and reduce the rates of unintended pregnancy, abortion, and infection with sexually transmitted diseases. Contraceptive use saves public health dollars. For every dollar spent to increase funding for family planning programs under title X of the Public Health Service Act, $3.80 is saved.

(7) Contraception is basic health care that improves the health of women and children by enabling women to plan and space births.

(8) Women experiencing unintended pregnancy are at greater risk for physical abuse and women having closely spaced births are at greater risk of maternal death.

(9) A child born from an unintended pregnancy is at greater risk than a child born from an intended pregnancy of low birth weight, dying in the first year of life, being abused, and not receiving sufficient resources for healthy development.

(10) The ability to control fertility allows couples to achieve economic stability by facilitating greater educational achievement and participation in the workforce.

(11) Without contraception, a sexually active woman has an 85 percent chance of becoming pregnant within a year.

(12) The percentage of sexually active women ages 15 through 44 who were not using contraception increased from 5.4 percent to 7.4 percent in 2002, an increase of 37 percent, according to the CDC. This represents an apparent increase of 1,430,000 women and could raise the rate of unintended pregnancy.

(13) Many poor and low-income women cannot afford to purchase contraceptive services and supplies on their own. In 2003, 20.5 percent of all women ages 15 through 44 were uninsured.

· · ·

(27) Teens who receive comprehensive sexuality education that includes discussion of contraception as well as abstinence are more

likely than those who receive abstinence-only messages to delay sex, to have fewer partners, and to use contraceptives when they do become sexually active.

(28) Government-funded abstinence-only-until-marriage programs are precluded from discussing contraception except to talk about failure rates. An October 2006 report by the Government Accountability Office found that the Department of Health and Human Services does not review the materials of recipients of grants administered by such department for scientific accuracy and requires grantees to review their own materials for scientific accuracy. The GAO also reported on the Department's total lack of appropriate and customary measurements to determine if funded programs are effective. In addition, a separate letter from the Government Accountability Office found that the Department of Health and Human Services is in violation of Federal law by failing to enforce a requirement under the Public Health Service Act that federally-funded grantees working to address the prevention of sexually transmitted diseases, including abstinence-only-until-marriage programs, must provide medically accurate information about the effectiveness of condoms.

(29) Recent scientific reports by the Institute of Medicine, the American Medical Association, and the Office on National AIDS Policy stress the need for sexuality education that includes messages about abstinence and provides young people with information about contraception for the prevention of teen pregnancy, HIV/AIDS, and other sexually transmitted diseases.

(30) A 2006 statement from the American Public Health Association ('APHA') 'recognizes the importance of abstinence education, but only as part of a comprehensive sexuality education program . . . APHA calls for repealing current federal funding for abstinence-only programs and replacing it with funding for a new Federal program to promote comprehensive sexuality education, combining information about abstinence with age-appropriate sexuality education.'

. . .

TITLE II—EQUITY IN PRESCRIPTION INSURANCE AND CONTRACEPTIVE COVERAGE

TITLE III—EMERGENCY CONTRACEPTION EDUCATION AND INFORMATION

TITLE IV—COMPASSIONATE ASSISTANCE FOR RAPE EMERGENCIES

TITLE V—AT-RISK COMMUNITIES TEENAGE PREGNANCY PREVENTION ACT

TITLE VI—ACCURACY OF CONTRACEPTIVE INFORMATION

TITLE VII—UNINTENDED PREGNANCY REDUCTION ACT

TITLE VIII—RESPONSIBLE EDUCATION ABOUT LIFE ACT

(Source: Library of Congress Thomas http://thomas.loc.gov/.)

Current State Laws Regulating Abortion

Regulations of Abortion Practice

Constitutional Framework: States have no authority to prohibit abortion practice prior to viability, with the possible exception of partial birth procedures, but they can regulate the medical conditions of the procedure to promote women's health. After viability, states may proscribe abortion except to protect a woman's life or health.

Overview: Thirty-nine states require abortion to be performed by a licensed physician and thirty-six prohibit abortions after viability, at 24 weeks, or in the third trimester. After a specified point in the pregnancy, nineteen states require that the procedure be performed in a hospital, and eighteen mandate the involvement of a second physician as seen in Table 6.1, page 193.

Limits on Public Funding

Constitutional Framework: It is constitutional for states to prohibit the use of public funds and facilities for abortion. The federal Hyde Amendment prohibits the states from using federal Medicaid funds for abortions for poor women. The states have authority to use their own funds.

Overview: Table 6.2, page 195, shows that most states follow the federal policy and fund only those abortions necessary because of threats to life or because of rape or incest. Seventeen states fund all or nearly all medically necessary abortions.

Parental Involvement

Constitutional Framework: States have the authority to require parental consent or notification for minors' abortions as long as a judicial bypass is available. Some states have their own constitutional requirements that limit the power of government to allow parents to impede abortions for their minor daughters.

Overview: Table 6.3, page 197, tallies the state regulations. Thirty-four states require either notification, consent, or both, but all of these states have provisions for judicial bypass. Other

TABLE 6.1
State Regulations of Abortion Practice

State	Must Be Performed by Licensed Physician	When the Procedure Must Be Performed in Hospital	When a Second Physician Is Required	When the Procedure Is Prohibited Except When the Woman's Health/Life Are in Danger*
Alabama	X	Viability	Viability	Viability
Alaska	X			
Arizona	X		Viability	Viability
Arkansas	X		Viability	Viability
California	X			Viability
Colorado	X			
Connecticut	X	Viability		Viability
Delaware				**
District of Columbia				
Florida	X		24 weeks	24 weeks
Georgia	X		3rd trimester	3rd trimester
Hawaii	X			
Idaho	X	Viability	3rd trimester	Viability
Illinois	X		Viability	Viability
Indiana	X	2d trimester	Viability	Viability
Iowa	X			3rd trimester
Kansas			Viability	Viability
Kentucky		2d trimester		Viability
Louisiana	X		Viability	Viability
Maine	X			Viability
Maryland	X			Viability
Massachusetts	X	12 weeks		24 weeks
Michigan	X			Viability
Minnesota	X	2nd trimester	**	**
Mississippi	X			
Missouri	X	Viability	Viability	Viability
Montana			Viability	Viability
Nebraska	X			Viability
Nevada	X	12 weeks		24 weeks
New Hampshire				
New Jersey	X	14 weeks		
New Mexico				
New York			24 weeks	24 weeks
North Carolina	X	20 weeks		20 weeks
North Dakota	X	12 weeks	12 weeks	Viability
Ohio	X		**	**
Oklahoma	X	2nd trimester	Viability	Viability
Oregon				

continues

TABLE 6.1   Continued

State	Must Be Performed by Licensed Physician	When the Procedure Must Be Performed in Hospital	When a Second Physician Is Required	When the Procedure Is Prohibited Except When the Woman's Health/Life Are in Danger*
Pennsylvania	X	Viability	Viability	24 weeks
Rhode Island	X			24 weeks
South Carolina	X	3rd trimester	3rd trimester	3rd trimester
South Dakota	X	24 weeks		24 weeks
Tennessee	X			Viability
Texas	X			3rd trimester
Utah	X	90 days		**
Vermont				
Virginia	X	2nd trimester	Viability	3d trimester
Washington				Viability
West Virginia				
Wisconsin	X	12 weeks		Viability
Wyoming	X			Viability
Total	39	19	18	36

*There may be other exceptions for rape, incest, or restrictions to life endangerment only; check specific state laws at www.guttmacher.org.

**Permanently enjoined law by court order.

Source: The Alan Guttmacher Institute, www.guttmacher.org.

exceptions are often permitted, such as medical emergency or in cases of abuse, assault, incest, or neglect.

Mandatory Counseling and Waiting Periods

Constitutional Framework: States have the authority to require counseling and waiting periods for women seeking abortions as long as the regulations are not deemed to be undue burdens on women and do not prevent women from obtaining abortions within the law. The Supreme Court has ruled that it is constitutional for states to adopt policies that favor birth over abortion.

Overview: A majority of states require counseling. Table 6.4, page 199, shows that in twenty-three states, the department of health develops materials that must be used. Some legislatures

TABLE 6.2
Limits on State Funding for Abortions

State	Follows Federal Standard of Life Endangerment, Rape, and Incest	Other Exceptions	Funds Most Abortions
Alabama	X		
Alaska			By court order
Arizona			By court order
Arkansas	X		
California			By court order
Colorado	X		
Connecticut			By court order
Delaware	X		
District of Columbia	X		
Florida	X		
Georgia	X		
Hawaii			Voluntarily
Idaho	X		
Illinois			By court order
Indiana	X	Physical health	
Iowa	X	Fetal abnormality	
Kansas	X		
Kentucky	X		
Louisiana	X		
Maine	X		
Maryland			Voluntarily
Massachusetts			By court order
Michigan	X		
Minnesota			By court order
Mississippi	X	Fetal abnormality	
Missouri	X		
Montana			By court order
Nebraska	X		
Nevada	X		
New Hampshire	X		
New Jersey			By court order
New Mexico			By court order
New York			Voluntarily
North Carolina	X		
North Dakota	X		
Ohio	X		
Oklahoma	X		
Oregon			By court order
Pennsylvania	X		
Rhode Island	X		
South Carolina	X		

continues

TABLE 6.2   Continued

State	Follows Federal Standard of Life Endangerment, Rape, and Incest	Other Exceptions	Funds Most Abortions
South Dakota	*		
Tennessee	X		
Texas	X		
Utah	X	Physical health/Fetal abnormality	
Vermont			By court order
Virginia	X	Fetal abnormality	
Washington			Voluntarily
West Virginia			By court order
Wisconsin	X	Physical health	
Wyoming	X		
Total	33		17

*State only pays when abortion is to save woman's life.

Source: The Alan Guttmacher Institute, www.guttmacher.org.

mandate specific information to be included such as assistance available so women can give birth rather than choose abortion or a list of pregnancy support centers. These centers are controversial because pro-choice abortion providers claim they are fronts for intimidating women against choosing abortion. A few states mandate information that is of questionable scientific merit, including a reputed link between abortion and breast cancer and allegations that a fetus feels pain, offering anesthesia to the fetus (see the next section for more information). Twenty-four states require a waiting period between the time of the counseling and the procedure.

Medical Accuracy of Mandated Counseling Materials

Constitutional framework: The Supreme Court has upheld laws that require specific information about abortion as part of overall "informed consent" policies. They have said these are acceptable under the law if the information provided is accurate and not misleading. In addition, medical ethics standards prohibit doctors or anyone else from using personal opinion in lieu of scientifically accepted information. States have the constitutional

TABLE 6.3
Parental Involvement Requirements

State	Requires Parental Involvement*	Judicial Bypass	Medical Emergency Exceptions	Abuse, Assault, and Incest Exceptions
Alabama	Consent	X	X	X
Alaska	**			
Arizona	Consent	X	X	X
Arkansas	Consent	X	X	X
California	**			
Colorado	Notification	X	X	
Connecticut				
Delaware	Notification	X	X	
District of Columbia				
Florida	Notification	X	X	
Georgia	Notification	X	X	
Hawaii				
Idaho	**			
Illinois	**			
Indiana	Consent	X	X	
Iowa	Notification	X	X	X
Kansas	Notification	X	X	X
Kentucky	Consent	X	X	
Louisiana	Consent	X		
Maine				
Maryland	Notification	X		
Massachusetts	Consent	X		
Michigan	Consent	X	X	
Minnesota	Notification of both parents	X	X	X
Mississippi	Consent of both parents	X	X	
Missouri	Consent	X		
Montana	**			
Nebraska	Notification	X	X	X
Nevada	**			
New Hampshire	**			
New Jersey	**			
New Mexico	**			
New York				
North Carolina	Consent	X	X	
North Dakota	Consent of both parents	X	X	
Ohio	Consent	X		
Oklahoma	Consent and notification	X	X	X
Oregon				
Pennsylvania	Consent	X	X	
Rhode Island	Consent	X	X	
South Carolina	Consent	X	X	X
South Dakota	Notification	X	X	

continues

TABLE 6.3   Continued

State	Requires Parental Involvement*	Judicial Bypass	Medical Emergency Exceptions	Abuse, Assault, and Incest Exceptions
Tennessee	Consent	X	X	X
Texas	Consent	X	X	
Utah	Consent and notification	X	X	X
Vermont				
Virginia	Consent	X	X	X
Washington				
West Virginia	Notification	X	X	
Wisconsin	Consent	X	X	X
Wyoming	Consent	X	X	
Total	34	34	28	13

*Except where indicated requires involvement of one parent only.

**Permanently enjoined law by court order.

Source: The Alan Guttmacher Institute, www.guttmacher.org.

authority to develop their own materials and require abortion providers to use them. Twenty-three states do this. How accurate are these counseling materials?

Overview: Table 6.5, page 201, is based on work by Richardson and Nash who compared the state requirements with medical literature and found that most of the materials produced by state health departments are accurate. In a few egregious cases, however, states require women to be informed of certain risks of abortion that are not confirmed by scientific research. Following are some of those unconfirmed risks:

1. *Link between abortion and breast cancer.* Some states require patients to be told that abortion greatly increases the risk of breast cancer. In 2003, however, the National Cancer Institute issued an official denial of such a link. Other states require women be given accurate information that there is no link.

2. *Postabortion psychological trauma.* Pro-life activists claim that women who have abortions are plagued by long-lasting psychological consequences, and some states include this warning in their materials. Experts on psychology and psychiatry deny this claim, and their research shows that there is no causal relationship.

TABLE 6.4
Mandatory Counseling and Waiting Periods

State	Counseling Required	Information on Pro-birth Care	Information on Abortion Alternatives	Length of Waiting Period
Alabama	X		X	24 hours
Alaska	X		X	
Arizona				
Arkansas	X	X	X	Prior day
California	X			
Colorado				
Connecticut	X			
Delaware	X		X	
District of Columbia				
Florida	**			
Georgia	X	X		24 hours
Hawaii				
Idaho	X		X	24 hours
Illinois	X			
Indiana	X	X		18 hours
Iowa				
Kansas	X	X	X	24 hours
Kentucky	X	X	X	24 hours
Louisiana	X	X	X	24 hours
Maine	X			
Maryland				
Massachusetts				**
Michigan	X	X		24 hours
Minnesota	X	X		24 hours
Mississippi	X	X		24 hours
Missouri	X		X	24 hours
Montana	**			**
Nebraska	X	X		24 hours
Nevada	X			
New Hampshire				
New Jersey				
New Mexico				
New York				
North Carolina				
North Dakota	X	X		24 hours
Ohio	X		X	24 hours
Oklahoma	X	X	X	24 hours
Oregon				
Pennsylvania	X	X	X	24 hours
Rhode Island	X	X		
South Carolina	X	X	X	1 hour
South Dakota	X	X		24 hours

continues

TABLE 6.4   Continued

State	Counseling Required	Information on Pro-birth Care	Information on Abortion Alternatives	Length of Waiting Period
Tennessee	X			**
Texas	X	X	X	24 hours
Utah	X	X	X	24 hours
Vermont				
Virginia	X	X	X	24 hours
Washington				
West Virginia	X	X		24 hours
Wisconsin	X	X		24 hours
Wyoming				
Total	32	21	17	24

**Permanently enjoined law by court order.

Source: The Alan Guttmacher Institute, www.guttmacher.org.

Some states assert the existence of a "postabortion trau-matic stress syndrome." This syndrome is also not rec-ognized by the experts.

3. *Fetuses feel pain:* Antiabortion experts also insist that women be told that their fetuses will feel pain and that they can choose anesthesia for them. In fact, at best there is disagreement among scientists about this claim; most argue that there is no evidence for the assertion that fetuses "feel" pain. Five states include incorrect materials about this.

State Policies if *Roe* Fell

Constitutional framework: If the Supreme Court completely reversed the *Roe* decision, the authority to regulate abortion—allow it, prohibit it, regulate it—would return to the states.

Overview: Even in 2006 and 2007, some state legislatures have passed or considered bills that directly oppose the *Roe* guarantees of women's liberty in seeking abortions before the fetus is viable. Others have left the pre-*Roe* bills on the books. See in Table 6.6, page 202, that sixteen states have laws that could be used to limit access to abortion if *Roe* is no longer binding on them and five oth-ers have expressed their intent to enact such laws. Seven states have laws that protect choice in abortion. Ten states have consti-

TABLE 6.5
Accuracy of State-Developed Abortion Counseling Materials

State	Breast Cancer and Abortion	Psychological Effects of Abortion	Information on Fetal Pain
Alabama		Correct	
Alaska	False	Correct	
Arkansas		Correct	X
Georgia		Correct	X
Idaho		Correct	
Kansas	False	Correct	
Kentucky			
Louisiana			
Michigan		False	
Minnesota	Correct	Correct	X
Mississippi	False		
Nebraska		False	
North Dakota			
Ohio			
Pennsylvania		Correct	
South Carolina		False	
South Dakota		False	X
Texas	False	False	X
Utah		False	
Virginia		Correct	
West Virginia	False	False	
Wisconsin		Correct	
Total	5 False	7 False	5
	1 Correct	11 Correct	

Source: Richardson, Chinué Turner, and Elizabeth Nash. 2006. "Misinformed Consent: The Medical Accuracy of State-Developed Abortion Counseling Materials." *Guttmacher Policy Review* 9 (Fall): 6–11.

tutions that have explicit privacy provisions in their constitutions that could limit a complete crackdown on legal abortion.

Abortion Practice: Incidence and Services

The incidence of abortion is typically measured three ways:

- Absolute number of abortions
- Abortion ratio: number of abortions per 1,000 live births
- Abortion rate: number of abortions for 1,000 women of childbearing age (15–44 years)

TABLE 6.6
State Policies after *Roe*

Abortion Policy	States
States with criminal abortion laws intended to ban abortion if *Roe* is overturned	Louisiana South Dakota Utah
States where pre-*Roe* ban is still on the books; some have exceptions for life, health, pregnancy due to rape or incest, or chance of fetal defect	Alabama Arizona Arkansas Colorado Delaware Massachusetts Michigan Mississippi New Mexico Oklahoma Vermont West Virginia Wisconsin
States where legislatures have expressed intent to limit abortion to the maximum extent after *Roe*	Arkansas Illinois Kentucky Missouri North Dakota
States with laws protecting the right to abortion	California Connecticut Hawaii Maine Maryland Nevada Washington
States with explicit privacy provisions in the constitution that could serve to protect the right to abortion	Alaska Arizona California Florida Hawaii Illinois Louisiana Montana South Carolina Washington

Source: The Alan Guttmacher Institute, www.guttmacher.org.

Incidence of Abortion in the United States—CDC Data

The Centers for Disease Control and Prevention (CDC), an agency in the U.S. Department of Health and Human Services, has conducted its "abortion surveillance" studies since 1969. Surveillance data are compiled from reports about the number of legal induced abortions from central health agencies in the states, the District of Columbia, and New York City. Although there are questions about the extent to which these health agencies receive the reports of all abortions, the data covered all fifty states until 1997. Between 1998 and 2003, California and New Hampshire did not report. Oklahoma did not report during 1998–1999, and Alaska did not report until 2003. Thus, the latest figures underreport the number of abortions. Nevertheless, they do show trends over time, as seen in Table 6.7, page 204.

Incidence of Abortion in the United State—AGI Data

Recognizing the limits of the CDC surveillance data, the Alan Guttmacher Institute (AGI) does a periodic survey of all known abortion providers. The most recent reports cover 1999–2000 as shown in Table 6.8, page 205. Based on this survey, the figures show a higher incidence of abortion than the CDC studies but the general pattern is the same. Abortions were highest in 1990 and have been declining in number, rate, and ratio ever since.

Comparative Incidence of Abortion—UNECE Data

Comparative data from the United Nations Economic Commission for Europe (UNECE) in Table 6.9, page 205, show the abortion ratio of the United States compared with the rates in other countries where abortion is legal. These U.S. figures also differ from CDC and AGI figures. However, the comparison shows that the U.S. abortion ratio is high in relation to Western Europe, but the highest rates are in Central and Eastern Europe where Soviet-style abortion laws are still mostly in place.

TABLE 6.7
CDC Reports of Number, Ratio, and Rate of Abortions 1970–2003—Selected Years

	1970	1972	1980	1983	1990	1993	1998*	2003**
No. of Abortions	193,491	615,831	1,297,606	1,268,987	1,429,247	1,330,414	883,273	838,163
Ratio per 1,000 births	52	196	359	349	344	333	264	243
Rate per 1,000 women aged 15–44 years	5	14	25	23	24	23	17	15

*Figures do not include abortions in Alaska, California, New Hampshire, and Oklahoma.

**Figures do not include abortions in California and New Hampshire.

Source: Abortion Surveillance—United States, 2003. Lilo T. Strauss, Sonya B. Gamble, Wilda Y. Parker, Douglas A. Cook, Suzanne B. Zane, Saeed Hamdan. *Surveillance Summaries,* CDC, November 24, 2006, 55(SS11), 1–32. www.cdc.gov/mmwr/preview/mmwrhtml/ss5511a1.htm.

TABLE 6.8
AGI Estimates of Abortions in the United States, 1973–2003—Selected Years

	1973	1980	1983	1990	1993	1998	2003
No. of abortions	744,600	1,553,900	1,575,000	1,609,000	1,495,000	1,319,000	1,287,000
Ratio per 1,000 births	193	303	304	280	274	251	238
Rate per 1,000 Women aged 15–45 years	16.3	29.3	28.5	27.4	25.0	21.5	20.8

Source: Finer, Lawrence B., and Stanley K. Henshaw. 2006. "Estimates of U.S. Abortion Incidence, 2001–2003." Alan Guttmacher Institute. www.guttmacher.org/pubs/2006/08/03/ab_incidence.pdf.

TABLE 6.9
Comparative Data on European Countries for
Ratio of Legal Abortions per 1,000 Live Births

Country	1980	1990	1995	2000
United States	430	387	350	327
Denmark	407	325	254	234
Finland	238	187	157	193
France	—	254	255	—
Germany	290	200	128	176
Italy	325	278	256	258
The Netherlands	117	93	110	132
Sweden	359	302	304	343
United Kingdom	231	247	239	291
Canada	430	387	350	327
Czech Republic	448	852	515	381
Hungary	544	719	687	607
Russia	2046	2063	2028	1688
Iceland	116	150	189	219

— Data not available.

Source: United Nations Economic Commission for Europe. "Families and Households." 2003. www.unece.org/stats/trends/ch2.htm.

Characteristics of Women Having Abortions

The trends suggested by data from 1973, 1990, and 2003, as shown in Table 6.10, below, are that women over 25 years old have the largest percentage of abortions; the lowest percentage is among women under the age of 19 years. The rate of abortions among blacks has been growing, but the percent of abortions among women of Hispanic origin remains low. Less than 1.5 percent of abortions are performed after the twentieth week of gestation; however, if the total number of abortions is 1.3 million that is still a large number—18,200.

TABLE 6.10

Characteristics of Women Having Abortions in 1973, 1990, and 2003 in Percents

Characteristic	1973	1990	2003
Age			
<19 years	32.7	22.4	17.4
20–25 years	32.0	33.2	33.5
>25 years	35.3	44.4	49.1
	100.0%	100%	100%
Race			
White	72.5	64.8	55.0
Black	27.5	31.9	35.1
Other	NA	3.3	7.9
	100%	100%	100%
Ethnicity			
Hispanic	NA	11.4	18.1
Non-Hispanic	NA	88.6	81.9
		100%	100%
Marital status			
Married	27.4	21.7	17.9
Unmarried	72.6	78.3	82.1
	100%	100%	100%
Weeks of gestation			
<10	65.5	76.9	78.5
11–20	32.8	22.1	20.1
>29	1.7	1.0	1.4
	100%	100%	100%

Note: NA = not available.

Source: Abortion Surveillance—United States, 2003. Lilo T. Strauss, Sonya B. Gamble, Wilda Y. Parker, Douglas A. Cook, Suzanne B. Zane, Saeed Hamdan. *Surveillance Summaries;* CDC, November 24, 2006, / 55(SS11), 1–32. www.cdc.gov/mmwr/preview/mmwrhtml/ss5511a1.htm.

Abortion-Related Deaths

The CDC has collected information from state agencies on the number of deaths from legal and illegal abortions since the early 1970s. The pattern shows declines in the number of deaths and the ratio of deaths to all abortions. Table 6.11, below, shows the figures for selected years.

Unintended Pregnancies and Their Consequences—2001

The primary source of information on the number and rates of unintended pregnancies in the United States is the National Survey of Family Growth, which is conducted by the National Center for Health Statistics. As seen in Table 6.12, page 208, Finer and Henshaw (2006) combine that information with government sources of information on births, abortions, and fetal losses. They found that nearly half (48 percent) of 6.4 million pregnancies in 2001 were unintended—that is, the mother did not aim to have a baby of that time. How many babies were "unwanted"? This is

TABLE 6.11
Number of Deaths from Abortions and Case Fatality Ratio,
Selected Years, 1972–2002

Year	Legal Abortion	Illegal Abortion	Unknown*	Total	Case Fatality Ratio
1972	24	39	2	65	4.1
1974	26	6	1	33	3.4
1980	9	1	2	12	.7
1985	11	1	1	13	.8
1990	9	0	0	9	.6
1993	4	0	0	4	.3
2002	9	0	0	9	NA
Total	377	94	15	486	1.1**

Note: NA = not applicable.

*Not known whether this refers to induced or spontaneous abortions.

**This figure is only available for 1972–1997.

Source: Abortion Surveillance—United States, 2003. Lilo T. Strauss, Sonya B. Gamble, Wilda Y. Parker, Douglas A. Cook, Suzanne B. Zane, Saeed Hamdan. *Surveillance Summaries;* CDC, November 24, 2006, / 55(SS11), 1–32. www.cdc.gov/mmwr/preview/mmwrhtml/ss5511a1.htm.

TABLE 6.12
Intended and Unintended Pregnancies and Outcomes, 2001

Pregnancies and Outcomes	Intended Pregnancies and Outcomes	Unintended Pregnancies and Outcomes
6.4 million pregnancies	3.3 million intended pregnancies	3.1 million unintended pregnancies
4.0 million (62.5%) resulted in births	2.64 million (80%) resulted in births	1.36 million (44%) resulted in births
1.3 million (20%) resulted in abortions	0 resulted in abortions	1.30 million (42%) resulted in abortions
1.1 million (17%) resulted in fetal losses (e.g., miscarriages)	.66 million (20%) resulted in fetal losses	.43 million (14%) resulted in fetal losses

Source: Finer, Lawrence B., and Stanley K. Henshaw. 2006. "Disparities in Rates of Unintended Pregnancy in the United States, 1994–2001." *Perspectives on Sexual and Reproductive Health* 38 (2): 90–96.

difficult to know because parents' attitudes change during the course of pregnancy and childbirth. Unintended pregnancies resulted in births and abortions on a roughly equal percentage. The rate of unintended pregnancies varies among population subgroups.

Abortion Services in the United States

The decline in the number of abortion providers has been steady since the early 1990s. The drop is nationwide, although it is greater in the South and West than in the Northeast, as shown in Table 6.13, page 209. At the end of the twentieth century, 87 percent of U.S. counties had no abortion provider. Even a majority of metropolitan counties (61 percent) had no provider, and 70 percent had no large provider, defined as one that performs more than 400 abortions per year. Ninety-one percent of rural women live in counties with no services compared with 21 percent of women in metropolitan counties.

Abortion Clinic Violence

The Feminist Majority Foundation has conducted a survey of abortion clinics since the early 1990s and publishes a tally of how

TABLE 6.13
Number of Abortion Providers by Region, 1992–2000

Region	1992	1996	2000	% Change 1996–2000
Northeast	620	562	536	−5%
Midwest	260	212	188	−11%
South	620	505	442	−12%
West	880	763	653	−14%
Total	2380	2042	1819	−11%

Source: Finer, Lawrence B., and Stanley K. Henshaw. 2003. "Abortion Incidence and Services in the United States in 2000." *Perspectives on Sexual and Reproductive Health* 35 (1): 6–15.

many and what percent experience various forms of violence. Since the high point in 1994, the incidence of clinic violence has steadily declined, as shown in Table 6.14, below. One reason is the enactment of the federal Freedom of Access to Clinic Entrances Act in 1994 as well as the adverse publicity of the assassination of doctors who worked in the clinics. Most pro-life organizations have denounced extreme violence as a way of stopping abortions. Nevertheless, among the 337 clinics, bomb

TABLE 6.14
Reported Clinic Violence, 1993–2005

Year	Percent Experiencing Extreme Violence (N=337)	Number Reporting Staff Resignations Due to Violence
1993	50	23
1994	52	9
1995	39	9
1996	28	4
1997	25	7
1998	22	5
1999	20	10
2000	20	5
2002	23	7
2005	18.4	4

Source: Feminist Majority Foundation. 2006. *2005 National Clinic Violence Survey.* www.feminist.org/research/cvsurveys/clinic_survey2005.pdf.

threats, death threats, and obstruction remain a part of providing services, as shown in Table 6.15, below.

Public Opinion Polls on Abortion Issues

Following is a sample of polls taken in 2006–2007 on various aspects of abortion. (Source: PollingReport. www.pollingreport.com/abortion.htm.)
For the past 10 years, public opinion on the legality of abortion has remained nearly unchanged. Fifty-four to fifty-seven percent of registered voters think abortion should be legal in all or most cases while 40 to 48 percent think abortion should be illegal in most or all cases. A tiny percentage of the registered voters are unsure.

The Pew Research Center survey attempts to get at some of the nuances in public opinion about the abortion issue and distinguishes between legality, availability, and personal views. Responses to the survey questions show that a minority of respondents—about 30 to 35 percent—have the view that abortion should be generally available. At the same time a minority believes abortion is always a moral issue while about half see it as a moral question only sometimes. Overall, a majority of respondents are looking for a national solution that finds a middle ground. See Tables 6.17, 6.18, and 6.19, pages 212–213.

TABLE 6.15
Percent of Clinics Reporting Types of Attacks in 2005

Type of Attack	Percent of Clinics
Stalking	3.6
Death threats	2.4
Blockades	8.3
Bomb threats	4.2
Invasions	2.1
Physical violence	1.5
Gunfire	.6
Chemical attack	.3
Arson	2.1
Bombing	.6
Arson threat	1.6

Source: Feminist Majority Foundation. 2006. *2005 National Clinic Violence Survey.* www.feminist.org/research/cvsurveys/clinic_survey2005.pdf.

TABLE 6.16
Survey Respondents' (N=1,082 Adults) Answers (in percent) to
Question about When Abortion Should Be Legal*

Survey Question
Do you think abortion should be legal in all cases, legal in most cases, or illegal in all cases?

Date	Legal in All Cases	Legal in Most Cases	Illegal in Most Cases	Illegal in All Cases	Unsure
2/22–25/07	16	39	31	12	2
12/15–18/05	17	40	27	13	3
4/21–24/05	20	36	27	14	3
12/04	21	34	25	17	3
5/04	23	31	23	20	2
1/03	23	34	25	17	2
8/01	22	27	28	20	3
6/01	22	31	23	20	4
1/01	21	38	25	14	1
9/00**	20	35	25	16	3
7/00	20	33	26	17	4
9/99	20	37	26	15	2
3/99	21	34	27	15	3
8/96	22	34	27	14	3
6/96	24	34	25	14	2

*Margin of error ± 3.

**Survey of registered voters.

Source: Washington Post Poll, published February 22–25, 2007. Fieldwork by TNS Intersearch.

Another poll looks at attitudes about *Roe v. Wade*. Table 6.20, page 213, shows that in January 2007 a strong majority (62 percent) did not want to see the Supreme Court overturn this decision.

Yet when people are asked about the provisions that were guaranteed by *Roe v. Wade* there is less support. This Harris poll (Table 6.21, page 214) shows that nearly half (47 percent) oppose the central holding in the case that leaves the abortion decision in the first 3 months in the zone of privacy.

The pro-choice movement gets sympathy of a majority of respondents in the polls, but there are distinct party differences as Table 6.22, page 215, indicates. Republicans continue to be the pro-life party while Democrats and Independents are more welcoming to pro-choice views.

The last two tables are compiled from the General Social Survey, which, since 1972, has asked questions of a random sample of American citizens about their attitudes toward abortion under certain conditions. Table 6.23, page 215, shows the pattern of support for legal

TABLE 6.17
Survey Respondents' (N=996 Adults) Answers (in percent) to a
Question about the Availability of Abortion*

Survey Question
Which comes closer to your view? Abortion should be generally available to those who want it.
Abortion should be available but under stricter limits than it is now. Abortion should be against
the law except in cases of rape, incest, and to save the woman's life. Abortion should not be
permitted at all.

Date	Generally Available	Stricter Limits	Rape, Incest, Woman's Life Only	Not Permitted at All	Unsure
7/6–19/06	31	20	35	11	3
12/7–11/05	35	20	31	11	3
11/9–27/05	30	19	31	16	4
7/13–17/05	35	23	31	9	2

*Margin of error ± 3.5.

Source: Pew Research Center for the People and the Press and Pew Forum on Religion and Public Life Survey conducted by Schulman, Ronca, and Bucuvalas. July 6–19, 2006. (Data from December 2005 and earlier conducted by
Princeton Survey Research Associates International.)

TABLE 6.18
Survey Respondents' (N=996 Adults) Answers (in percent) to a
Question about Whether Abortion Is Morally Wrong*

Survey Question
Regardless of whether or not you think abortion should be legal, do you personally believe that
having an abortion is morally wrong in nearly all circumstances, morally wrong in some
circumstances, or is it not a moral issue?

	Nearly Always Morally Wrong	Sometimes Morally Wrong	Not a Moral Issue	Unsure
7/6–19/06	24	49	24	3
7/13–17/05	29	41	26	4

*Margin of error ± 3.5.

Source: Pew Research Center for the People and the Press and Pew Forum on Religion and Public Life Survey conducted by Schulman, Ronca, and Bucuvalas. July 6–19, 2006. (Data from December 2005 and earlier conducted by
Princeton Survey Research Associates International.)

TABLE 6.19

Survey Respondents' (N=996 Adults) Answers (in percent) to
Questions about the Abortion Issue*

Survey Question 1
Which comes closer to your view about the abortion issue? The country needs to find a middle
ground on abortion laws or there's no room for compromise when it comes to abortion laws.
(Options are rotated.)

Finding a Middle Ground on Abortion Laws*

	Middle Ground	No Room for Compromise	Unsure
7/6–19/06	66	29	5

Survey Question 2
Do you think the question of whether abortion should be legally permitted is something that
should be decided at the national level, or is it something that each state should decide for itself?

	National Level	Each State	Unsure
7/6–19/06	55	39	6

*Margin of error ± 3.5.

Source: Pew Research Center for the People and the Press and Pew Forum on Religion and Public Life Survey conducted by Schulman, Ronca, and Bucuvalas. July 6–19, 2006. N=996 adults nationwide. (Data from December and earlier conducted by Princeton Survey Research Associates International.)

TABLE 6.20

Survey Respondents' (N=1,008 adults) Answers (in percent) to a
Question about Overturning *Roe v. Wade**

Survey Question
Would you like to see the Supreme Court overturn its 1973 *Roe v. Wade* decision concerning
abortion or not?

	Would	Would Not	Unsure
1/19–21/07	29	62	9

*Margin of error ± 3.

Source: CNN/Opinion Research Corporation Poll, January 19–21, 2007.

TABLE 6.21

Survey Respondents' (N=1,016 adults) Answers (in percent) to a Questions about the Abortion Issue*

Survey Question 1

In 1973, the U.S. Supreme Court decided that states laws that made it illegal for a woman to have an abortion up to three months of pregnancy were unconstitutional, and that the decision on whether a woman should have an abortion up to three months of pregnancy should be left to the woman and her doctor to decide. In general, do you favor or oppose this part of the U.S. Supreme Court decision making abortions up to three months of pregnancy legal?

	Favor	Oppose	Unsure
4/4–10/06	49	47	4

Survey Question 2

In general, do you favor permitting a woman who wants one to have an abortion in all circumstances, some circumstances, or no circumstances?

	All	Some	No	Unsure
4/4–10/06	24	53	20	4

Survey Question 3

Do you favor laws that would make it more difficult for a woman to get an abortion, favor laws that would make it easier to get an abortion, or should no change be made to existing abortion laws?

	More Difficult	Easier	No Change	Unsure
4/4–10/06	40	15	40	6

*Margin of error ± 3.

Source: The Harris Poll, April 4–10, 2006. N=1,016 adults nationwide.

abortion by conditions. Throughout the years the vast majority of people support abortion on the basis of women's health, fetal defect, or rape. There is less than majority support for abortion on women's choice or economic circumstances. The pattern of support varies only slightly by race and gender, as shown in Table 6.24, page 216.

TABLE 6.22

Survey Respondents' (N=1,002 adults) Answers (in percent) to a
Questions about the Abortion Issue*

Survey Question
Which side of the political debate on the abortion issue do you sympathize with more: the right-to-life movement that believes abortion is the taking of human life and should be outlawed, or, the pro-choice movement that believes a woman has the right to choose what happens to her body, including deciding to have an abortion?*

	Right-to-Life	Pro-Choice	Neither	Unsure
All adults	39	53	3	5
Republicans	62	31	4	3
Democrats	25	69	2	4
Independents	35	57	4	4
Trend:				
11/10–11/05	34	57	5	4
10/29–30/98	39	51	5	5

*Options rotated; margin of error ± 3 (for all adults).

Source: Newsweek Poll conducted by Princeton Survey Research Associates International, October 26–27, 2006.

TABLE 6.23

Support for Abortion under Conditions—Percent Answering Yes

Abortion Is Okay if:	1972	1989	2004
There is a strong chance of defect in the baby	78.6	81	72.9
A woman is married and doesn't want any more children	39.7	44.5	41.8
A woman's health is seriously endangered	86.9	90.1	86.0
A woman is low income and can't afford any more children	48	47	41
A woman is pregnant as the result of rape	79.1	83.2	76.2
A woman is unmarried	43.5	45.4	40.9
A woman wants the abortion for any reason	NA	40.3	40.6

Note: NA = not available.

Source. General Social Survey, NORC, http://gss.norc.org.

TABLE 6.24
Support for Abortion under Conditions—
Percent Answering Yes by Gender and Race for 2004

Abortion Is Okay if:	All Women	All Men	All Blacks
A woman's health is seriously endangered	85.2	86.9	85.5
There is a strong chance of defect in the baby	73.0	72.7	69.2
A woman wants the abortion for any reason	38.6	42.9	40.6

Source: General Social Survey, NORC, http://gss.norc.org.

7

Directory of Organizations

Introduction

Because the pro-choice and pro-life movements are such an important part of the abortion debate story, this section provides descriptions of an equal number of organizations from the two sides. Although a few of these are no longer in existence or have reorganized in later years, they are included because they are an essential part of understanding the trajectory of the policy debates on abortion since the early 1970s. Information on government agencies that have programs related to reproductive health precedes the section on U.S. organizations; a list of groups on the international scene follows. Relatively fewer pro-life organizations are working internationally than pro-choice ones.

Government Agencies

Centers for Disease Control and Prevention (CDC)
www.cdc.gov/

The mission of the CDC, a division of the Department of Health and Human Services, is to prevent and control infectious and chronic diseases, injuries, workplace hazards, disabilities, and environmental health threats. The CDC also keeps records on mortality and morbidity; as part of that function it conducts an annual surveillance of abortion practice. The report is based on surveys of health departments in the states, but it remains incomplete because of limits on the data in some locales.

Congressional Pro-Choice Caucus
Rep. Louise M. Slaughter 202-225-3615

This quasi-governmental body is composed of members of Congress who support the pro-choice position. The caucus is chaired by Representative Louise Slaughter (D-NY) .

Congressional Pro-Life Caucus
Rep. Chris Smith 202-225-3715

This quasi-governmental body is composed of members of Congress who support the pro-life position. Congressional caucuses receive no funding, and the pro-life group is no exception. Chaired by Chris Smith (R-NJ), the caucus allows members of Congress to take a public stand on the issue.

Food and Drug Administration (FDA)
www.fda.gov

The FDA is an agency in the Department of Health and Human Services that has been charged with protecting consumers since 1906. Today its mission includes ensuring the safety of drugs, medical devices, food, and cosmetics. Through its Center for Drug Evaluation and Research, FDA receives applications for approval of drugs for sale in the United States. The FDA has had a significant role in affecting reproductive health through its reviews of birth control pills, intrauterine devices, and mifepristone, the abortion pill.

Office of Family Planning (OFP)
http://opa.osophs.dhhs.gov/titlex/ofp.html

Part of the massive Department of Health and Human Services, the OFP administers Title X, the only federal program to support family planning services. The agency makes annual grants to nearly 5,000 clinics that serve about 5 million people a year (out of a population of 300 million). The services are primarily contraceptives and counseling, but there are also preventive health services such as breast and pelvic exams, sexually transmitted disease and HIV/AIDS tests, and cervical cancer tests. Under Presidents George H. W. Bush, Ronald Reagan, and George W. Bush, these programs have been forbidden to give any information or advice about abortion options and services.

Office of Women's Health (OWH)
www.4woman.gov/owh/about/

Since 1991, the OWH has been working to advance the women's health agenda inside the vast Department of Health and Human Services. To that end it coordinates OWH offices in the major agencies such as the Food and Drug Administration (FDA), the National Institutes of Health, and the CDC. When the FDA director stalled a decision allowing emergency contraception to be sold over the counter, the director of the FDA's OWH Susan Wood resigned in protest. The OWH also maintains an information website—www.womenshealth.gov—to address a wide variety of questions about the women's health , including a detailed description of all sorts of methods of birth control. Currently, under the Bush administration, www.womenshealth.gov does not mention abortion at all. In the early years of the Bush administration, pro-choice activists complained that the site had an article claiming that abortion causes breast cancer. Such a posting is no longer there.

United Nations Division for the Advancement of Women (UNDAW)
www.un.org/womenwatch/daw/

This agency oversees United Nations (UN) policy relating to gender equality. It supports the UN Commission on the Status of Women (CSW) and CEDAW (Convention for the Elimination of All Forms of Discrimination Against Women). Compliance with the 1995 Beijing Platform for Action is also under the UNDAW's supervision. Thus, the agency provides an international forum for the world's women to sustain efforts for gender equality and to advance the status of women worldwide. Questions dealing with abortion and other matters of reproductive health are delicate, however, because of the opposition of the Roman Catholic Church to contraception and abortion. At the same time, the agency sees these as important health matters for women.

United Nations Population Division
www.un.org/esa/population/unpop.htm

Like UNDAW, the Population Division is part of the UN's Department of Economic and Social Affairs. In the past decades it has been involved in two ways in the abortion question. First, the

division keeps track of the abortion policies in all the member states
of the UN and provides an important resource for students and policy practitioners. Second, the division sponsors conferences; the
most significant one—the International Conference on Population
and Development—was held in Cairo in 1994. That conference saw
major debate over the legalization of abortion and the problems of
illegal abortion. Pro-choice and pro-life activists assembled from
around the world, including a high-level delegation from the Vatican. The final statement reflected the compromises:

> In no case should abortion be promoted as a method of
> family planning. All Governments and relevant inter-
> governmental and non-governmental organizations are
> urged to strengthen their commitment to women's
> health, to deal with the health impact of unsafe abortion
> as a major public health concern and to reduce the
> recourse to abortion through expanded and improved
> family planning services. Prevention of unwanted preg-
> nancies must always be given the highest priority and
> all attempts should be made to eliminate the need for
> abortion. Women who have unwanted pregnancies
> should have ready access to reliable information and
> compassionate counselling. Any measures or changes
> related to abortion within the health system can only be
> determined at the national or local level according to
> the national legislative process. In circumstances in
> which abortion is not against the law, such abortion
> should be safe. In all cases women should have access to
> quality services for the management of complications
> arising from abortion. Post-abortion counselling, educa-
> tion and family planning services should be offered
> promptly which will also help to avoid repeat abortions
> (Source: www.iisd.ca/Cairo.html).

U.S. Agency for International Development (USAID)
www.usaid.gov

USAID is the agency charged with distributing U.S. foreign aid.
Since 1965 that aid has included funds for family planning. In
1984, President Ronald Reagan's Mexico City policy prohibited
the use of these funds for providing services or information
about abortion. During President Bill Clinton's administration,

USAID was again able to fund many more family planning organizations because he rescinded that policy. President George W. Bush put the policy back in effect, and it has been difficult to find family planning groups that don't have to deal with the abortion question. Instead, USAID focuses on integrating aid for preventing HIV/AIDS with family planning.

United States Organizations

Abortion Rights Mobilization (ARM)

Lawrence Lader, a leading member of the abortion reform/repeal movement of the 1960s, founded ARM in 1975. A tiny group with no staff or members, ARM was a resource for Lader to promote his various goals for abortion policy. It was especially active in the 1980s and 1990s in the campaign to legalize mifepristone, also known as RU-486 or the abortion pill. With support from the John Merck Foundation, among others, ARM produced a version of the drug and with Food and Drug Administration permission conducted trials to meet requirements for more general usage. ARM also followed a litigation strategy. With others, it brought lawsuits to challenge the tax-exempt status of the Roman Catholic Church claiming that the church's abortion activism violated the federal law. With Lader's death in 2006, ARM is no longer in existence.

American Civil Liberties Union (ACLU) Reproductive Freedom Project
www.aclu.org/reproductiverights/index.html

The ACLU established its Reproductive Freedom Project in 1974, a year after *Roe v. Wade* decriminalized abortion. A pro-choice organization, ACLU strives to protect the individual's right to make informed decisions about whether to become a parent by advancing the broad spectrum of reproductive policies. The project is especially concerned that rights not be limited by income, age, race, or where people live. The project has its own staff of attorneys, paralegals, and support personnel, and its main activities are lobbying at federal and state legislatures, litigation in state and federal courts, and public education through press releases, conferences, meetings, and publications. Many state ACLU chapters have counterparts to the national Reproductive Freedom Project.

American Coalition of Life Activists (ACLA)

This pro-life group was associated with the spike in pro-life violence in the early 1990s. It authored a series of wanted-style posters that portrayed doctors and others who worked in abortion practice as criminals. ACLA offered a $5,000 reward for success in driving such doctors out of the business. The "Nuremburg" files posted on the Internet got the group in real trouble. Dossiers about scores of doctors and clinic personnel were offered to show their "crimes against humanity." Subsequently, some of these practitioners were the victims of assassinations. When anyone was attacked ACLA drew a line through the photos on the website. Planned Parenthood sued the group and won a $100 million judgment but this was overturned on appeal, based on First Amendment grounds. The group has disbanded apparently and no longer has its website.

American Law Institute (ALI)
www.ali.org

The ALI was founded in 1923 to bring those with the best legal minds together to work on improving the law. The ALI is composed of 3,000 judges, practicing attorneys, and legal scholars asked to join on the basis of their experience and interest in law reform. Through committees, the ALI focuses on special problems to produce model codes and reinstatements of law through "thoughtful and impartial analysis," according to their website. ALI made a major contribution to the abortion reform movement by including a conditional abortion law in its model penal code, which was drafted in 1959 and adopted in 1962. This served as a model for reform in many state legislatures and remains a part of the debate over abortion law.

American Life League (ALL)
www.all.org

ALL was founded in 1979 by Paul and Judie Brown and is led today by Judie Brown. The organization professes strong pro-life views, declaring that the life of every human being is sacred from conception to natural death, and that all such life must have equal rights. ALL is one of the most absolutist of the pro-life groups, as they say, "without compromise, without exception, without apology." For ALL the pro-life movement is a moral crusade. Its projects include *Celebrate Life* magazine; Rock for Life youth activism; STOPP International, which directly attacks Planned Parenthood; and the Crusade for Defense of Our Catholic Church. In the Crusade, Judie and her group proclaim their fundamentalist Catholic ideals, urging bishops to unite in actively opposing abortion and denying communion to all elected Catholic officials who do not support extreme pro-life positions.

American Society for Reproductive Medicine (ASRM)
www.asrm.org/whatsnew.html

Founded in Chicago in 1944, ASRM has a membership of physicians, nurses, researchers, and other medical and health professionals in fifty states and 100 countries. The mission is to develop all aspects of reproductive medicine and serve as an advocate for patient care, research, and education. ASRM has programs to support continuing education for physicians in every area of reproductive health. The Benjamin Young Office of Public Affairs is the lobbying arm of ASRM and promotes, among other goals, reproductive rights. Abortion is not central to the activities today, but the ASRM has been part of pro-choice coalitions during times of policy debates in Congress.

Americans United for Life (AUL)
www.unitedforlife.org/

AUL calls itself a "non-profit public-interest bioethics law firm." The group was founded in 1971 to focus on lawmaking and litigation to achieve pro-life goals. AUL attorneys call the 1973 ruling in *Roe v. Wade* abortion on demand—a judge-created social experiment. Their goal is to reverse this decision and its effects through joining in litigation and, especially, offering their legal expertise to propose model legislation to Congress and the states. The organization claims that abortion destroys two lives—the child who is killed and the woman who suffers "devastating physical and psychological harm." In fact, making the case that abortion is a particular threat to women's health has been part of AUL's agenda since its formation. AUL also claims that legal abortion has led to increases in illegitimacy and child abuse. Instead of privacy and choice, women have suffered through loss of moral integrity and failure to find committed relationships.

Roe v. Wade created a "culture of death," which AUL wants to replace with a "culture of life" through law reform.

Army of God
www.armyofgod.com/

The Army of God takes up where the American Coalition of Life Activists left off in carrying the militant pro-life banner. At its website one can find disturbing photographs of alleged abortions and links to the "Nuremburg" files, websites for assassins Paul Hill and Eric Rudolph, and the Baby Liberation Army. It remains an underground organization committed to the use of violence to stop abortion.

Black Women's Health Imperative (formerly National Black Women's Health Project)
www.blackwomenshealth.org/

This organization was founded in 1983 by Byllye Y. Avery to promote "empowerment of African American women as educated health care consumers and a strong voice for the improved health status of African American women." It is an education, research, and advocacy organization, focusing primarily on reaching and informing black women about their health options and encouraging self-help and responsibility. Reproductive issues are a small part of their overall program; they advocate access to a broad range of reproductive health options, recognizing that black women have high levels of unintended pregnancy. These options include prenatal care, complete and accurate family planning information and services, safe childbirth, fertility services, adoption, safe abortion, and disease prevention.

Catholics for a Free Choice (CFFC)
www.catholicsforchoice.org/

Frances Kissling founded CFFC in 1973 to challenge the assumption that the Vatican and the bishops speak for all Catholics on the issue of reproductive rights. Since then, CFFC has offered a way for Catholics who support a woman's right to "follow her conscience in the matters of sexuality and reproductive health" to come together to support pro-choice policies. CFFC advocates full access to contraception, safe and legal abortion, prenatal and postnatal care, and adoption. With these goals, the organization seeks to establish links with the Catholic traditions of social justice, instead of the more patriarchal natural-law tradition. CFFC focuses on networking and educational activities, forming coalitions with other pro-choice organizations within the United States as well as Latin America, Europe, and Africa and at the United Nations.

Center for Bio-Ethical Reform (CBR)
www.cbrinfo.org/

The CBR is based in California and was founded in 1990 to seek "prenatal justice, and the right to life of the unborn, disabled and aged." To accomplish its pro-life agenda, CBR's strategy is to portray images of abortions and bloody aborted fetuses to the public through many media, based on the assumption that the reason abortion remains legal is because people have not confronted what CBR says is the true nature of the procedure. Following are three of CBR's recent campaigns: the Reproductive Choice Campaign, where CBR sends many large tractor-trailers painted with aborted fetuses along highways and through cities; the Genocide Awareness Campaign, which places displays of aborted fetuses next to recognized images of genocide to make the case that abortion is similar to the Holocaust; and the Abortionno campaign, which offers free copies of a video showing an abortion. The CBR has been heavily criticized for its genocide campaign because it implies that women who have abortions are like Nazis.

Center for Reproductive Rights (CRR)
www.reproductiverights.org/

CRR was founded in 1992 as the Center for Reproductive Law and Policy. The group's mission is to use the law to achieve its goals of reproductive rights in the United States and around the world. To CRR, the idea of reproductive rights includes safe and affordable contraception; safe, accessible, and legal abortion; and safe, healthy pregnancies. The group pays special attention to reproductive health and support of adolescents and low-income women and to countering violence against women's freedom to exercise their rights. CRR took the lead in the successful challenge to the constitutionality of state bans on partial-birth abortions in *Stenberg v. Carhart* (2000). CRR has extensive activities abroad, especially helping lawyers in Latin American countries who want to change their restrictive abortion and contraceptive laws. This organization is a prominent and reliable participant in the pro-choice movement.

Christian Coalition of America
www.cc.org/

Christian TV preacher Pat Robertson founded the Christian Coalition in 1989, the year after he ran for president. For Robertson and his colleague, Ralph Reed, the Coalition was a means by which Christian fundamentalists could "take over" the Republican party through grassroots organizing. Strong pro-life views linked the coalition to other Christian conservative groups, such as Focus on the Family. The Coalition was a national player during the 1990s, but its political activism got it in trouble with the Internal Revenue Service, which revoked its tax-exempt status. Robertson left the organization in 2000, and it reorganized as the Christian Coalition of America under the presidency of Roberta Coombs. The Christian Coalition calls itself the "largest and most active conservative grassroots political organization in America," claiming more than 2 million members. Although the group maintains its pro-family, pro-life agenda, without the media star Robertson, many think the Christian Coalition has lost much of its influence.

Committee for Abortion Rights and Against Sterilization Abuse (CARASA)

CARASA was founded in 1977 in the wake of the passage of the Hyde Amendment, which denied the use of federal Medicaid funds to poor women for abortions. The group brought together a broad coalition of activists from mainstream to socialist feminist groups focusing on the poor, the young, and women of color. The activists formed committees to promote their goals, which placed abortion rights in a wider context of overall social justice for poor women. Important to CARASA is the material context for reproductive rights—welfare rights, child care, workplace safety, and especially, an end to sterilization abuse. The issue of sterilization brought in membership from the Committee to End Sterilization Abuse (CESA). CESA had been active in black and Puerto Rican communities, where they charged doctors with sterilizing women without their knowledge. The aim of CARASA was to create a popular movement to counter the grassroots Right to Life movement that was gaining momentum in the late 1970s and early 1980s. What distinguished CARASA from other pro-choice groups such as the National Organization for Women and NARAL was its focus on class and color, and its stand against racism. To this end CARASA helped found the Reproductive Rights National Network in 1979. Both groups declined in the 1980s.

Common Ground Network for Life and Choice
www.sfcg.org/

Between 1993 and 2000—during a time of extreme polarization in the abortion conflict and pro-life violence—the Search for Common Ground, an organization that promotes conflict resolution, formed the Common Ground Network for Life and Choice. The goal was to shift the ground in the divisive debate over legal abortion. The steering committee, which comprised pro-choice and pro-life activists, set out the steps that would bring a solution to the divisive conflict: first bring each side into dialogue where the goal is to understand the other's points of view; second, find common values and beliefs; and third, look for ways to move together toward common goals. The common goals that arose through the dialogue were preventing teenage pregnancy, making adoption more accessible, avoiding violence, increasing options for women, and reducing conditions that increase abortion rates. The intense discussion took place in Buffalo, NY, and Pensacola, FL, and produced manuals for use in other conflict situations.

Concerned Women for America (CWFA)
www.cwfa.org/main.asp

CWFA was founded in 1979 by fundamentalist Christian activist Beverly LaHaye, who remains the chairman of the board. CWFA claims to be the largest public policy women's organization in the United States. The central theme of the organization's mission is to bring "Biblical principles" to government through activism of "women and like-minded men." CWFA derives its agenda from its fundamentalist view of the Bible and Christianity and its goal to return the nation to the traditional values of the founders. Sanctity of life is a top-priority issue for CWFA, placing it firmly in the pro-life camp—against abortion, fetal tissue experimentation, embryonic research, euthanasia, population control, and human genetic engineering. CWFA also advocates for sexual abstinence and the natural distinctions between men and women in marriage. CWFA is a reliable partner in the pro-life movement, and its president, Wendy Wright, is a frequent guest on talk shows and other news programs about abortion and other "life" issues.

Democrats for Life of America (DLA)
www.democratsforlife.org/

DLA was formed in 1999 after several prominent pro-life Democrats were denied the chance to speak at the Democratic Party's presidential conventions. The organization seeks to attract those in the Democratic Party who do not support the party's pro-choice stand. Like other pro-life organizations, DLA opposes abortion and euthanasia, but it also opposes capital punishment, a position not usually on the pro-life agenda. These pro-life Democrats agree that abortion should be illegal, but overturning *Roe v. Wade* is not their top priority; instead, they focus on programs that would reduce abortion through preventing unplanned pregnancy and helping pregnant women to find options other than abortion. The group's signature proposal in the 2000s has been pregnant women support acts, both federal and state, which combine a number of programs to provide support for childbirth while dissuading women from choosing abortion. Members of the DLA argue that the Democratic Party has been hurt in elections because of its rigid pro-choice position and has swung support to a number of pro-life representatives and senators—including Senate Majority Leader Harry Reid. DLA counts as many as thirty-seven pro-life democrats in the 110th Congress. Emily's List and other pro-choice feminists are highly critical of DLA. At the same time, many in the pro-life movement, especially the Republicans, criticize the pro-life Democrats for remaining in a party that is pro-choice and for opposing capital punishment, which most pro-life organizations accept.

Eagle Forum (EF)
www.eagleforum.org/

Phyllis Schlafly is the founder and president of EF, which calls itself the "leader of the pro-family movement." EF was formed in 1972 as a vehicle for Schlafly's conservative agenda and made its mark by successfully rallying support to stop ratification of the equal rights amendment (ERA). Much of its success is attributable to Schlafly's political savvy and a strategy that organized little EF's at the state level, especially where ERA was on the legislative agenda. Since the early 1980s, EF has moved on to other conventional conservative issues, such as maintaining American sovereignty, private enterprise, and strict construction of the Constitution by judges. At 81 years, Schlafly has not tempered her battle against feminism, however, which includes championing the full-time homemaker in marriage and a strong pro-life, antichoice stand.

Elliott Institute
www.afterabortion.org/

The Elliott Institute was founded in 1988 to support the research and outreach of Dr. David Reardon, a biomedical ethicist who claims to have conducted research on the impact of abortion on women since 1983. The Institute bills itself as a mission and ministerial organization, dedicated to helping women who have been injured by abortion. The group's claim is that both pro-life and pro-choice groups ignore women; their assumption is that all women are adversely affected by abortion and many are exploited and injured. The Institute collects testimonies of women to use in its "Poor Choice" campaign. It proposes laws that would make it easier for women to hold abortion providers liable for psychological and physical effects of abortion. It uses its website—www .afterabortion.org—for its Internet information and outreach projects. In addition, the Institute promotes Reardon's books and a variety of pamphlets and position papers.

Family Research Council (FRC)
www.frc.org

The FRC is a think tank and lobbying organization that promotes policy that "values human life and upholds the institutions of marriage and the family." FRC was founded in 1983 with the goal of shaping the debate over families and politics in a conservative Christian direction. According to its website, FRC considers the right to life the most fundamental human right. FRC is a major component of the pro-life movement, lobbying against legal abortion, for abstinence-only education, and against government-supported family planning. However, FRC is also well known for its strong opposition to gay rights. Its leaders have been prominent in right-wing circles, especially Gary Bauer who ran for U.S. president in 2000, and eventually became president of FRC in 2007, and Tony Perkins, a frequent guest on conservative talk shows and in debates about social issues.

Feminists for Life of America (FFL)
www.feministsforlife.org

FFL, formed in 1972, has the goal of meeting the needs of women who are pregnant or parenting and to help them find alternatives to abortion. To FFL, abortion represents society's failure and the victimization of women; their goal is to "eliminate the root causes that drive women to abortion" and promote what they call the core values of feminism: "justice, nondiscrimination, and nonviolence." The organization's primary activities involve outreach to college campuses where they support the formation of collegiate FFL groups and give speeches to show students they can be both pro-life and pro-feminist. They gain much of their inspiration from the lives and politics of women's rights pioneers Susan B. Anthony and Elizabeth Cady Stanton, who opposed abortion because they considered it a form of violence against women. They are not reliable pro-life coalition members, however, as they are not interested in lobbying to promote other conservative values nor will they take a stand on contraception and abstinence.

Feminist Majority and Feminist Majority Foundation
www.feministmajority.org and www.feminist.org/

The Feminist Majority and its sister organization, the Feminist Majority Foundation, were formed in 1987. The name "Feminist Majority" came in response to a *Newsweek* poll in the 1980s that showed a majority—56 percent—of women self-identified as feminists and that most men supported the women's rights movement. The Feminist Majority focuses on mobilization and lobbying before state and federal governments while the foundation funds research, educational programs, and forums on public issues. Eleanor Smeal, former president of NOW, is president of the foundation. Both organizations are dedicated to women's equality, reproductive health, and nonviolence, and the Feminist Majority especially promotes empowerment and influence of feminists. The Feminist Majority has taken leadership roles in activities of the pro-choice coalition, including the March for

Women's Lives in 1992, the campaign for Freedom of Access to Clinic Entrances (FACE) Act in 1994, and the appointment of justices to the Supreme Court to save *Roe v. Wade.*

Focus on the Family (FOF)
www.focusonthefamily.com/

FOF is best described as a ministry and media organization established to promote "biblical principles to help families." Dr. James Dobson founded the organization in 1977 and continues as chairman of the board. Dobson has a daily radio broadcast that has a central place in the world of "conservative talk radio." FOF publishes ten magazines and lots of books, many written by Dobson, and it sells CDs and videos to distribute its version of Biblical values and family life. Dobson has been a major leader of the religious right in the United States for nearly 30 years. He has served as an adviser to the U.S. president on family issues and on many boards and commissions. FOF and Dobson adhere to a strict pro-life point of view, strongly opposing legal abortion, gay rights, and anything other than abstinence-only sex education.

Guttmacher Institute
www.guttmacher.org

The Guttmacher Institute's mission is to promote "sexual and reproductive health" through social science research, policy analysis, and public education. Founded in 1968 as an offshoot of Planned Parenthood Federation of America (PPFA) called the Center for Family Planning Program Development, it was guided by PPFA president Alan Guttmacher and named after him following his death in 1974. The Institute has a pro-choice perspective as shown in its policy goals: to help people avoid unplanned pregnancy, prevent and treat sexually transmitted diseases, exercise the right to choose abortion, maintain healthy pregnancies and childbirth, and maintain healthy sexual relationships. Nevertheless, advocates on both sides of the abortion debate rely on the objectivity of the data on abortion practice produced by the Institute's researchers. The Institute publishes three journals: *International Family Planning Perspectives, Guttmacher Policy Review,* and *Perspectives on Sexual and Reproductive Health.* Copies of their articles are available at the website.

Lambs of Christ

The Lambs of Christ formed what its founder Norman Weston called a "rapid deployment force" to support antiabortion militancy. Founded in 1989 by Weston, a Roman Catholic priest and former army paratrooper, and Operation Rescue's Randall Terry, the Lambs was one of the names given to a small group of militants—some called them nomads—who roamed about the country, ready to target abortion providers through harassment, blockades, and invasions. Their tactic was to do what it took to get arrested and then refuse to give their names—calling themselves either Baby John Doe or Baby Jane Doe. This was intended to tie up the resources of local law enforcement and hamper their ability to deal with the pro-life activists. Related groups include the Victim Souls of the Unborn Christ Child, Prolife Police, and Rescue Outreach.

March for Life Education and Defense Fund
www.marchforlife.org

The March for Life Fund organizes and the supports the annual pro-life March for Life in Washington, DC. The first march was held January 22, 1974, on the one-year anniversary of the Supreme Court's decision in *Roe v. Wade* legalizing abortion. The event proved to be an effective rallying and mobilizing event for the pro-life movement; leaders formed the March for Life Education and Defense fund as a nonprofit organization to organize the march annually ever since. The group adheres to a set of "Life Principles," which call for the enactment of a Human Life Amendment. The theme of the 2007 march was "Thou Shalt Protect the Equal Right to Life of Each Innocent Human in Existence at Fertilization. *No Exception! No Compromise!*" The symbols of the march are the red roses delivered to each member of Congress along with a pro-life "Red Rose Letter."

Medical Students for Choice (MSFC)
www.ms4c.org/

MSFC responds to the recognized shortage in trained abortion providers in the United States and Canada by mobilizing medical students to work to increase training opportunities. The mission is to "destigmatize abortion provision among medical students and residents." MSFC student groups are found at more than 120 medical schools; they lobby their schools to provide courses and other training in both the context and the practice of abortion. Because most medical school graduates do internships in hospitals, where fewer than 5 percent of abortions are conducted, rather than clinics, MSFS runs an internship program to match students with reproductive health clinics where they can develop necessary skills to contribute to abortion practice. At their annual convention, students have opportunities to take clinical training as well as learn about the place of abortion in the practice of medicine.

Moral Majority Coalition
www.moralmajority.us

Evangelical preacher Jerry Falwell organized the Moral Majority in 1979 as a mechanism to bring evangelical leaders together to "engage the culture" to the pro-life, pro–traditional family message. In the coalitions of the religious right, the Moral Majority was a key component in promoting pro-life politics, especially the successful campaigns of Ronald Reagan for president. Falwell disbanded the Moral Majority in 1989 to devote his attention to establishing Liberty University. He brought the group back in 2004 in the form of the Moral Majority Coalition with a commitment to lead it for 4 years. The Coalition's main goal is to mobilize voters for candidates of the religious right and to fight against what Falwell called "out-of-control lawmakers and radical judges—working at the whims of society—to alter the moral foundations of America." Falwell died in May 2007.

NARAL Pro-Choice America
www.prochoiceamerica.org/

Formed in 1969 as the National Association for Repeal of Abortion Laws, NARAL remains the leading advocacy organization in the pro-choice movement. It has kept a single focus on maintaining legal abortion, despite expansion of its mission to include reproductive rights more generally. To that goal, the name changed to National Abortion and Reproductive Rights Action League in 1993 and then NARAL Pro-Choice America in 2003. NARAL has been at the center of the pro-choice victories and defeats: the campaign for legal abortion that ended in *Roe v. Wade*, countering the pro-life resurgence in the 1980s with its Abortion Rights: Silent No More campaign, promoting the Freedom of Choice Act in Congress in the early 1990s, as a leading sponsor of the March for Women's Lives in 1989 and 2004, and opposing appointments of anti-*Roe* justices to the Supreme Court. As a tireless advocate for "privacy and women's right to choose" NARAL mobilizes activists through NARAL organizations in many states, lobbies Congress and state legislatures, and uses its political action committee funds to endorse pro-choice candidates regardless of political party.

National Abortion Federation (NAF)
www.prochoice.org/

The NAF is a professional association of abortion providers, organizing about 400 facilities in forty-seven states. The NAF's agenda is to maintain abortion as a safe, legal, and accessible procedure. The group's URL claims the pro-choice label, as does their belief statement: "We believe that women should be trusted to make private medical decisions in consultation with their health care providers." NAF sponsors training and education programs, but it is especially active in monitoring and fighting against restrictive state laws. Of special interest in recent years have been the so-called "TRAP" bills—Targeted Regulation of Abortion Providers. With these, state legislators try to put special restrictive regulations on abortion clinics only; examples include special building codes—down to the size of janitors' closets—special additional licensing requirements, collection of records, and frequent intrusive inspection of facilities. These are in addition to the regulations already in place for providers as forms of outpatient clinics. NAF asserts that these laws are based on erroneous claims that abortion procedures are unsafe and unregulated.

National Coalition of Abortion Providers (NCAP)
www.ncap.com

The NCAP brought together "independent" abortion providers in the 1990s to form a national trade organization that would support and defend their members. NCAP's slogan is "We Trust Women." Along with providing information about abortion services of their members, they have launched a program called "Need for a New Conversation." This move is to counter the success of the pro-life movement in demonizing abortion as an immoral act and stigmatizing the women who have them. As abortion providers, NCAP claims their members know first hand the circumstances of women seeking abortions. Because of the stigma, many women face delays, guilt, and remorse. Abortion alienates and isolates them. This can be rectified, says NCAP, by challenging the notion that abortion is immoral and spreading the stories of real women. It's time to learn from the patients and lift the veil of secrecy to show the ethical core of abortion: "relief, conflict, confusion, sadness and empowerment."

National Latina Institute for Reproductive Health (NLIRH)
www.latinainstitute.org/

The Latina Institute formed in 1994 under the auspices of Catholics for a Free Choice as part of its initiative to bring Latinas into the discussion about reproductive rights. The self-stated goal is "to ensure the fundamental human right to reproductive health care for Latinas, their families and their communities through education, policy advocacy and community mobilization." They call themselves a "social justice organization," which means they tend to get involved in the larger social, economic, and political situation of Latinas that may affect their access to reproductive health. The Institute runs training sessions for leadership development and works to build local and regional networks. Policy goals include repealing the Hyde Amendment, fighting against abortion restrictions, improving availability of emergency contraception, achieving comprehensive sex and sexuality education, and promoting immigration reform.

National Pro-Life Action Center (NPLAC)
www.nplac.org/

The NPLAC bought a house on Capitol Hill in Washington, DC, a few years ago and from there seeks to keep government officials aware of the pro-life position on issues through "information, contacts and spiritual encouragement." It publishes a newsletter and links to National Pro-life Radio, which broadcasts on the Internet 24 hours a day. The Center works for and with three other pro-life organizations: Priests for Life, Catholics United for Life, and Faith and Action.

National Network of Abortion Funds (NNAF)
www.nnaf.org

NNAF is a national umbrella organization for locally based abortion funds. These funds arose in response to the denial of federal and state Medicaid funds to poor women. These are voluntary organizations, relying on shoestring budgets to raise money for grants and loans to needy clients. Working on one case at a time, these fund organizations can arrange price cuts at clinics in cases of extreme need. In 2006, NNAF joined with other groups in the campaign to counter the Hyde Amendment, which denies use of federal Medicaid funds for abortion: "30 Years is Enough!"

National Organization for Women (NOW)
www.now.org

In 1967, NOW was the first national organization to advocate repeal of criminal abortion laws; Betty Friedan was president of the group, and this took place at NOW's first annual convention. Other top priorities for NOW in 1967 were publicly supported child care and the equal rights amendment. Forty years later, in 2007, constitutional equality and reproductive rights remain the top priorities for NOW, along with antiracism, lesbian rights, countering violence against women, and economic justice. In between, NOW has been at the center of the pro-choice movement promoting an agenda of safe and legal abortion, birth control, emergency contraception, health services, and education for all women. With its 500,000 members and 500 affiliates across the country, NOW claims to be the voice of those who support equality. To NOW, reproductive rights are "issues of life and death for women, not just choice."

National Right to Life Committee (NLRC)
www.nrlc.org/

The place of NLRC in the pro-life movement is as a single-issue, nonreligious, and nonpartisan organization. Indeed, it took a leadership position in June 1973, when the NLRC came together to counter the decision in *Roe v. Wade.* The national body is composed of fifty state representatives; NLRC claims to have 3,000 chapters in all fifty states and the District of Columbia. Some say it is the largest pro-life grassroots organization. In 1999, *Fortune* magazine ranked it as the ninth most powerful lobbying organization on Capitol Hill. The goal of the organization is "to restore legal protection to innocent human life." Fighting legal abortion is its primary mission, but it also takes positions on stem cell research, euthanasia, and infanticide. NLRC does not take a position or even comment on questions of contraception, sex education, or capital punishment, so it is unlikely to form any coalitions with pro-choice groups to stop unintended pregnancies as a way to limit abortion. The legality of the practice is its sole concern.

National Women's Law Center (NWLC)
www.nwlc.org/

The NWLC was established by women lawyers from the Center for Law and Social Policy as a public-interest law group that would "make law and public policy work for women and their families." Although one of its first projects was to protect poor women from coercive contraception and sterilization, reproductive issues are a small part of the center's activities. NWLC has four major areas of action: education, employment, economic security, and health. Health activities include "fighting to protect reproductive rights and contraceptive coverage." A recent NWLC position paper warned that the appointments of justices John Roberts and Samuel Alito to the Supreme Court in 2005 and 2006, respectively, were a threat to legal abortion guarantees in *Roe v. Wade.*

National Women's Political Caucus (NWPC)
www.nwpc.org/

The NWPC promotes its agenda through efforts to increase women's participation in politics. Its stated mission is to create a women's power base by recruiting, training, and supporting pro-choice women candidates of both parties. The caucus dates back to the early days of the women's rights movement—1973—when women in the Republican and Democratic parties found common ground in supporting women's equality. As the Republican Party became the anti-ERA and pro-life party, the caucus found it difficult to connect with Republican women on pro-choice issues. In 1999, however, the caucus was led, once again, by a Republican president. Its agenda remains strongly pro-choice: maintaining women's access to abortion, comprehensive sex education, and availability of RU-486 and emergency contraception.

Operation Rescue
www.operationsaveamerica.org; www.operationrescue.org

The original Operation Rescue was formed by Randall Terry in 1988 to use a religious strategy and tactics of civil disobedience to shut down abortion clinics. Terry left the organization in 1989, and the organization's tactics have been limited by the federal FACE regulations. In 2007, two groups lay claim to the Terry legacy. Operation Rescue's primary focus is an abortion clinic in Wichita, Kansas—the one that was the scene of Terry's longest campaign in the 1980s. The other group—Operation Rescue/Operation Save America—presents "Jesus as the standard" and seeks repentance through street action for what they term the abortion holocaust in America.

Physicians for Life
http://physiciansforlife.org

Although the organization invites pro-life physicians to join, Physicians for Life is primarily a website with many links to commentary and research papers about issues from a pro-life point of view. The group's goal is to draw attention to issues of abortion, euthanasia, stem cell research, cloning, infanticide, sexually transmitted diseases, and out-of-wedlock sexual activity. Through the website the organizers hope to build support for physicians who have taken a pro-life stand.

Physicians for Reproductive Choice and Health (PRCH)
www.prch.org/

The name identifies the members and purpose of this group founded in 1992. PRCH is "committed to providing and advocating the best possible care for patients." Such care includes a full range of reproductive choices. "We believe that all people should have the knowledge, equal access to quality services and freedom of choice to make their own reproductive health care decisions." To achieve its goals, the organization has three areas of action: public policy and community organization, communication, and medical education. PRCH supports comprehensive sexuality education. Another project is Voices of Choice, which documents the experience of doctors who practiced abortion before it was legalized in *Roe v. Wade.*

Pharmacists for Life International (PFLI)
www.pfli.org/

PFLI was founded in Ohio in 1984, but it has a national and even international mission. Its founding statement declares a clear pro-life belief: "PFLI defends, upholds and protects the sanctity of all human life from conception to natural death, regardless of age, biological stage, handicap or place of residence." PFLI seeks to promote this goal by persuading pharmacists and other medical personnel to resist the use of any medication that is or could be an abortifacient—an agent that causes an abortion, which PFLI defines as preventing a fertilized egg from implanting in the uterus. PFLI urges pharmacists to refuse to fill prescriptions for any of these drugs—including RU-486, emergency contraception, and many hormone birth control pills—and defend their legal rights to do so as part of their rights of conscience. Two of their mottos are: "Let the gift of medicines promote life, not destroy life" and "Rights of conscience outweigh rights to abortifacient chemicals."

Planned Parenthood Federation of America (PPFA)
www.plannedparenthood.org/

Planned Parenthood traces its origins to Margaret Sanger's first birth control clinic in Brooklyn in 1916. In 2007, it calls itself the "nation's leading sexual and reproductive health care advocate and provider." Certainly, Planned Parenthood has been a central player in the abortion debate since the 1950s, advocating reform of criminal laws in the 1960s and then defending legal abortion since 1973. Much of its advocacy work is done through its affiliates, which have been litigants in major cases challenging restrictive laws (e.g., *Planned Parenthood v. Casey*); 860 clinics and health care centers provide services, all supporting PPFA's creed that the individual right to manage fertility is fundamental. Planned Parenthood, the chief nemesis of most pro-life organizations, is a member of the International Planned Parenthood Federation, which takes the family planning message to international conferences and other forums.

Priests for Life (PFL)
www.priestsforlife.org/

Established in 1991, PFL presents itself as an organization for anyone who wants to stop abortion and euthanasia. Its special approach is to educate priests to unite and do all they can to give top priority to the life issues, keeping them at the center of their ministries. This organization is primarily a vehicle for the work and writings of Father Frank Pavone who travels the country giving talks and seminars as well as networking with major organizations in the pro-life movement. In 2004, Pavone started assembling a community of priests devoted to missionary work on life issues. Two other top projects relate to claims that women who have abortions suffer from lifelong psychological and emotional damage: Rachel's Vineyard retreats and the Silent No More Awareness Campaign.

Pro-Choice Public Education Project (PEP)
www.protectchoice.org/

PEP is less an organization than an education project with close links to some major pro-choice organizations, such as the Feminist Majority, NARAL, Planned Parenthood, and the Religious Coalition for Reproductive Choice. PEP is dedicated to educating young women about reproductive freedom issues and choice, based on the assumption that many young women, women of color, and low-income women have been marginal to the pro-choice movement. The group may also be reacting to polling data that show dwindling support for choice among people younger than 25 years. PEP focuses on publications, outreach, and leadership training. One recent publication is *She Speaks: African American and Latina Young Women Speak on Reproductive Health and Rights*.

Pro-Life Action League (PLAL)
www.prolifeaction.org/

The Pro-Life Action League formed in 1980 and has been led by its founder Joseph M. Scheidler ever since. PLAL has a prominent place in the pro-life movement through its use of direct but nonviolent action to stop abortions. One of its most important techniques is sidewalk counseling. People are trained, almost as missionaries, to intercept women and men coming to abortion clinics and try to dissuade them from going through with a planned abortion. PLAL members also picket clinics and sponsor "Face the Truth" tours where they show large photos of aborted fetuses. Scheidler and his organization were the object of a decade-long lawsuit by NOW seeking damages under the federal antiracketeering statutes. The case was finally resolved in 2003 in Scheidler's favor.

Pro-Life Alliance of Gays and Lesbians (PLAGAL)
www.plagal.org/

PLAGAL occupies the margins of both the pro-choice and pro-life movements. Most gays and lesbians are thought to be associated with the ideas of pro-choice, that is, privacy, individual rights, and sexual freedom. The pro-life philosophy, on the other hand, often goes hand in hand with a fundamentalist view of sexuality that condemns homosexuality and fights against gay rights. PLAGAL confounds both sides by claiming that legal abortion is just like homophobia. For example, the group asserts, abortion denies fundamental humanity and rids societies of human beings who are considered undesirable, just like homophobia. The organization, formed in 1990, was originally called Gays Against Abortion, but it expanded to reflect its membership of lesbians (about one-third). This is a small group, but it distributes position pamphlets and participates in activities such as the March for Life.

Religious Coalition for Reproductive Choice (RCRC)
www.rcrc.org/

With the mission of using the moral power of religious communities to ensure reproductive choice, RCRC was founded in 1973. It seeks to provide a network for churches and religious people who support reproductive rights and to counter the religious claims of the pro-life movement. The Call to Justice Campaign, for example, is to "fight *against* the 'Religious' Right's assault on mainstream America and *for* our pro-choice ideals." Other initiatives focus on people of color—in African-American and Latina churches, for example—and the poor. RCRC sponsors several state affiliates and a group called Clergy for Choice, which support a wide range of reproductive rights including family planning and contraceptive services; comprehensive sex education; safe, legal, and affordable abortion; affordable health; and child care and adoption.

Reproductive Health Technologies Project (RHTP)
www.rhtp.org/

The RHTP was founded in the late 1980s to provide information about the French "abortion pill," RU-486, and to make it more likely that the United States would approve distribution of the drug. Since then, RHTP has expanded its mission to gain public acceptance of current and new technologies affecting reproductive matters. Its stated goal is "to advance the ability of every woman of any age to achieve full reproductive freedom with access to the safest, most effective, appropriate and acceptable technologies for ensuring her own health and controlling her fertility." RHTP works to counter efforts to limit access to technologies, for example, with respect to emergency contraception, and to develop supportive networks with pharmacists and sellers of medical devices. These campaigns have brought the organization into coalitions that support the place of scientific research in federal policymaking.

Republican Majority for Choice
www.gopchoice.org/

Like its sister organization, Republicans for Choice Political Action Committee (PAC), the Republican Majority for Choice works to protect reproductive rights by challenging the official pro-life platform of the Republican Party. They contend that pro-life ideas run counter to the Republican goals of limited government and personal freedoms and the current stance is "intrusive and alienating." This organization boasts a large number of prominent moderate Republicans as members of its boards and committees. Its policy agenda includes supporting stem cell research and emergency contraception for rape victims.

Republican National Coalition for Life (RNCLIFE)
www.rnclife.org

Conservative activist Phyllis Schlafly formed this organization in 1990 to counter the attempts by the two Republican pro-choice organizations to change the Republican pro-life platform. Floor flights occurred at the conventions in 1992 and 1996, but the pro-life coalition prevailed then and through the 2004 convention. Between conventions the organization is little more than a blog with occasional position papers to connect with the faithful. The network remains in place, no doubt, to be ready for the next convention battle in the Republican Party over the abortion issue.

Republicans for Choice Political Action Committee (RCPAC)
www.republicansforchoice.com

Ann E. W. Stone founded Republicans for Choice in the wake of the Supreme Court's 1989 decision *Webster v. Reproductive Services*, which showed that the majority of justices in favor of maintaining legal abortion was dangerously close to disappearing. As a PAC, the organization funds Republican candidates who support legal abortion and women's privacy. Stone argues that this platform is central to traditional Republican principles of limited government and individual liberty. The strong pro-life stance of the Republican Party in the 1990s has hurt the party, she claims, alienating women voters especially. Republicans for Choice tries to help so-called "moderate" Republicans who do not subscribe to the pro-life views of the religious right. As Stone says, pro-choice voters should look beyond party labels: some Democrats are anti-choice; while some Republicans are pro-choice. She works to protect the latter.

Sex Information and Education Council of the United States (SIECUS)
www.siecus.org/

SIECUS was founded in 1964 by Dr. Mary S. Calderone. Then and now its primary mission has been to promote sexuality education for all, including reproductive health and services. Its main contribution to the abortion conflict occurred in the 1960s when it provided a forum for raising awareness about the limits of criminal abortion laws and promoted law reform. Abortion is no longer at the center of its mission, but related issues are, such as emergency contraception, comprehensive sex education, and gay rights. SIECUS uses its website to offer research and policy updates on sexuality and sex education for educators, policy-makers, journalists, and religious leaders. One such project for school personnel is the School Health Clearing House Online.

Traditional Values Coalition (TVC)
www.traditionalvalues.org/

The TVC, founded in 1980 as a "non-denominational, grassroots church lobby," claims to speak for 43,000 churches of all faiths and races. TVC is a component of the pro-life movement with a goal of restoring values for strong families based on guidance from a literal reading of the Bible. At the top of the list of values is the right to life from conception to natural death, but TVC also supports the power of government to execute murderers through capital punishment. Other values on the traditional list are fidelity in marriage, abstinence before marriage, and condemnation of all sex outside of heterosexual marriage. The TVC is also against pornography and for patriotism and refuses to be tolerant of behaviors they believe destroy families. In 2007, the highest priority is the fight against homosexuality.

United States Conference of Catholic Bishops (USCCB)
www.usccb.org/

The USCCB is the official hierarchy of the Roman Catholic Church in the United States. It organizes itself into a series of committees and secretariats to work on special topics. The Pro-life Secretariat and Committee is one of the most active in assembling educational materials, developing campaigns to promote a pro-life agenda, and engaging in public policy efforts. The policies they support include the following:

- Passage of a constitutional amendment that will protect unborn children's right to life to the maximum degree possible, and pursuit of appropriate strategies to attain this goal
- Federal and state laws and administrative policies that restrict the practice of abortion as much as possible
- Prohibition of support of human cloning, and research that destroys human embryos
- Seeking to get the U.S. Supreme Court to reverse its decisions regarding the legalization of abortion
- Support for legislation that provides morally acceptable alternatives to abortion, including funding to expand education, health, nutrition, and other services for disadvantaged parents and their children
- Support for federal and state legislation that promotes effective palliative care for those who are chronically ill or dying
- Support for efforts to prevent legalization of euthanasia and assisted suicide by legislation or referendum
- Support for efforts to end the death penalty

"As U.S. citizens and religious leaders, we see a critical moral imperative for public policy efforts to ensure the protection of human life. We urge our fellow citizens to see the justice of this cause and to work with us to achieve these objectives." The USCCB is a major component and provides resources for the pro-life movement.

International Organizations

Human Life International (HLI)
www.hli.org

Father Paul Marx founded HLI to promote the teachings of Roman Catholicism about contraception and abortion around the world. HLI calls itself the largest international, pro-life, pro-family, pro-woman organization in the world. The organization uses the language of missionary work to describe its efforts to inspire, organize, train, and support pro-life activists in countries in Europe, Latin America, Asia, and Africa. HLI claims to have ninety offices in seventy-five countries and opposes family planning, legal abortion, and sex education. These organizations separately attend international conferences to enhance their antiabortion clout. HLI has no official connection with the Roman Catholic Church, although Pope John Paul II did endorse the work of its founder, Father Marx. HLI presents itself as a sort of David to the pro-choice, family planning Goliath—namely the Ford Foundation. "They have money; we have God."

International Right to Life Federation
www.lifeissues.org/international/index.html

This federation brings leaders of national pro-life organizations together to promote their common agenda. The federation publishes a newsletter at www.lifeissues.org. The President, Dr. Jack Willke, gives talks all over the world, especially emphasizing the message of the 1968 papal encyclical, *Humanae Vitae*. At the 2007 meeting of right-to-life leaders in Manila, the Philippines, the group issued the following statement:

> "We call on citizens throughout the world to demand that innocent human life, from conception until natural death, be protected from intentional killing in their nations' laws; we call on citizens throughout the world to demand that only marriage between a man and a woman be recognized in their nations' laws; we call on citizens throughout the world to demand that the inalienable rights of parents as primary educators and protectors be respected in their nations' laws." (www.spuc.org.uk/news/releases/2007/january8)

International Women's Health Coalition (IWHC)
www.iwhc.org

The premise of IWHC is that "women's health and rights are central to economic justice and global wellbeing." To achieve its goal the organization supports local organizations in Africa, Asia, and Latin America. It also serves as an advocate for women's health rights at international conferences such as the UN Population Fund, the World Health Organization, and the World Bank. Adrienne Germaine and Joan Dunlop formed IWHC in 1984. They had both worked with the Population Council and saw an opportunity to develop a similar organization on behalf of women worldwide. Germaine is the current president. She was a U.S. delegate to both the Cairo Conference on population in 1994 and the Beijing Conference on women in 1995.

Marie Stopes International (MSI)
www.mariestopes.org.uk

Named for the British birth control pioneer Marie Stopes, MSI seeks to provide sexual and reproductive health services. It was established in 1976 in London and is still based in the United Kingdom. MSI reaches out to thirty-eight other countries through its global partnership program and has centers in Africa, Asia, Latin America, the Middle East, and Europe.

Population Council
www.popcouncil.org

One of the leaders in the movement to curb population growth, the Population Council has always had both a national and an international focus. John D. Rockefeller III founded the Council in 1952, and he used it to promote the legalization of abortion in the United States in the 1960s and 1970s. More recently the organization has focused on research on matters of reproductive health to achieve a balance between people and resources. It has programs in sixty countries and offices in eighteen. With more than $70 million in the budget, the Council funds research in biomedicine for safe pregnancies, gender and family issues, HIV and AIDS, infants and children, and reproductive health, especially contraception, postabortion care, and unsafe abortions.

Society for the Protection of Unborn Children (SPUC)
www.spuc.org.uk

In 1966, when the act to legalize abortion was being considered in the British parliament, SPUC formed because its members were convinced that the new law would mean abortion on demand. The group failed to prevent its passage but has been active ever since as a "voice for the unborn." SPUC argues that the unborn child has a right to protection guaranteed by the 1959 UN Declaration of Rights of the Child. To advance its cause the organization monitors and lobbies in the British and European parliaments. SPUC also has an education charity called "How You Began." Along with leafleting and talks, they use fetal models showing stages of development to convince people that the fetus is a child. They do not take direct action to picket or blockade abortion clinics.

Women on Waves
http://womenonwaves.org

This Dutch organization's goal is "to prevent unwanted pregnancy and unsafe abortion around the world." It runs informative websites in several languages to talk about contraceptives, abortion access, and news stories about these topics, and it provides a link to online medical abortion services. The organization is probably most famous for its sea voyage campaigns. In these it sends its ship, *Borndiep,* staffed with medical personnel, to a country where abortion is illegal and anchors off shore. Then it runs tenders from shore to the ship and performs medically safe abortions. The ship's presence stirred up much discussion about criminal abortion when it visited Ireland in 2001, and, in 2004, Portugal.

Women's Global Network on Reproductive Rights (WGNRR)
www.wgnrr.nl

This small NGO intends to offer a way to provide support to local groups working on behalf of women's reproductive rights on all continents. It was originally based in Costa Rica but is now working from Amsterdam, The Netherlands. This organization defines reproductive rights as human rights—connected to the global human rights movement—and advocates for access to safe, legal abortion. However, laws do not confer rights on their own without changes in the social, economic, and political conditions that affect the capability of women to enjoy their rights. One of their goals is to establish May 28 as International Day on Women's Health. They claim 2,000 members, mostly in the regions of Latin America and the Caribbean, Asia Pacific, and Africa and the Middle East.

World Population Fund (WPF)
www.wpf.org

The WPF is based in the Netherlands and works at the national (Dutch), European (EU), and international (UN) levels and in developing countries. Their goal is to promote sexual and reproductive health and rights. The group considers that freedom of choice is essential to economic well-being and the end of poverty. Along with alerting networks of activists to threats to sexual and reproductive health and rights, the fund builds and supports NGOs at local levels, especially in the developing countries. They consider it important to increase the number of what they call "stakeholders" in securing and maintaining rights.

8

Resources

Introduction

Because the abortion issue has been on the public agenda for so long, and because it is so contentious, there are more print and nonprint materials than it is possible to keep track of, let alone list in one place. So this list represents those I have found especially useful in my work over the past 30 years following the abortion debates in the United States and internationally. Only a few articles are listed because it is my experience that books give the most complete versions of the various points of view in the debate. Some of the resources are edited volumes that include essays and articles; thus, they seem to be much more useful and accessible than relying on a list of magazine or journal articles. The nonprint sources are also the most well-known DVDs/ videos and websites.

Print Sources

General United States: Books

Belkin, Jack C. *What* Roe v. Wade *Should Have Said*. New York: New York University Press, 2005.

Legal scholars got a chance to change history—hypothetically— by rewriting the decision in *Roe v. Wade*. They were allowed to use their experiences since 1973 but had to rely only on materials available when the justices made the original ruling making abortion legal in the first 6 months of pregnancy. The result is a series of opinions, concurring opinions, and dissenting opinions both for and against the right to abortion.

Blank, Robert, and Janna C. Merrick. *Human Reproduction, Emerging Technologies, and Conflicting Rights.* **Washington, DC: CQ Press, 1995.**

To feminists, the idea of reproductive rights means the ability of women to get sex education, contraception, abortion, and health care as well as the right not to be sterilized. The authors here present a more detailed perspective of the concept of reproductive rights to include the right not to have children, the right to have children, and the right to choose the quality and characteristics of one's children. They then relate these rights to policymaking contexts. New at the time the book was published were the analyses of assisted reproduction and the survey of state policies being developed to regulate the consequences—intended and unintended—of in vitro fertilization, artificial insemination, surrogacy, and the like.

Burns, Gene. *The Moral Veto: Framing Contraception, Abortion, and Cultural Pluralism in the United States.* **Cambridge: Cambridge University Press, 2005.**

For readers interested in an in-depth analysis of the framing processes surrounding abortion debates in the United States, this book is a good choice. It explores frames about abortion and contraception in public debate since the nineteenth century and examines how these frames developed through the policy debates of the twentieth century. The title reflects the author's conceptualization of the significance of framing. The frames of the pro-life movement that express great moral passion make it difficult for the movement actors to obtain their goals. At the same time these frames prevent—that is, veto—the goals proposed by the pro-choice activists. As a result, policy change is stymied.

Butler, J. Douglas, and David F. Walbert, eds. *Abortion, Medicine, and the Law,* **4th ed. New York: Facts on File, 1992.**

For this series on abortion law, the editors selected what they considered to be the most important essays and articles from the fields of law, medicine, and ethics to provide a comprehensive reference work on all aspects of the issue. These essays are still useful for understanding the debate in the 1980s and early 1990s.

Craig, Barbara Hinkson, and David M. O'Brien. *Abortion and American Politics.* **Chatham, NJ: Chatham House Publishers, 1993.**

The purpose of Craig and O'Brien's book is to describe and analyze the impact of abortion controversies on American politics. At the same time, the authors review the events in policymaking, both at the federal and state levels, from the 1970s to the 1990s. Chapters are devoted to interest groups, state politics, Congress, presidential politics, the courts, and public opinion. Three major cases structure the time frame of the descriptions: *Roe v. Wade* in 1973, *Webster v. Reproductive Services* in 1989, and *Planned Parenthood v. Casey* in 1992.

Critchlow, Donald T. *Intended Consequences: Birth Control, Abortion, and the Federal Government in Modern America.* **New York: Oxford University Press, 1999.**

Critchlow is the founding editor of the *Journal of Public History* and brings a historian's eye to the changes in public policy affecting contraception and abortion from the 1950s through the 1990s. The goal is to describe the formation of the federal family planning policy and how the legalization of abortion changed the debate over birth control. Key to the change was the growth of the feminist movement, which moved the issue from the purview of population control experts to the combative movements in the abortion debate.

Garrow, David J. *Liberty and Sexuality: The Right to Privacy and the Making of* **Roe v. Wade. Berkeley: University of California Press, 1994, 1998.**

Here is the definitive legal history of *Roe v. Wade*, the result of meticulous research by Garrow, a professor of law at Emory University. Garrow finds the origins of the decision in the birth control campaigns of Katherine Houghton Hepburn in Connecticut in the early part of the twentieth century. These politics eventually led to the ruling that the decision whether or not to have a child was fundamental and within a zone of constitutional privacy. The book goes on to take the reader step by step through the litigation that resulted in the legalization of abortion and the Supreme Court's rejection of conditional abortion laws. This is an essential resource for anyone following the abortion debate.

Ginsburg, Faye. *Contested Lives: The Abortion Debate in an American Community.* **Berkeley: University of California Press, 1998.**

The abortion clinic in Fargo, North Dakota, is the setting for anthropologist Ginsburg's ethnography of abortion debates. The women's health center in that Plains community has been one of the most embattled in the United States. The study here delves into the narratives of the participants on both sides of the divide and places them in historic context. Like Gorney's 1998 book on a clinic in Missouri, it covers the period of the 1980s.

Gorney, Cynthia. *Articles of Faith: A Frontline History of the Abortion Wars.* **New York: Simon & Schuster, 1998.**

Gorney tells the tale of the conflict over abortion between 1973 and 1989 from the point of view of impassioned advocates on both sides. The scene is an abortion clinic in Missouri, but she relates the events to the broader picture of abortion politics and policy in the nation. The story ends with the decision in *Webster v. Reproductive Services.* For a similar approach see Ginsburg (1998).

Herring, Mark Y. *The Pro-Life/Choice Debate.* **Westport, CT: Greenwood Press, 2003.**

Part of Greenwood's series called Historical Guides to Controversial Issues in America, Herring's book provides an introduction to the debate through a historical survey of major periods. His goal is to offer a nonpartisan approach so the guide will be of use to students and the general public. It includes a bibliography and a list of web sources on the issue.

Hull, N. E. H., Williamjames Hoffer, and Peter Charles Hoffer, eds. *Abortion Rights Controversy in America: A Legal Reader.* **Chapel Hill: University of North Carolina Press, 2004.**

Assembled by three law professors, this book collects primary source documents about the abortion debate beginning in the nineteenth century, including legal briefs, speeches, oral arguments, court opinions, and newspaper articles. Each item has an introduction that places it in a historical context. One item of special interest is an excerpt from a conference among Supreme Court justices in which they discuss their views before deciding the *Roe v. Wade* and *Doe v. Bolton* cases. This book is designed for instructors and students who are exploring the abortion issue.

Levine, Phillip B. *Sex and Consequences: Abortion, Public Policy, and the Economics of Fertility.* **Princeton, NJ: Princeton University Press, 2004.**

Levine wants to step away from what he terms the "ideological extremes" provoked by abortion and bring in the cool rationality of economic modeling. His model predicts that when abortion is initially legalized, the rate of abortions will increase, and the rate of both unwanted births and fertility will decline. However, as access expands, the costs of abortion decrease, contraceptive use declines, and more pregnancies result. Finally, when there are limited restrictions on access to legal abortion, such as administrative hurdles and limits on Medicaid funding, there will be a reduction in abortion demand, thus decreasing the number of abortions without increasing the number of births. People will increase their use of contraceptives when abortion is more costly.

Luker, Kristin. *Abortion and the Politics of Motherhood.* **Berkeley: University of California Press, 1984.**

By the 1980s, the conflict over the abortion issue had arrived at its fully polarized form between the pro-life and pro-choice movements. Luker's classic study of the abortion issue places this debate in a historical context, following the formation of the issue from the early nineteenth century to the early 1980s. The descriptions of her interviews with pro-choice and pro-life activists capture the early days of both movements and provide valuable insights into the perspectives and motivations of the people on both sides.

Maxwell, Carol J. *Pro-Life Activists in America: Meaning, Motive, and Direct Action.* **Cambridge: Cambridge University Press, 2002.**

This book is another example of ethnographic studies of abortion activism, in this case the pro-life supporters who engaged in direct action at clinics. Maxwell interviewed many of them to search for the motives for their activism. She found more diversity than might be expected, and the book details the profound impact their activism had on their lives. This study covers the campaigns in the 1990s.

McDonagh, Eileen L. *Breaking the Abortion Deadlock: From Choice to Consent.* **Oxford: Oxford University Press, 1996.**

In the early 1990s, McDonagh began a campaign to reframe the rationale for legal abortion in a way that would combine the goals of both sides. She argued that advocates for legal abortion should accept the pro-life claim of equal personhood of the fetus. Then, she reasoned that law would support the right of a woman to consent to accept the embryo in her body for gestation and birth and, at the same time, the right to withdraw that consent through terminating the pregnancy. The legal principle is that no person can live off the body of another without her consent. In this book McDonagh elaborates her provocative argument.

McFarlane, Deborah R., and Kenneth J. Meier. *The Politics of Fertility Control: Family Planning and Abortion Policies in the American States.* **New York: Chatham House Publishers, 2001.**

Using techniques of comparative state policy analysis, McFarlane and Meier examine claims that high levels of conflict and more restrictive policies on contraception and abortion are ineffective in addressing high rates of unintended pregnancy and have even contributed to high pregnancy rates. They find that states with lower levels of family planning have higher abortion rates. However, they conclude that with the moral component so important in the debates on fertility control, it is unlikely that workable policies will be developed soon.

Mohr, James C. *Abortion in America: The Origins and Evolution of National Policy, 1800–1900.* **Oxford: Oxford University Press, 1978.**

Probably the first detailed history of the politics and culture of abortion criminalization in the nineteenth century, Mohr's book is an essential source used by all who study the abortion issue in the United States. It is a very interesting read and the book includes some wonderful photographs of abortion ads of the period and newspaper stories of government enforcement of laws. Although out of print, it is available in the used book market and is well worth the search.

Mooney, Christopher Z., ed. *The Public Clash of Private Values: The Politics of Morality Policy.* **New York: Chatham House Publishers, 2001.**

The politic of moral issues is not limited to contraceptives, sex education, and abortion policies. As shown in this edited collection, these issues include gay rights, gambling, death penalty, drugs, and pornography. Readers will find case studies of all of these here, as well as some cross-national studies and a review of Catholic bishops' statements from 1792 to 2000.

Morgen, Sandra. *Into Our Own Hands: The Women's Health Movement in the United States, 1969–1990.* **New Brunswick, NJ: Rutgers University Press, 2002.**

The women's health movement developed at the same time as feminists began demanding legal abortion: both efforts challenged male control over women's health. This book describes the origins of the movement and follows its development, focusing especially on the grassroots efforts through clinics and self-help groups. The movement faced many challenges but can look to the increased funding for women's health initiatives at federal and state levels as real victories.

Olasky, Marvin. *Abortion Rites: A Social History.* **Wheaton, IL: Crossway Books, 1992.**

Journalism professor Olasky explored documentary sources in the Library of Congress to challenge Mohr's view of nineteenth-century history in *Abortion in America* (1978). Mohr claimed that the mid-century increase in abortions included many white, middle-class, Protestant women and was the stimulus for the campaign to criminalize the procedure. Olasky begins his book by making the case that three groups of women—prostitutes, those who had been seduced and abandoned, and the followers of free love (in other words, women who were not respectable)—were the main clients for abortionists. Overall, Olasky's book is more agreeable to pro-life advocates than Mohr's book.

Press, Eyal. *Absolute Convictions: My Father, a City, and the Conflict that Divided America.* **New York: Henry Holt, 2006.**

Press is the son of an abortion doctor who practiced in Buffalo, New York, in the 1970s and 1980s. An antiabortion activist murdered his father's colleague, Barnett Slepian, in 1998, and Press's father was warned he would be next. The author returned to Buffalo to discover the reasons behind such violence and rage and to try to understand the motives of those who had blockaded his father's office for years. The result combines an interesting case study with research on the rise of the evangelical antiabortion movement.

Reagan, Leslie J. *When Abortion Was a Crime: Women, Medicine, and Law in the United States, 1867–1973.* **Berkeley: University of California Press, 1997.**

Historian Reagan combines information about the private life of women with problem pregnancies during the period when criminal abortion laws were in place with descriptions of the public campaigns against abortion and for law reform. An important contribution of this book is to open up the period from the 1900s to the 1960s when most thought the abortion issues was completely dormant. Her book brings to light evidence that the period was anything but silent as far as abortion politics was concerned.

Riddle, John M. *Eve's Herbs: A History of Contraception and Abortion in the West.* **Cambridge, MA: Harvard University Press, 1997.**

This history of medicine shows that women have used herbs to regulate fertility ever since ancient times. Riddle has done the research to uncover these practices and name the herbs. This ancient knowledge has been passed down to women through the years. However, the Catholic Church forbid these practices after the fifteenth century, and condemned practitioners of these arts as witches. Regular medicine then criminalized the use of these herbs through law. Nevertheless, Riddle argues, these herbs are still available and are still used today around the world.

Rubin, Eva. *The Abortion Controversy: A Documentary History.* **Westport, CT: Greenwood, 1994.**

This book contains excerpts from some very interesting documents from the early nineteenth century up to the early 1990s.

Although the book is out of print, it is available through several e-book services on the Internet or at libraries.

Rudy, Kathy. *Beyond Pro-Life and Pro-Choice: Moral Diversity in the Abortion Debate.* **Boston: Beacon Press, 1996.**

Rudy recounts the views of four groups on the abortion debate: liberals, feminists, Roman Catholics, and evangelicals. Given the diversity of the views of these groups, the author considers the current legal doctrine of absolute rights to be part of the problem in settling the issue. What courts provide is an abstract right of abortion to a single individual. What is needed, she claims, is to take account of the circumstances of pregnant women in all their diversity. Let communities work out ways to care for women and provide the conditions for real choice. She recommends the repeal of all abortion laws.

Saletan, William. *Bearing Right: How the Conservatives Won the Abortion War.* **Berkeley: University of California Press, 2003.**

This book delves into the process whereby issues are defined and how these definitions affect outcomes. For his example, Saletan focuses on the alliance between pro-choice activists and antigovernment conservatives in the 1990s. The women's rights frame did nothing but lose support for legal abortion, especially in the South. A particular referendum campaign in Arkansas showed how packaging a pro-choice position in terms of opposition to government interference was successful despite a high percentage of pro-life voters. This led to NARAL's "Who Decides?" campaign, which sought to connect with those who did not want government to interfere in private family decisions. Saletan claims that although the pro-choice movement has saved legal abortion, it has lost the most important power: to define the issue in pro-choice women's rights terms.

Schroedel, Jean Reith. *Is the Fetus a Person? A Comparison of Politics across the Fifty States.* **Ithaca, NY: Cornell University Press, 2000.**

Schroedel explores the emerging issue of fetal personhood in law, politics, and state policymaking. The book begins with a chapter on the history of the concept and how it has changed in English and U.S. law. Chapters on state policymaking follow, covering abortion, prenatal drug exposure, and third-party fetal killings. In these chapters, the author frames the policy alternatives and then summarizes the types of policies in the states. The effect of the issue of fetal personhood on women's abortion rights is central to the analysis in the book.

Segers, Mary C., and Timothy A. Byrnes, eds. *Abortion Politics in American States.* **Armonk, NY: M. E. Sharpe, 1995.**

Despite the media focus on *Roe v. Wade* and national debates about partial-birth abortion, the issue is primarily a state matter and the Constitution charges state legislatures with establishing abortion policy. This book assembles a number of state-focused studies, including studies in Pennsylvania, Massachusetts, and California, where scholars describe their state's involvement with the issue. Most of these studies are still useful because they show the social and political background of a state's approach to the issue, whether the state is pro-life, as is Louisiana, or the state has seen a pro-choice outcome through initiative, as in Washington State.

Shapiro, Ian, ed. *Abortion: The Supreme Court Decisions.* **Indianapolis: Hackett Publishing, 1995.**

Before the expansion of the Internet, many used books like this one as reference sources. It contains abridged versions of the major Supreme Court cases, beginning with *Griswold v. Connecticut* in 1965 through *Planned Parenthood v. Casey* in 1992. Today the full text of all the cases is available on the Internet from sources like Findlaw.com (see nonprint sources). Still, given the length and technical presentation of many of the decisions that come directly from the Court, having the essential parts in a small paperback is still useful.

Staggenborg, Suzanne. *The Pro-Choice Movement: Organization and Activism in the Abortion Conflict.* **New York: Oxford University Press, 1991.**

The author uses social movement theory to study the emergence and activism of the pro-choice movement. The structure and analysis reflects the work's origins as a PhD dissertation. The author conducted interviews with many activists in the movement in national organizations as well as with those in state and local activities, mostly in Illinois. The research shows the different ways the movement gained access to policymakers. Staggenborg counters the media claims that the pro-choice movement was dormant during the 1980s, yielding the ground to pro-life activists. What was important, she claims, was that when needed, as in response to the *Webster* decision, movement leaders could rally grass roots activists to wage effective campaigns.

Tribe, Laurence H. *Abortion: The Clash of Absolutes*. New York: W.W. Norton, 1990.

With his title and his book, legal expert Tribe, professor of law at Harvard Law School, gave a cogent name to the nature of the abortion debate in the United States—that it is a battle between beliefs that defy compromise. The book appeared in the wake of the controversy over the *Webster* decision where some justices invited challenges to legal abortion. Using his knowledge of jurisprudence, Tribe considers this divide, beginning with a historical and world context and then delving into the claims about the law coming from both sides. His discussion of rights to privacy and personhood in constitutional law are especially compelling. He concludes that both sides can find common ground: "If advocates on both sides of the abortion debate would just pause, they would recognize at least one broadly shared interest, that of working toward a world of only wanted pregnancies. Better education, the provision of contraception, indeed the creation of a society in which the burden of raising a child is lighter are all achievable goals that are lost in the shouting about abortion" (p. 228).

General United States: Plays

Heffron, Elizabeth. *Mitzi's Abortion*. Seattle, WA: ACT Theatre, 2003.

Playwright Heffron struggled with the title for her play because the term *abortion* has become such a controversial word in the midst of the polarizing pro-life/pro-choice debate. But, she reasoned, if one can't speak about something there will be great difficulty in finding closure. Her play tells the story of one woman's experience with a problem pregnancy and her struggle to make the right choice. All the arguments about abortion find a place in the words of one or another of the characters. The conclusion is that, like any life experience, the experience of problem pregnancy is personal, and neither wholly positive or wholly negative.

General World and Comparative Studies: Books

David, Henry P., ed., with assistance of Joanna Skilogianis. *From Abortion to Contraception: A Resource to Public Policies and Reproductive Behavior in Central and Eastern Europe from 1917 to the Present.* Westport, CT: Greenwood Press, 1999.

Using a common framework, experts on policy and demography in Central and Eastern European countries from Albania to Yugoslavia describe fertility behavior, family and abortion policies, and "the woman question." The book is, thus, a detailed reference work. The first chapters place the country reports in general context and pay special attention to what the authors call the "abortion culture" in the region.

Ferree, Myra Marx, William Anthony Gamson, Jürgen Gerhards, and Dieter Rucht. *Shaping Abortion Discourse: Democracy and the Public Sphere in Germany and the United States.* Cambridge: Cambridge University Press, 2002.

In the late 1990s, the authors conducted a large and complex study to describe, analyze, and compare the public discourse on abortion in the United States and Germany. They created a database of newspaper articles from the two countries and used content analysis to uncover the form and substance of the debates. This approach also enabled them to compare constitutional and political patterns. They found, among other things, that abortion has historically been a gendered issue in Germany while it has more likely been framed in medical terms in the United States.

Githens, Marianne, and Dorothy McBride Stetson, eds. *Abortion Politics: Public Policy in Cross-Cultural Perspective.* New York: Routledge, 1996.

This book brings together distinguished scholars of abortion politics in comparative contexts and yields some interesting studies that remain timely. Examples include the "stability of compromise" in Western Europe, the pressures of European Union membership on restrictions in Ireland, and feminist perspectives on abortion and reproductive technologies.

Haussman, Melissa. *Abortion Politics in North America.* **Boulder, CO: Lynn Rienner, 2005.**

It is unusual to find a study of policy that compares Mexico with the United States and Canada, but the politics surrounding the North American Free Trade Agreement encouraged Haussman to look beneath the surface to find a common framework from which to analyze the differences. There are two similarities: all have federal constitutions and all face a paradox between the law on the books and the law in practice. In addition, access to abortion services is increasingly limited in all three countries.

Htun, Mala. *Sex and the State: Abortion, Divorce, and the Family under Latin American Dictatorships and Democracies.* **Cambridge: Cambridge University Press, 2003.**

This book focuses on policies in Argentina, Brazil, and Chile during the last third of the twentieth century. Forces of democratization and modernization were in play, energizing new political voices, such as feminists and other social groups. The states responded with some gender-related policy reform but uniformly rejected any attempt to change criminal abortion laws. The answers to the puzzle are complex, but the key is the growing influence of the Catholic Church on social policy. The book is based on historical research and many interviews with policy activists, religious leaders, and academics.

Kulczycki, Andrzej. *The Abortion Debate in the World Arena.* **New York: Routledge, 1999.**

The title promises a more global perspective than what the book actually delivers: three case studies of the abortion debate in Poland, Kenya, and Mexico. The case studies provide alternative views of the issue from the non-Western perspective; as the author points out, sometimes the conflict is hidden, even unspoken, in places where there are no concepts or vocabulary to describe abortion as a public problem. Information about the Kenyan case is especially useful because few studies of abortion politics in Africa are available.

Latham, Melanie. *Regulating Reproduction: A Century of Conflict in Britain and France.* Manchester, UK: Manchester University Press, 2002.

This book provides a very useful and comprehensive source of information about reproduction law and politics in two European countries. The book is organized according to the three component issues: contraception, abortion, and assisted conception. For each, a chapter describes the parallel development of law in the UK and France since the early 1900s. In all these chapters on law the author focuses on the different aspects of the common law/statute law legal system in Britain and the code/civil law system in France to explain variations in the patterns of change and the content of the laws. Each of these law chapters is followed by a chapter that details the policy conflicts and interest-group politics related to the development of the statutes and case law in the two countries.

Lee, Ellie, ed. *Abortion Law and Politics Today.* New York: St. Martin's Press, 1998.

The first part of this book is a collection of articles on abortion politics in Great Britain, including an interesting memoir of the 1960s by Madeleine Simms, one of the leaders behind campaign for abortion law reform. The second part of the book puts British policy in a larger context with discussions on Ireland, Poland, the United States, and France. Finally, the book ends with articles on newer issues such as reproductive technology and men's rights.

McBride Stetson, Dorothy, ed. and contributing author. *Abortion Politics, Women's Movements and the Democratic State: A Comparative Study of State Feminism.* Oxford: Oxford University Press, 2001.

This book is both a collection of case studies of the development of abortion politics in Western Europe and North America as well as a comparative research project on the influence of women's movements and women's policy agencies on abortion policies. No other work covers the sweep of movement activism and policy outcomes among the Western democracies. The studies reveal the complex paths policy actors have taken to come to similar outcomes, that is, the legalization of abortion in the first weeks of pregnancy. The exception is Ireland, where the dominant culture makes feminists reluctant to campaign on the issue and instead accept the "escape route" to England.

Rolston, Bill, and Anna Eggert, eds. *Abortion in the New Europe: A Comparative Handbook.* **Westport, CT: Greenwood Press, 1994.**

In this collection, the "new Europe" refers to the effect of the end of Soviet domination over parts of the continent and the recognition of the potential "Europeanness" of Russia, Poland, Hungary, and the Czech and Slovak Republics. Along with Western European countries, each rates a separate chapter in this book prepared according to a common outline: history of abortion law, current abortion law and practice, and future debates. The book remains a useful reference for tracking down policies in individual countries.

Tatalovich, Raymond. *The Politics of Abortion in the United Sates and Canada: A Comparative History.* **Armonk, NY: M. E. Sharpe, 1997.**

Tatalovich has published widely on moral debates in the United States and Canada, but this is his most in-depth analysis of an issue in the two countries. It places the highly divisive American debate in perspective and shows the effects of institutional similarities—federalism—and differences—parliamentarism versus presidentialism—on the abortion policy and its implementation in the two countries.

United Nations Department of Economic and Social Affairs. Population Division. *Abortion Politics: A Global Review.* **Volumes I–III. New York: United Nations, 2001.**

This three-volume series provides nuggets on all the countries in the United Nations, listing the grounds on which abortion is permitted, data on reproductive health in the country, and a description of the background for the abortion policy and politics. These useful guides are also available on the United Nations website: www.un.org/esa/population/publications/abortion/.

General World and Comparative Studies: Articles

Yishai, Yael. "Public Ideas and Public Policy: Abortion Politics in Four Democracies." *Comparative Politics* 25 (1993): 207–228.

This is one of the first systematic comparative studies of abortion politics and policy. The democracies included are the United States, Ireland, Sweden, and Israel. Yishai questions what the pattern of abortion politics has to say about the status of women in a country. The answer is very little. Despite women's movement activism, the official definitions of abortion policies rely on traditional public ideas: individualism in the United States, Catholic doctrine in Ireland, the welfare state in Sweden, and demographic constraints in Israel.

Pro-Choice Books

Baer, Judith. *Historical and Multicultural Encyclopedia of Women's Reproductive Rights in the United States.* Westport, CT: Greenwood Press, 2002.

Want a book that will provide not only a definition but an analysis of just about every legal and political term you can imagine pertaining to reproductive issues? Want it from a feminist perspective? Then this is an excellent reference work. From undue burden standard to fetal protection policies to the squeal rule, you'll find it here. Baer recruited a large number of experts to contribute entries, giving the encyclopedia a solid scholarly foundation.

Baird-Windle, Patricia, and Eleanor J. Bader. *Targets of Hatred: Anti-Abortion Terrorism.* New York: Palgrave, 2001.

The goal of this work is to raise the press and the public's awareness that terrorism in the United States is not limited to Timothy McVeigh and the attacks of September 11, 2001. It reads like a documented diary of the threats and violence abortion providers have experienced since the 1960s. Here is a typical entry: "December 28, 1991: Springfield Missouri: A man in a ski mask walked into the Central Health Center for Women and asked to see a doctor. When he was told that the physician had already gone for the day, the man pulled out a sawed-off shotgun and fired it. He seriously wounded the clinic receptionist and the owner of the building. The gunman was not apprehended, and the clinic closed its doors in early 1992. The pair were the first victims of an abortion-related shooting" (p. 167)

Dombrowski, Daniel A., and Robert Deltete. *A Brief, Liberal, Catholic Defense of Abortion.* **Urbana: University of Illinois Press, 2000.**

The authors review Catholic thought from the time of Augustine and Thomas Aquinas, showing that the current official Catholic view on abortion does not have an ancient history. In fact, neither of these philosophers considered the embryo to be a person. Today's restrictive Catholic doctrine was established only in the seventeenth century. The authors go on to show that the Catholic Church's view that moral sexual relations occur only for procreation within marriage is too narrow and has devastating negative consequences for people's lives.

Ehrlich, J. Shoshanna. *Who Decides? The Abortion Rights of Teens.* **Westport, CT: Praeger, 2006.**

Relatively little has been written on the effects of parental involvement laws that the Supreme Court has ruled are constitutional. This book explores the development of these rules and their effects on the lives of young women. Ehrlich studied the stories of twenty-six women to reveal the burdens of these laws on their lives and choices.

Feldt, Gloria. *The War on Choice: The Right-Wing Attack on Women's Rights and How to Fight Back.* **New York: Bantam Books, 2004.**

In the introduction to this book, Sally Blackmun, the daughter of Justice Harry Blackmun, recalls what life was like at home when her father was making his historic decision in *Roe v. Wade*. The body of the book, is faithful to the promises in the title; each chapter describes the status of an area of reproductive policy with bullet points to make the message easy to understand. Topics include restrictions on abortion, family planning, sex education and abstinence, fetal personhood, right wing attacks on science, and the fate of legal abortion.

Hadley, Janet. *Abortion: Between Freedom and Necessity.* **Philadelphia: Temple University Press, 1996.**

The goal here is to look beneath the abortion wars to see how women's lives are affected. The first chapters look at countries where the debates over legal abortion remain contentious: the United States, Ireland, and Germany. The author then expands her lens to cover prenatal diagnosis and sex selection in India, China, and Britain, and the relation of contraception to abortion in Russia, Holland, and Britain. She answers critics who say abortion is immoral and makes the case that the right to abortion is really about women's rights to reproductive health.

Joffe, Carol. *Doctors of Conscience: The Struggle to Provide Abortion Before and After* **Roe v. Wade. Boston: Beacon Press, 1995.**

The motivation for this study was to counter the image of those who practiced abortion before it was legalized as "butchers." Joffe set out to interview doctors and others who helped women get abortions and found that the practitioners were largely motivated by their personal experience with the horrible effects of botched abortions. They tried to help women because they believed it was right, despite the risks of arrest and imprisonment. She also found that the stresses on abortion providers were only slightly lessened after abortion became legal because of the continued portrayal of abortion doctors as "baby killers," even by medical colleagues.

Kaplan, Laura. *The Story of Jane: The Legendary Underground Feminist Abortion Services.* **New York: Pantheon Books, 1995.**

From 1969 to 1973, a group of Chicago women developed an informal network to help women in need of abortions. At first they handled referrals to willing doctors, but word soon spread and the demand grew. Eventually, despite the law, they learned to perform the procedure themselves. They also provided counseling to women using the service. This is their story as told by one of the members of the network.

Lader, Lawrence. *Abortion.* **Boston: Beacon Press, 1966.**

Like its author, this book played an important part in the abortion reform movement. Through his investigative research, Lader revealed the extent to which women sought abortions and doctors performed them, despite the restrictive criminal laws. Even more important was the evidence of the large number of illegal abortions that threatened women's health. With the study, Lader provided the evidence of the need to reform these laws.

Lader, Lawrence. *Abortion II: Making the Revolution.* **Boston: Beacon Press, 1973.**

Abortion II is Lader's story of his experience with the abortion reform/repeal movement. It was written in the wake of the *Roe v. Wade* decision, which he saw as a victory for those demanding a radical rejection of both the Catholic Church and the medical bureaucracies. The book did not foresee the backlash against the movement and the rise of the pro-life forces that stopped Lader's "revolution" in its tracks.

Maguire, Daniel C. *Sacred Choices: The Right to Contraception and Abortion in Ten World Religions.* **Minneapolis: Fortress Press, 2001.**

For those in the pro-choice movement who consider religion their enemy, Maguire finds pro-choice sympathies in all of the world's religions alongside the antiabortion and anti–family planning beliefs. Pro-life Catholics are especially critical of Maguire's work as it challenges the official doctrine and provides support for groups such as Catholics for Choice. His main point is that beliefs in most religions are pluralistic, not absolute, and one does not have to reject one's faith altogether to support the goals of abortion rights.

Mason, Carol. *Killing for Life: The Apocalyptic Narrative of Pro-Life Politics.* **Ithaca, NY: Cornell University Press, 2002.**

Mason analyzes narratives that arose from the militants in the pro-life movement in the 1990s and into the anthrax scares of 2001. Rather than the fringe ranting of a few dispossessed criminals, the author makes the case that the narrative is the culmination of a 30-year expansion of right wing thought that claims American moral society is under threat from forces of evil, in fact, following the steps toward Armageddon as predicted in the Bible. The antiabortion warrior depicted is male, Christian, and white.

Michelman, Kate. *With Liberty and Justice for All: A Life Spent Protecting the Right to Choose.* **New York: Hudson Street Press, 2005.**

Michelman combines her personal biography with her political activism as long-time president of NARAL Pro-Choice America. It begins with the story of her own abortion back in the pre-*Roe* days, which required the consent of a hospital board of men as well as the husband who had recently abandoned her and her three daughters. She describes her role and her views of the politics of pro-choice campaigns from 1985 to 2004. The book provides a useful record of NARAL's place in the pro-choice movement.

Nelson, Jennifer. *Women of Color and the Reproductive Rights Movement.* **New York: New York University Press, 2003.**

Many who want to know "what were minority women doing during the abortion debates?" turn to Nelson's study of the campaign for legal abortion. It covers activism by women of color beginning in the 1960s. Nelson documents the success of these activists in expanding the campaign from a narrow idea of abortion rights held by women's liberation and other mainstream feminist groups to addressing a broad spectrum of reproductive rights, including sterilization, child care, health care, and poverty.

Page, Cristina. *How the Pro-Choice Movement Saved America: Freedom, Politics, and the War on Sex.* **New York: Basic Books, 2006.**

Page claims to uncover a covert war by the pro-life movement against sex education, birth control, and in fact sexual freedom itself. The effect of its campaign is to increase, not decrease, the number of abortions by making it impossible for women to prevent unplanned pregnancies. Thus, to Page, who is a top official with NARAL Pro-Choice America, the abortion wars are not about women's privacy versus the unborn; the war is on sex itself, that is, any sexual behavior that is not within heterosexual marriage and for the purposes of procreation. Her conclusion is that the pro-choice movement is doing the most to reduce abortions.

Petchesky, Rosalind Pollack. *Abortion and Woman's Choice: The State, Sexuality, and Reproductive Freedom.* **Boston: Northeastern University Press, 1984.**

Socialist feminism is not popular among feminist writers in the 2000s, so Petchesky's analysis of the abortion issue in the early 1980s using a socialist feminist perspective is especially interesting. The success of the pro-life attack on abortion rights prompted her to write the book, in which she defends women's need for safe, legal abortion and develops a theory of social relations and reproduction. Her approach is based on the assumption that historical and cultural conditions shape ideas; the book traces the abortion debate from the nineteenth century to the 1980s. Her arguments presage contemporary arguments that feminists must claim the moral argument for women's rights.

Powers, Meghan, ed. *The Abortion Rights Movement.* **Detroit: Greenhaven/Thomson/Gale, 2006.**

Part of the American Social Movements series, this book uses speeches and articles by activists and academics to describe the origins, goals, strategies, and outcomes of the abortion rights movement. Included are writings by Margaret Sanger, Betty Friedan, and Gloria Feldt among others.

Sanger, Alexander. *Beyond Choice: Reproductive Freedom in the 21st Century.* **New York: Public Affairs Press, 2004.**

The grandson of Margaret Sanger takes a page from the ideology of the family planning movement to offer a solution to the divisive abortion debate: people should and will make decisions to improve the chances for raising healthy children to adulthood. Pro-choice ideas ignore the moral dimension of these decisions, while the pro-life approach ignores the family well-being dimension. Sanger's goal is to frame the matter of reproductive freedom to show contraception and abortion as moral choices because without them parents will not be able to reproduce the next healthy generation. Only individuals, not the government, can decide whether they should become parents, so a pregnant woman who does not have the will to be a parent is making a moral choice by terminating a pregnancy. Sanger makes a provocative argument for a new way of looking at the debate.

Schrage, Laurie. *Abortion and Social Responsibility: Depolarizing the Debate.* **Oxford: Oxford University Press, 2003.**

The solution to the polarization of the abortion debates, according to philosophy professor Schrage, is to reframe the debate to bring in the moral issues and the social conditions that influence women's lives. She lays blame on the frame of debate left by the *Roe v. Wade* court—abortion on demand for the first 6 months of pregnancy—which inflamed divisions on the issue rather than healed them. The pro-life side has dominated not only the debate but also the images of the debate, and the author suggests that it is time for feminists to retake this territory, that is, "to move out of the journals and museums and into newspapers, bus terminals, the internet, film and TV" (p. 130). The author includes many illustrations of feminist artwork and makes concrete suggestions, such as limiting the time for nontherapeutic abortions along with removing administrative and funding hurdles.

Silliman, Jael, Marlene Gerber Fried, Loretta Ross, and Elena R. Gutiérrez. *Undivided Rights: Women of Color Organize for Reproductive Justice*. Cambridge, MA: Southend Press, 2004.

Like Nelson's 2003 book, *Undivided Rights* documents the role of women of color in developing what the authors call "reproductive justice." The material is organized according to organizations and their activities, such as the National Black Women's Health Project, and the health organizations for Asian, Native American, and Latina women.

Solinger, Rickie, ed. *Abortion Wars: A Half Century of Struggle, 1950–2000*. Berkeley: University of California Press, 1998.

Solinger has brought together eighteen articles that look at parts of the abortion debate. Many of these are written by those who participated in the events, such as the description of *Jane*, the feminist clandestine abortion network, while others are more scholarly works. All examine abortion politics from a feminist perspective.

Pro-Choice Article

Thomson, Judith Jarvis. "A Defense of Abortion." *Philosophy and Public Affairs* 1 (1971): 47–66.

This controversial essay is a classic logical argument in favor of legal abortion or, more accurately, against the denial of all abortion. In it, Thomson responds to the difficulties in drawing a line during pregnancy before which it is okay to kill a fetus because it is not yet a person or a human being but after which it is not okay. Instead, she grants that the embryo is a person and then analyzes the problems related to its "right to life." Does agreeing that a fetus is a person mean abortion is always wrong? Does a fetus have the right to occupy and threaten the life of another without consent? To make her case she says, imagine "you wake up in the morning and find yourself back to back in bed with an unconscious violinist. A famous unconscious violinist. He has been found to have a fatal kidney ailment, and the Society of Music Lovers has canvassed all the available medical records and found that you alone have the right blood type to help. They have therefore kidnapped you, and last night the violinist's circulatory system was plugged into yours, so that your kidneys can be used to extract poisons from his blood as well as your own. The director of the hospital now tells you, "Look, we're sorry the Society of Music Lovers did this to you—we would never have permitted it if we had known. But still, they did it, and the violinist is now plugged into you. To unplug you would be to kill him. But never mind, it's only for nine months." The question is whether you would have to accept this or could deny the use of your body to save the violinist. She goes on to conclude that a woman can defend her life against the threat posed by an unborn child. McDonagh picks up this argument in her book *Breaking the Abortion Deadlock: From Choice to Consent.*

Pro-Life Books

Bachiochi, Erica, ed. *The Cost of Choice: Women Evaluate the Impact of Abortion.* **San Francisco: Encounter Books, 2004.**

The authors of the twelve essays in this book have one theme: legal abortion has harmed women socially, medically, psychologically, and culturally. This harm began with *Roe v. Wade* and *Doe v. Bolton,* which struck down laws that balanced the life of the unborn with the rights of women. The problems have been furthered by the feminist pro-choice idea that abortion constitutes a form of emancipation for women. These laws and ideas have robbed women of support from the culture for bearing and rearing children. One article promises to show the relationship of breast cancer to abortion. Most of the authors in this book are well-known critics of contemporary feminism, for example, Mary Ann Glendon and Elizabeth Fox-Genovese.

Baird, Robert M., and Stuart E. Rosenbaum, eds. *The Ethics of Abortion: Pro-Life vs. Pro-Choice,* 3rd ed. Amherst, NY: Prometheus Books, 2001.

Although the title suggests a balanced presentation of views on the abortion debate, the articles in this book are overwhelmingly in support of the pro-life position. Even the articles by feminists are pro-life. Designed as a textbook, the articles are all reprinted from journals and newspapers. The authors are professors of philosophy at Baylor University, a department that focuses on a pro-life moral philosophy.

Beckwith, Francis J. *Politically Correct Death: Answering Arguments for Abortion Rights.* Grand Rapids, MI: Baker Books, 1994.

From the perspective of logic and not religion, Beckwith offers an argument against abortion based on "moral reasoning." To the author, the pro-life side has failed to convince the public that the issue is not a matter of religious belief, but instead it is a matter of absolute and defensible truth. Following are the essential parts of the argument:

1. "the unborn entity, from the moment of conception is fully human;
2. it is prima facie wrong to kill an entity which is fully human;
3. almost every act of abortion is intended to kill the unborn entity, which is fully human;
4. therefore almost every act of abortion is prima facie wrong" (p. 12)

The logic is impeccable if one accepts the assumption that the fertilized egg is "fully human." This assumption is a matter of belief, and disagreement about that belief is the source of most abortion conflicts. Thus, although Beckwith valiantly takes on all pro-choice arguments, he does not provide evidence that would convince everyone of the truth of his arguments.

Critchlow, Donald. *Phyllis Schlafly and Grassroots Conservatism: A Woman's Crusade.* Princeton, NJ: Princeton University Press, 2005

This biography of the founder of Eagle Forum is included here not because it focuses on the abortion issue, but because it tells how Schlafly and her colleagues mobilized activists for conservative causes, beginning with her campaign against the equal rights amendment in the 1970s. Her political biography shows the shift the Republican Party made toward the right, beginning with the presidential nomination of Barry Goldwater in 1964 and culminating with the election of President Ronald Reagan in 1980. This shift brought the pro-life movement to a powerful place in the nation's party politics.

Dyer, Frederick. *Physicians' Crusade Against Abortion.* Sagamore Beach, MA: Science History Publishers, 2005,

In 1996, Dyer published a detailed biography of the life and work of Dr. Horatio Robinson Storer. In this 2005 book he focuses more directly on Storer's role as lead advocate for criminalizing abortion in the nineteenth century. The book is presented as a challenge to assumptions that the people in the nineteenth century wanted abortions to be illegal because they were dangerous to women or because doctors wanted to drive "irregulars" who performed them out of business. This book makes the case that the primary reason was the protection and defense of the unborn children. Thus, pro-life advocates today can show that their crusade has strong roots in American history.

Hendershott, Anne. *The Politics of Abortion.* New York: Encounter Books, 2006.

Although the author claims that this book is a scholarly study of the abortion debate, it turns out to be highly critical of pro-choice positions on the issue and sympathetic to the pro-life argument. The presentation is based on the assumption that the *Roe* decision polarized the abortion debate, denying pro-life advocates a public hearing in legislatures and sparked a cultural divide that has lasted for over 30 years. The author devotes several chapters to showing the success of pro-life Catholic activists in regaining control of the abortion debate.

Kreeft, Peter. *Three Approaches to Abortion: A Thoughtful and Compassionate Guide to Today's Most Controversial Issue.* **San Francisco: Ignatius Press, 2002.**

This is one of several books by professors of philosophy attempting to argue one or the other side of the abortion debate with logic, not emotion. At the same time, the first pro-life essay starts with an assumption (as all pro-life arguments based on logic do) that we know what a human being is, just as we know what an apple is, and from there the case against abortion follows. The second essay tries to explain pro-life motives to pro-choice people while the third is a script of a debate as imagined by a pro-life philosopher.

Nathanson, Bernard. *Aborting America.* **New York: Doubleday, 1979.**

In this book, Nathanson, the former clinic director and founder of NARAL, described his rebirth as a Christian and pro-life advocate. He also told his story about his life as an advocate for legal abortion in the 1960s. This book is oft quoted by pro-life activists, especially the author's confession that pro-choice people made up statistics to make their case, in particular claiming that thousands of women died because of backstreet illegal abortions. The danger to women's health of illegal abortion was fundamental to the pro-choice case and, according to this author, it was all based on a lie. Nathanson went on to produce the film *Silent Scream.*

Ramesh, Ponnuru. *The Party of Death: The Democrats, the Media, the Courts, and the Disregard for Human Life.* **Washington, DC: Regnery Publishing, 2006.**

Ramesh, senior editor of the conservative *National Review* magazine, selected a provocative title for his book describing how the Democratic Party went from being primarily a pro-life party to being a pro-choice party. He warns that abortion was the means by which left-wing radicals took over the party, and now they want to add euthanasia and embryo destruction to their agenda. As a result, rights of humans will apply to a smaller and smaller group while many of these radicals support animal rights. He names Hillary Rodham Clinton as the most dangerous Democrat in her campaign to bring the "party of death" to the White House.

Reagan, Ronald. *Abortion and the Conscience of the Nation.* **Sacramento, CA: New Regency Publishing, 2000.**

In this essay, originally published in 1983 to mark the tenth anniversary of *Roe v. Wade,* President Reagan uses this medium to denounce the decision to allow "abortion on demand through nine months of pregnancy" (p. 37) and to call the pro-life faithful to action. He states that the question is not when human life begins, but: "What is the value of human life?" He uses the language of equality to argue for the rights of the unborn and endorses the human life amendment and human life bill then under discussion in Congress. The Introduction is written by Wanda Franz, president of the National Right to Life Committee.

Scheidler, Joseph M. *Closed: 99 Ways to Stop Abortion,* **rev. ed. Rockford, IL: Tan Books and Publishers, 1993.**

This book is a guide to tactics for the pro-life true believer, that is, the ordinary individual who, convinced that abortion is the same as murder, wants to act to stop every single such "murder." Scheidler, the founder of the Pro-Life Action League, describes ninety-nine nonviolent actions. The first is sidewalk counseling—"a method of saving babies by talking to their parents in front of the abortion clinic" (p. 19). The book describes each action, such as leafleting, getting the story to the press, getting on talk shows, exposing abortionist lies, and filing counter charges for false arrest, along with organization contacts and other resources.

Wagner, Teresa, ed. *Back to the Drawing Board: The Future of the Pro-Life Movement.* **South Bend, IN: St. Augustine Press, 2003.**

The editor of this book served for years as a lobbyist for the National Right to Life Committee, so she was in a central place to collect a series of essays from pro-life leaders for this book. The purpose is to assess the status of the movement 30 years after *Roe v. Wade.* Included are writings by James Dobson, Congressman Chris Smith (R-NJ), Phyllis Schlafly, and Paul Weyrich. They and others provide food for thought for the next generation of pro-life leaders.

Nonprint Sources

Video/DVD

Abort73.com. Laxafamosity Ministries, 2003. http://abort73.com.

Mike Spielman and his group have established the website and the video that is available there to make a case against abortion. Although they have fundamentalist principles, they base their case on secular evidence, not religious belief. That evidence consists of graphic photos of aborted fetuses from 7 to 24 weeks. Spielman and his group say that millions of children are dying by a brutal act of violence and invite viewers to look at the video. They also warn of the graphic nature of the pictures.

Abortion Denied: Shattering Young Women's Lives. Feminist Majority Foundation, 1990. www.feminist.org

Feminist Majority founder Eleanor Smeal cowrote this video, which aims to show that parental consent and notification laws discourage teens from getting help when they are pregnant. It tells the story of Becky Bell and her parents; Bell had been so reluctant to tell her parents she was pregnant that she fled to another state for an illegal abortion and died as a result. This video was shown on TV in 1990 and is available today primarily in libraries.

Abortion for Survival. Feminist Majority Foundation, 1989. www.feminist.org.

This video makes the case for legal abortion. It begins by showing a woman comfortable and confident before, during, and after a vacuum aspiration abortion at 6 weeks. The film goes on to contrast the status of women under legal abortion and illegal abortion, first through conversations with doctors who experienced both in the United States. and then by comparing the situation in countries with criminal abortion laws, for example, Brazil. The video is currently available at the Feminist Majority website.

Can I Live? Cannon, Nick. 2005. www.nickcannon.com.

In this music video, rap singer Nick Cannon's song tells the story of his mother's decision not to have an abortion when she was pregnant with him, at age 17. The music video portrays Cannon trying to persuade his mother not to have the abortion, as she comes to an abortion clinic in 1979. After the ultrasound shows her unborn child, Cannon's mother leaves the clinic and decides to have her baby. At the end of the song, Cannon thanks his mother for letting him live. Cannon sells "Can I Live?" T-shirts on his website.

Cider House Rules. **Miramax Home Entertainment, 1999.**

This movie is based on the novel by John Irving. It tells the story of a young man raised in an orphanage in the backwoods of Maine. His surrogate father is the chief doctor who performs abortions illegally on pregnant women in distress and passes on his knowledge to his protégé. He believes he is doing the Lord's work by helping desperate young women. However, his "son" believes it is immoral. When he glimpses another, more prosperous life, he leaves the orphanage, but is called upon to perform an abortion himself. Eventually he returns to the orphanage as director.

If These Walls Could Talk. **Home Box Office, 1996.**

Using the stories of three women—in 1952, 1974, and 1996—this film strongly portrays the complex interplay between the realities of women with unintended pregnancies and the social and legal environments that constrain them. The first episode shows the frustration and moral condemnation of a widow and the danger of clandestine abortion. In the third story, the woman's confusion grows in the context of threatening pro-life blockades at legal clinics. Only in the second does the woman face a choice that she could exercise without violence, although the effects of that choice on her family and her own life are very serious. The video is available for purchase.

The Last Abortion Clinic. **Public Broadcasting System, 2005. www.pbs.org.**

In the summer of 2005, documentary filmmakers spent several months in southern states examining the pro-life/pro-choice debate. They found that since the ruling in *Planned Parenthood v. Casey,* pro-life activists have taken advantage of the "undue burden" standard to press state legislatures to pass restrictions. They have been quite successful in the South, especially in Mississippi, which has enacted ten laws since 1992: fetal homicide prosecution, new clinic regulations, requirements to report abortion complications, rights of conscience, and a law that would prohibit the state's last abortion clinic from offering abortions beyond the first trimester. The effect is that abortion is legal but very difficult and expensive to get. This video is available for viewing on the PBS website.

A Private Matter. **HBO Productions, 1992.**

Based on the true story of Sherri Finkbine, this film portrays the media frenzy that followed the Romper Room host as she sought an abortion in 1962. Sissy Spacek stars as Sherri with Aidan Quinn as her husband. The two face the uproar that followed their realization that their fourth child would likely be horribly deformed by thalidomide. The story traces the Finkbines' ordeal all the way to Sweden where the abortion was finally performed after being denied in U.S. hospitals. Available through used video outlets.

The Silent Scream. **American Portrait Films, 1984. www.amport .com**

Widely available today for download or purchase, this video has been very important for the pro-life movement. In it, Dr. Bernard Nathanson narrates scenes portraying an abortion on an 11-week-old fetus, as seen on an ultrasound screen. The makers of the film claim that it demonstrates, unequivocally, the humanity of the fetus. Pro-choice activists charge that it is the Nathanson pro-life narration, not the images, that persuades the viewers they have witnessed an abortion where the fetus fights back. Available at www.silentscream.org/.

Turning Points in the Debate on Abortion and Birth Control. **CBS Reports, 1965.**

This historic documentary focuses on the legal, moral, social, and psychological aspects of abortion in the United States. Narrated by Walter Cronkite, it includes interviews with clergy, lawyers, and physicians and provides a glimpse of the campaign for legalization of abortion before it became a feminist issue. May be available in public and college libraries.

Vera Drake. New Homeline Video, 2005.

British actress Imelda Staunton was nominated for an Academy Award for her role in this film by Mike Leigh. Vera Drake is a middle-aged cleaning lady in 1950's London. She devotes herself to her family and visits shut-ins and invalids. She also readily helps young women with unwanted pregnancies by performing abortions despite strict criminal laws. The film evokes a way of life, a wife and mother, a family, and the destruction that ensues when the police show up.

When Abortion Was Illegal: Untold Stories. Concentric Media, 1992. www.concentric.org/projects/when.html.

Before *Roe v. Wade* legalized abortion, there was an aura of shame around anyone having anything to do with the procedure. Women, especially, were afraid to speak about their experiences and their hardships. This award-winning documentary provides an oral history of an unknown era. Women, many for the first time, talk about their experiences. There is also testimony from doctors, heath care workers, family, and friends.

Internet Sources

Centers for Disease Control and Prevention. Abortion Surveillance Report. www.cdc.gov/mmwr/.

This federal agency collects data on abortion rates and characteristics of women who get abortions from health departments in the states. They publish a surveillance report on the website of the *Morbidity and Mortality Weekly Report* (MMWR). Because some states do not report and others may not have accurate data, the Centers for Disease Control and Prevention data should be compared with Guttmacher reports.

Findlaw for Legal Professionals. www.findlaw.com/casecode/.com.

Although it takes a little practice, most readers will be able to use this website to find and download cases decided by the Supreme Court as well as the circuit courts. There are also links to the U.S. Code, the Code of Federal Regulations, and laws for every state.

Guttmacher Institute. **www.guttmacher.org.**

This is the premier source for data on practices relating to sexual and reproductive health matters, including abortion, birth control, HIV/AIDS, and pregnancy in the United States and internationally. The Institute staff collects and makes available to the public statistics as well as information on laws in all the states and in other countries. A page allows users to make tables from Guttmacher Institute data. In addition, articles from the Institute's three journals can be downloaded.

Human Life Review. **www.humanlifereview.com/.**

For those interested in scholarly writing from a pro-life perspective, this journal makes its articles available online. The journal's primary concern is abortion, but it also publishes articles dealing with family, moral relativism and its effects, and "what the 'abortion mentality' has done to our culture."

I'm Not Sorry. **www.imnotsorry.net/.**

This website posts stories from women who have had abortions. Most of the women are positive about the experience they relate and the relief they felt after it was over. The site was started by a Virginia woman in 2003. It also has a news update section and a guestbook where people can rate the site.

Kaiser Family Foundation. **http://kaisernetwork.org**

Kaisernetwork.org is a project of the Kaiser Family Foundation to provide up-to-date information on health policy and politics. One of the topics it monitors is women's health policy, where there are news stories on such matters as abortion rights, pregnancy and child birth, and breast cancer in the states, nationally, and in other countries. This is a very useful source for keeping up with the latest information on the topic of reproductive health.

Sex Respect. **www.sexrespect.com/.**

This website offers materials and advice to help parents and teachers offer abstinence-only sex education for teens. An entire curriculum plus videos and other materials are available. Guides such as "What do I tell my 10 year old girl about womanhood?" and "What do I tell my son?" are also offered. Guidebooks and manuals are available for teachers, parents, and students as well as "I'm worth waiting for" stickers. The program was developed by Colleen Kelly Mast. According to her website: "The curriculum defines human sexuality, recognizes influences on sexual decision making, identifies emotional, psychological, and physical consequences of teenage sexual activity; discusses dating guidelines; teaches how to say "no"; shows how to change former sexual behavior and explores the responsibilities of marriage and parenthood. It is being used at the seventh, eighth, ninth and tenth grade levels."

Glossary

abortifacient   Any drug or practice that terminates a pregnancy.

abortion manifesto   A pro-choice tactic whereby women admit to having had illegal abortions and challenge the police to arrest them; this has been effective when challenging criminal abortion laws.

abortion reform   A process to make small changes in existing laws, such as expanding the conditions for legal abortions.

abortion repeal   The removal of all government policies regulating abortion; treating abortion like any medical procedure.

case law   All the judicial decisions pertaining to a particular issue under litigation, such as states' power to regulate abortion or birth control.

civil law   The system of law derived from formal codes, such as the Roman Law Code, and found in European countries as well as many countries in Latin America, Africa, and Asia.

Comstock Act   The 1873 federal law that outlawed the provision of information about contraception and abortion.

common law   Also called "judge-made law"; it is the legal system found in England and many of its former colonies, including the United States.

compulsory pregnancy   A term used by feminists to characterize the effect of criminal abortion laws on women's lives.

conditional abortion law   A policy that regulates abortion according to the circumstances of pregnancy, such as threats to the life and health of the mother, fetal deformity, or pregnancies resulting from rape or incest. Also called an *indications law.*

constitutional law   The provisions of the U.S. Constitution and all judicial interpretations, especially those of the Supreme Court.

diagnosis   That portion of a pro-choice or pro-life collective action frame that defines the reasons a particular situation is a public problem.

frames Ways of giving meaning to a particular condition, question, or problem; social movements use frames to mobilize followers and achieve public policy goals.

gender regime The norms and customs that pertain to the relative status and roles of women and men in society.

"irregular" physicians A term used in the nineteenth century to refer to people who practiced medicine but who had no formal training.

Islamic law Also called *sharia*, this is a legal system found in some Muslim countries.

issue frame The terms of the debate on a public problem used by policymakers in government institutions.

judicial bypass The provisions in parental involvement laws that allow a judge to grant permission for an abortion to be performed on a minor if informing the parents would cause hardship to the young woman.

litigation strategy A plan to change policy by bringing challenges to existing laws to courts, urging them to declare the laws unconstitutional or interpret the laws is a particular way.

Medicaid The government health program for poor families and the destitute that is funded by both the federal and state governments.

menstrual regulation treatments Seen as an alternative to abortion, this procedure extracts the contents of the uterus before results of pregnancy tests are known.

mifepristone The drug used in the so-called abortion pill or medical abortion. It involves two doses, one of mifepristone and the second of misoprostol, which bring about miscarriage. In the 1980s, it was called RU-486.

nontherapeutic abortion terminating a pregnancy for other than health reasons, such as economic or personal reasons or inability to care for a child.

parental involvement laws Regulations in states requiring the notification or permission of parents before physicians can perform abortions on minors (usually defined as a girl younger than 18 years.

periodic abortion law A policy that regulates abortion according to stages of pregnancy, for example weeks of gestation or trimesters.

personhood The status of individuals under the U.S. Constitution, especially in reference to the rights to due process and equal protection under the Fourteenth Amendment.

policy debate A structured discussion about a public problem that takes place in a public arena, usually centered on a government institution.

postabortion syndrome The pro-life claim that women who have abortions suffer psychological trauma. There is little scientific evidence that this syndrome exists.

precedent Also called *stare decisis,* it is the practice in U.S. courts to decide current cases the same way previous cases were decided.

privacy, right to The constitutional limit on the government's power to make laws that interfere with an individual's decisions in a particular area of life; has been applied to the individual's decision whether to bear or beget a child.

prognosis That portion of a pro-life or pro-choice movement's collective action frame that sets forth the solution to a problem, in most cases, it refers to what they want government to do about a problem they have described.

quickening The point in a pregnancy where the mother can feel the fetus move; also called *animation.*

"regular" physicians A term used in the nineteenth century to refer to those practicing medicine who had received some formal training.

religiosity The degree to which religion is important in people's lives.

strategic frames The definition or diagnosis of a problem and the policy solution or prognosis offered by movement actors in particular policy debates.

therapeutic abortion Terminating a pregnancy for reasons of health of the mother or the fetus.

triad The pattern of relationships among the government, doctors, and women that results from any abortion policy.

undue burden standard States may limit abortion practice up to the point where the regulations constitute an insurmountable obstacle to a woman's liberty to exercise her right to seek abortion.

unintended pregnancy When a woman is pregnant but does not want to be pregnant at that time. It does not imply whether or not the woman wants the baby that results.

vacuum aspiration The preferred technique for surgical abortion in the early stages of pregnancy.

viability The state in the gestation of a fetus when it is able to live outside the mother's uterus either naturally or with artificial assistance.

Index

About the Author

Dorothy E. McBride (formerly Stetson) is Emeritus Professor of political science at Florida Atlantic University, where she was a founder of the women's studies program. As a professor, she has taught and written about the politics of abortion in the United States and internationally since the mid-1970s. She is co-convener (with Amy G. Mazur) of the Research Network on Gender, Politics and the State, a network of U.S. and European scholars who are studying the impact of women's movements on policy and the role of women's policy agencies. As part of this project, Dr. McBride was editor and contributing author of *Abortion Politics, Women's Movements and the Democratic State: A Comparative Study of State Feminism* (2001). She was also coeditor (with Marianne Githens) and a contributing author to *Abortion Politics: Public Policy in Comparative Perspective* (1996). She lives in Washington State and is a visiting professor at the University of Washington (2006–2008).